THIS BOOK IS THE PROPERTY
of
POPE JOHN PAUL II S.S

YEAR	NAME	GRADE
00/01	Shawn Balouch	9
01	Shain	9
01	Sonia Balouch	9
06	ELOISE BUCAIS	9
07	Jose Hernandez	9
	Beverly +	9
		9

Students are given this book on the
understanding that the book will not be damaged
in any way.
A charge will be made for damaged books.

CROSSROADS

Dom Saliani
Nova Morine

Gage Editorial Team
Joe Banel
Patrice Peterkin
Diane Robitaille

gage EDUCATIONAL PUBLISHING COMPANY
A DIVISION OF CANADA PUBLISHING CORPORATION
Vancouver·Calgary·Toronto·London·Halifax

Managing Editor: Darleen Rotozinski
Contributing Editor: David Friend
Contributing Writer: Chelsea Donaldson
Copy Editors: Sue Kanhai, Sheree Haughian
Permissions Editor: Elizabeth Long
Photo Researcher: Mary Rose MacLachlan
Researcher: Catherine Rondina
Bias Reviewer: Margaret Hoogeveen
Cover Illustration: Brian Deines
**Design, Art Direction
& Electronic Assembly:** Wycliffe Smith Design

Canadian Cataloguing in Publication Data

Main entry under title:

Gage crossroads 9

ISBN 0-7715-1324-0

1. Readers (Secondary). I. Saliani, Dom
II. Title: Gage crossroads nine. III. Title: Crossroads 9.

PE1121.G256 1999   428.6   C99-931437-8

We acknowledge the financial support of the Government of Canada through the Book Publishing Industry Development Program for our publishing activities.

ISBN 0-7715-**1324-0**
1 2 3 4 5 BP 03 02 01 00 99
Printed and bound in Canada

CROSSROADS SERIES REVIEWERS
Deborah Adams SD #4, Maple Ridge-Pitt Meadows, BC
June James Surrey SD #36, BC
Dale Wallace Calgary B of E, AB
Harry Wagner Parkland School Div. #70, AB
Irene Heffel Edmonton PSB, AB
Joan Alexander St. Albert PSSD #6, AB
Cindy Coffin Saskatoon Catholic B of E, SK
John Pilutti Peel District SB, ON
Cam MacPherson Toronto DSB, ON
Susan Loban Toronto DSB, ON
Alice Carlson Durham DSB , ON
Francine Artichuk SD 02/04, NB
Martin MacDonald Strait Regional SB, NS
Helena Butler Avalon East SB, NF

Lines
for a
Bookmark

by Gael Turnbull

You who read...
May you seek
As you look;
May you keep
What you need;
May you care
What you choose;
And know here
In this book
Something strange,
Something sure,
That will change
You and be yours.

TABLE OF CONTENTS

ALTERNATE TABLE OF CONTENTS

PERSONAL FOCUS

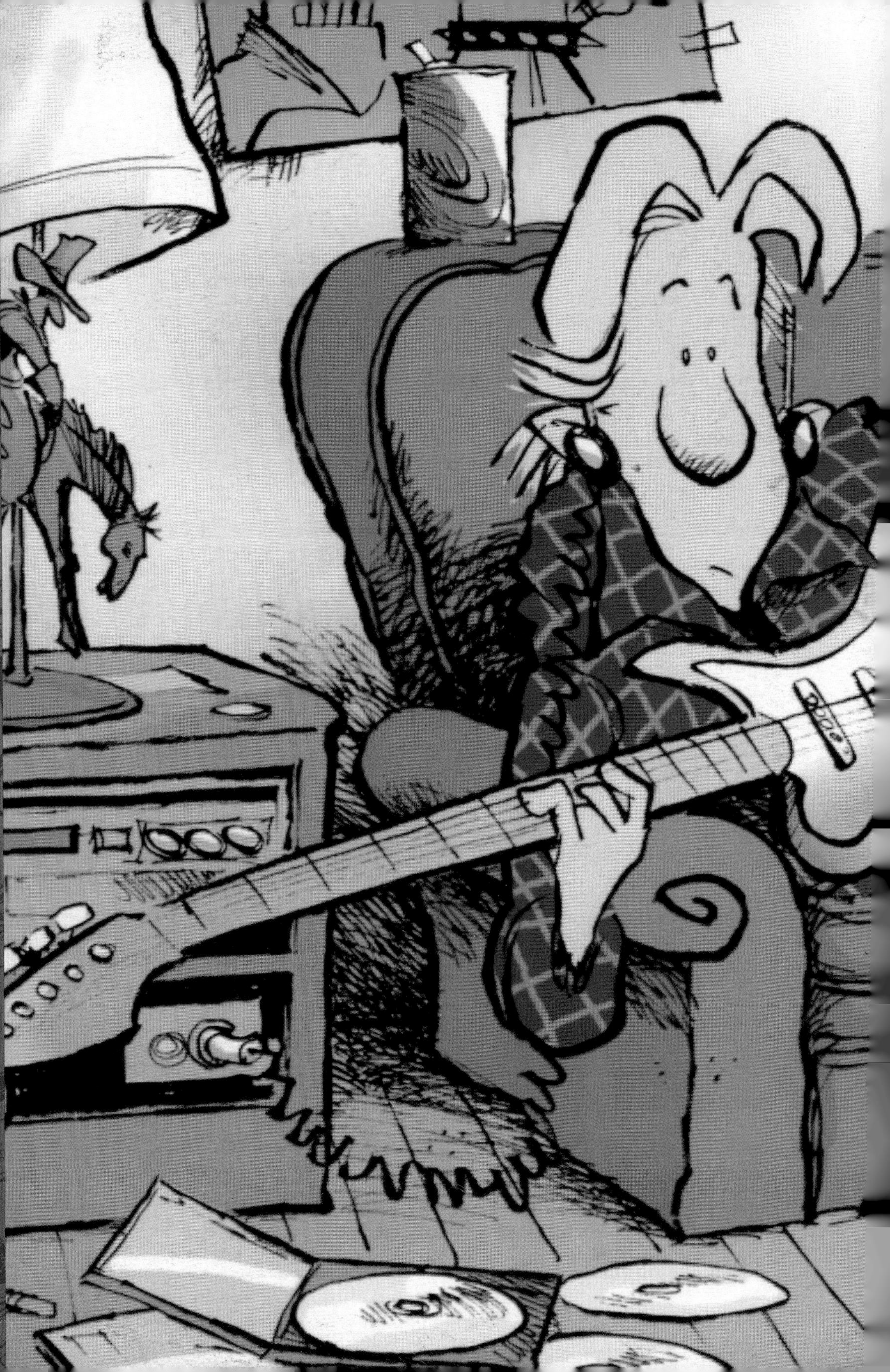

ALL THAT I AM

UNIT AT A GLANCE

What do you know about your brain and how it works? What would you do if you came face to face with the greatest…

Mystery of Mysteries

Anecdote by Robert Fulghum

The teacher is quiet. He is thinking, I can't believe I am doing this. He pulls on rubber gloves, reaches into a white plastic bag, and pulls out a human brain. A real human brain.

The students are quiet. They are thinking, I can't believe he is really doing this.

The students are thinking, If he hands it to me I will DIE, JUST DIE! Sure enough, he hands it to them. They do not die.

When the brain comes back to him, the teacher tosses it across the table to the rubber-gloved quarterback of the football team, and he tosses it to his rubber-gloved tight end. Laughter as the tight end drops the brain on the table. The brain bounces.

◆ ◆ ◆

To explain: In this beginning drawing class, I had been lecturing about the impact of brain research on the process of art, using pictures and diagrams and anatomy charts. We had tossed around a cantaloupe to get the feel of the size of a brain, but somehow brains remained a bit abstract. The students had that glazed expression on their faces that means this is getting b-o-r-i-n-g.

In that moment of educational *ennui*, a girl says, "I can bring a human brain to school if you want—my father has lots of them." *(Talk about a full-scale class alert: "She's going to do WHAT?!")*

GOALS AT A GLANCE

- Analyse the features of an anecdote.
- Respond critically.

Well, it turns out her daddy is a bona fide* research neurosurgeon at the medical school and has jars and jars of brains in his lab and he would be pleased to have us see the real thing. So, sure, I can handle this. "Bring a brain to school!" I shout at the departing class. "ALL of you."

Sure enough, a week later, the girl, Queen Forever of Show and Tell, shows up with a brain in a bag.

"Well, Mr. Fulghum, what do you think?"

If ever there was an appropriate use of the word "nonplussed,"** it is now. This is what the students call an "oooo-wow" moment of monumental proportion.

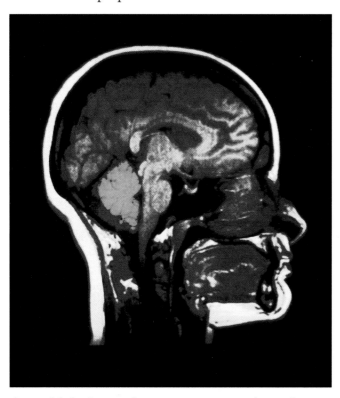

"I have one of these things between my ears," I said. "It is made up entirely of raw meat at the moment. It is fuelled by yesterday's bologna sandwich, potato chips, and chocolate milk. And everything I am doing at the moment—everything I have ever done or will do—passes through this lump. I made it; I own it. And it is the most mysterious thing on earth."

(This brain in my hand wasn't raw, mind you—it had been preserved in formaldehyde. And no, it was not in fact icky or gross. Light beige in colour, slightly damp, soft and rubbery, like clay. And just about the size of that cantaloupe we had passed around—only this one weighed almost one and a half kilograms.)

"Now I can kind of understand the mechanical work of the brain—stimulating breathing, moving blood, directing protein traffic. It's all chemistry and electricity. A motor. I know about motors.

---

* **bona fide:** genuine; real.

** **nonplussed:** to be puzzled.

"But this one-and-a-half-kilogram raw-meat motor also contains all the limericks I know, a recipe for how to cook a turkey, the remembered smell of my junior-high locker room, all my sorrows, the ability to double-clutch a pickup truck, the face of my wife when she was young, formulas like $E=MC^2$ and $A^2+B^2=C^2$, the Prologue to Chaucer's *Canterbury Tales*, the sound of the first cry of my first-born son, the cure for hiccups, the words to the fight song of St. Olaf's College, fifty years' worth of dreams, how to tie my shoes, the taste of cod-liver oil, an image of Van Gogh's *Sunflowers*, and a working understanding of the Dewey decimal system. It's all there in the MEAT.

"One cubic centimetre of brain contains ten billion bits of information and it processes five thousand bits a second. And somehow it evolved over a zillion years from a molten ball of rock, Earth, which will itself fall into the sun someday and be no more. Why? How?

"*That's* what I think."

"Oooo-wow," chorus the students. The teacher is in a groove—got 'em.

Once again the brain is passed around from hand to hand, slowly and solemnly. Once again it is very quiet. The Mystery of Mysteries is present, and it includes us.

----

1. RESPONDING TO THE ANECDOTE

a. The author begins the anecdote by showing a brain to his class. Why does the author begin the anecdote at this point?

b. How does having the "real thing" change the students' reactions to their assignment?

c. Which line in the anecdote has a double meaning? What are its two meanings?

d. What does the author mean when he states, "The Mystery of Mysteries is present, and it includes us"?

e. How does this ancedote fit into a theme on identity?

2. LITERATURE STUDIES THE FEATURES OF AN ANECDOTE

"Mystery of Mysteries" is an **anecdote**. Like a story, it can contain a beginning, middle, and end.

- Outline how the events in this anecdote are organized.
- Why did the author choose to tell the anecdote in this order? Was it an effective technique? Explain.
- With a partner, discuss the similarities and differences between an anecdote and a story.

> An **anecdote** is a brief story that retells a memorable personal event. Like a story, it could be sad, funny, or adventurous.

The Jade Peony

Does your family have any special traditions? Have you ever wondered how they developed and how they have affected you?

Short Story by **Wayson Choy**

When Grandmama died at eighty-three our whole household held its breath. She had promised us a sign of her leaving, final proof that her present life had ended well. My parents knew that without any clear sign, our own family fortunes could be altered, threatened. My stepmother looked endlessly into the small cluttered room the ancient lady had occupied. Nothing was touched; nothing changed. My father, thinking that a sign should appear in Grandmama's garden, looked at the frost-killed shoots and cringed: *no, that could not be it.*

My two older teenage brothers and my sister, Liang, age fourteen, were embarrassed by my parents' behaviour. What would all the white people in Vancouver think of us? We were Canadians now, *Chinese-Canadians*, a hyphenated reality that my parents could never accept. So it seemed for different reasons, we all held our breath waiting for *something*.

I was eight when she died. For days she had resisted going into the hospital...*a cold, just a cold*...and instead gave constant instruction to my stepmother and sister on the boiling of ginseng roots mixed with bitter extract. At night, between wracking coughs and deadly silences, Grandmama had her back and chest rubbed with heated camphor oil* and sipped a bluish decoction of an herb called Peacock's Tail. When all these failed to abate her fever, she began to arrange the details of her will. This she did with my father, confessing finally: "I am too stubborn. The only cure for old age is to die."

My father wept to hear this. I stood beside her bed; she turned to me. Her round face looked darker, and the gentleness of her eyes, the thin, arching eyebrows, seemed weary. I brushed the few strands of grey, brittle hair from her face; she managed to smile at me. Being the youngest, I had spent nearly all my time with her and could not imagine that we would ever be parted. Yet when she spoke, and her voice hesitated, cracked, the sombre shadows of her room chilled me. Her wrinkled brow grew wet with fever, and her small body seemed even more diminutive.

"I—I am going to the hospital, Grandson." Her hand reached out for mine. "You know, Little Son, whatever happens I will never leave you." Her palm felt plush and warm, the slender, old fingers bony and firm, so magically strong was her grip that I could not imagine how she could ever part from me. Ever.

Her hands *were* magical. My most vivid memories are of her hands: long elegant fingers, with impeccable nails, a skein of fine, barely-seen veins, and wrinkled skin like light pine. Those hands were quick when she taught me, at six, simple tricks of juggling, learnt when she was a village girl in Southern Canton; a troupe of actors had stayed on her father's farm. One of them, "tall and pale as the whiteness of petals," fell in love with her, promising to return. In her last years his image came back like a third being in our two lives. He had been magician, acrobat, juggler, and some of the things he taught her she had absorbed and passed on to me through her stories and games. But above all, without realizing it then, her hands conveyed to me the quality of their love.

Most marvellous for me was the quick-witted skill her hands revealed in making wind chimes for our birthdays: wind chimes in the likeness of her lost friend's only present to her, made of bits of string and scraps, in the centre of which once hung a precious jade peony. This wondrous gift to her broke apart years ago, in China, but Grandmama kept the jade pendant in a

---

*camphor oil: oil with a bitter taste and a strong odour made out of a compound from the camphor tree.

tiny red silk envelope, and kept it always in her pocket, until her death.

These were not ordinary, carelessly made chimes, such as those you now find in our Chinatown stores, whose rattling noises drive you mad. But making her special ones caused dissension in our family, and some shame. Each one that she made was created from a treasure trove of glass fragments and castaway costume jewellery, in the same way that her first wind chime had been made. The problem for the rest of the family was in the fact that Grandmama looked for these treasures wandering the back alleys of Keefer and Pender Streets, peering into our neighbours' garbage cans, chasing away hungry, nervous cats, and shouting curses at them.

"All our friends are laughing at us!" Old Brother Jung said at last to my father, when Grandmama was away having tea at Mrs. Lim's.

"We are not poor," Oldest Brother Kiam declared, "Yet she and Sek-Lung poke through those awful things as if—" he shoved me in frustration and I stumbled against my sister, "—they were beggars!"

"She will make Little Brother crazy!" Sister Liang said. Without warning, she punched me sharply in the back; I jumped. "You see, look how *nervous* he is!"

I lifted my foot slightly, enough to swing it back and kick Liang in the shin. She yelled and pulled back her fist to punch me again. Jung made a menacing move towards me.

"Stop this, all of you!" My father shook his head in exasperation. How could he dare tell the Grand Old One, his aging mother, that what was somehow appropriate in a poor village in China, was an abomination here? How could he prevent me, his youngest, from accompanying her? If she went walking into those alleyways alone she could well be attacked by hoodlums. "She is not a beggar looking for food. She is searching for—for..."

My stepmother attempted to speak, then fell silent. She, too, seemed perplexed and somewhat ashamed. They all loved Grandmama, but she was *inconvenient*, unsettling.

As for our neighbours, most understood Grandmama to be harmlessly crazy, others that she did indeed make lovely toys but for what purpose? Why? they asked, and the stories she told me, of the juggler who smiled at her, flashed in my head.

Finally, by their cutting remarks, the family did exert enough pressure so that Grandmama and I no longer openly announced our expeditions. Instead, she took me with her on "shopping trips," ostensibly for clothes or groceries, while in fact we spent most of our time exploring stranger and more distant neighbourhoods, searching for splendid junk; jangling pieces of a vase, cranberry glass fragments embossed with leaves, discarded glass beads from Woolworth necklaces… We would sneak them all home in brown rice sacks, folded into small parcels, and put them under her bed. During the day when the family was away at school or work, we brought them out and washed every item in a large black pot of boiling lye and water, dried them quickly, carefully, and returned them, sparkling, under her bed.

Our greatest excitement occurred when a fire gutted the large Chinese Presbyterian Church, three blocks from our house. Over the still-smoking ruins the next day, Grandmama and I rushed precariously over the blackened beams to pick out the stained glass that glittered in the sunlight. Small figure bent over, wrapped against the autumn cold in a dark blue quilted coat, happily gathering each piece like gold, she became my spiritual playmate: "There's a good one! *There!*"

Hours later, soot-covered and smelling of smoke, we came home with a grocery carton full of delicate fragments, still early enough to steal them all into the house and put the small box under her bed.

"These are special pieces," she said, giving the box a last push, "because they come from a sacred place." She slowly got up and I saw, for the first time, her hand begin to shake. But then, in her joy, she embraced me. Both of our hearts were racing, as if we were two dreamers. I buried my face in her blue quilt, and for a moment, the whole world seemed silent.

"My juggler," she said, "He never came back from Honan…perhaps the famine…" Her voice began to quake. "But I shall have my sacred wind chime…I shall have it again."

One evening, when the family was gathered in their usual places in the parlour, Grandmama gave me her secret nod: a slight wink of her eye and a flaring of her nostrils. There was *trouble* in the air. Supper had gone badly, school examinations were due, Father had failed to meet an editorial deadline at the *Vancouver Chinese Times*. A huge sigh came from Sister Liang.

"But it is useless this Chinese they teach you!" she lamented, turning to Stepmother for support. Silence. Liang frowned, dejected, and went back to her Chinese book, bending the covers back.

"Father," Oldest Brother Kiam began, waving his bamboo brush in the air, "you must realize that this Mandarin only confuses us. We are Cantonese speakers…"

"And you do not complain about Latin, French, or German in your English school?" Father rattled his newspaper, a signal that his patience was ending.

"But, Father, those languages are *scientific*," Kiam jabbed his brush in the air. "We are now in a scientific, logical world."

Father was silent. We could all hear Grandmama's rocker.

"What about Sek-Lung?" Older Brother Jung pointed angrily at me. "He was sick last year, but this year he should have at least started Chinese school, instead of picking over garbage cans!"

"He starts next year," Father said, in a hard tone that immediately warned everyone to be silent. Liang slammed her book.

Grandmama went on rocking quietly in her chair. She complimented my mother on her knitting, made a remark about the "strong beauty" of Kiam's brushstrokes which, in spite of himself, immensely pleased him. All this babbling noise was her family torn and confused in a strange land: everything here was so very foreign and scientific.

The truth was, I was sorry not to have started school the year before. In my innocence I had imagined going to school meant certain privileges worthy of all my brothers' and sister's complaints. The fact that my lung infection in my fifth and sixth years, mistakenly diagnosed as TB, earned me some reprieve, only made me long for school the more. Each member of the family took turns on Sunday, teaching me or annoying me. But it was the countless hours I spent with Grandmama that were my real education. Tapping me on my head she would say, "Come, Sek-Lung, we have *our* work," and we would walk up the stairs to her small crowded room.

There, in the midst of her antique shawls, the old ancestral calligraphy and multicoloured embroidered hangings, beneath the mysterious shelves of sweet herbs and bitter potions, we would continue doing what we had started that morning, the elaborate wind chime for her death.

"I can't last forever," she declared, when she let me in on the secret of this one. "It will sing and dance and glitter," her long fingers stretched into the air, pantomiming the waving motion of her ghost chimes. "My spirit will hear its sounds and see its lights and return to this house and say goodbye to you."

Deftly she reached into the grocery carton she had placed on the chair beside me. She picked out a fish-shaped amber piece, and with a long needle-like tool and a steel ruler, she scored it. Pressing the blade of a cleaver against the line, with the fingers of her other hand, she lifted up the glass until it cleanly snapped into the exact shape she required. Her hand began to tremble, the tips of her fingers to shiver, like rippling water.

"You see that, Little One?" She held her hand up. "That is my body fighting with Death. He is in this room now."

My eyes darted in panic, but Grandmama remained calm, undisturbed, and went on with her work. Then I remembered the glue and uncorked the jar for her. Soon the graceful ritual movements of her hand returned to her, and I became lost in the magic of her task: she dabbed a cabalistic* mixture of glue on one end and skilfully dropped the braided end of a silk thread into it. This part always amazed me: the braiding would slowly, *very* slowly, *unknot*, fanning out like a prized fishtail. In a few seconds the clear, homemade glue began to harden as I blew lightly over it, welding to itself each separate silk strand.

Each jam-sized pot of glue was precious; each large cork had been wrapped with a fragment of pink silk. I remember this part vividly, because each cork was treated to a special rite. First we went shopping in the best silk stores in Chinatown for the perfect square of silk she required. It had to be a deep pink, a shade of colour blushing toward red. And the tone had to match—as closely as possible—her most precious jade carving, the small peony of white and light-red jade, her most lucky possession. In the centre of this semi-translucent carving, no more than two and a half centimetres wide, was a pool of pink light, its veins swirling out into the petals of the flower.

"This colour is the colour of my spirit," she said, holding it up to the window so I could see the delicate pastel against the broad strokes of sunlight. She dropped her voice, and I held my breath at the wonder of the

---

* **cabalistic:** having a mystical meaning; secret.

colour. "This was given to me by the young actor who taught me how to juggle. He had four of them, and each one had a centre of this rare colour, the colour of Good Fortune." The pendant seemed to pulse as she turned it: "Oh, Sek-Lung! He had white hair and white skin to *his toes! It's true,* I saw him bathing." She laughed and blushed, her eyes softened at the memory. The silk had to match the pink heart of her pendant: the colour was magical for her, to hold the unravelling strands of her memory...

It was just six months before she died that we really began to work on her wind chime. Three thin bamboo sticks were steamed and bent into circlets; thirty exact lengths of silk thread, the strongest kind, were cut and braided at both ends and glued to the stained glass. Her hands worked on their own command, each hand racing with a life of its own: cutting, snapping, braiding, knotting... Sometimes she breathed heavily and her small body, growing thinner, sagged against me. *Death,* I thought, *He is in this room,* and I would work harder alongside her. For months Grandmama and I did this every other evening, a half-dozen pieces each time. The shaking in her hand grew worse, but we said nothing. Finally, after discarding hundreds, she told me she had the necessary thirty pieces. But this time, because it was a sacred chime, I would not be permitted to help her tie it up or have the joy of raising it. "Once tied," she said, holding me against my disappointment, "not even I can raise it. Not a sound must it make until I have died."

"What will happen?"

"Your father will then take the centre braided strand and raise it. He will hang it against my bedroom window so that my ghost may see it, and hear it, and return. I must say goodbye to this world properly or wander in this foreign devil's land forever."

"You can take the streetcar!" I blurted, suddenly shocked that she actually meant to leave me. I thought I could hear the clear-chromatic chimes, see the shimmering colours on the wall: I fell against her and cried, and there in my crying I knew that she would die. I can still remember the touch of her hand on my head, and the smell of her thick woollen sweater pressed against my face. "I will always be with you, Little Sek-Lung, but in a different way...you'll see."

Months went by, and nothing happened. Then one late September evening, when I had just come home from Chinese School, Grandmama was preparing supper when she looked out our kitchen window and saw a cat—a long, lean white cat—jump into our garbage pail and knock it over. She ran out to chase it away, shouting curses at it. She did not have her thick sweater on and when she came back into the house, a chill gripped her. She leaned against the door: "That was not a cat," she said, and the odd tone of her voice caused my father to look with alarm at her. "I can not take back my curses. It is too late." She took hold of my father's arm: "It was all white and had pink eyes like sacred fire."

My father started at this, and they both looked pale. My brothers and sister, clearing the table, froze in their gestures.

"The fog has confused you," Stepmother said. "It was just a cat."

But Grandmama shook her head, for she knew it was a sign. "I will not live forever," she said. "I am prepared."

The next morning she was confined to her bed with a severe cold. Sitting by her, playing with some of my toys, I asked her about the cat.

"Why did Father jump at the cat with the pink eyes? He didn't see it, you did."

"But he and your mother know what it means."

"What?"

"My friend, the juggler, the magician, was as pale as white jade, and he had pink eyes." I thought she would begin to tell me one of her stories, a tale of enchantment or of a wondrous adventure, but she only paused to swallow; her eyes glittered, lost in memory. She took my hand, gently opening and closing her fingers over it. "Sek-Lung," she sighed, "*he* has come back to me."

Then Grandmama sank back into her pillow and the embroidered flowers lifted to frame her wrinkled face. I saw her hand over my own, and my own began to tremble. I fell fitfully asleep by her side. When I woke up it was dark and her bed was empty. She had been taken to the hospital and I was not permitted to visit.

A few days after that she died of the complications of pneumonia. Immediately after her death my father came home and said nothing to us, but walked up the stairs to her room, pulled aside the drawn lace curtains of her window and lifted the wind chimes to the sky.

I began to cry and quickly put my hand in my pocket for a handkerchief. Instead, caught between my fingers, was the small, round firmness of the jade peony. In my mind's eye I saw Grandmama smile and heard, softly, the pink centre beat like a beautiful, cramped heart.

1. RESPONDING TO THE STORY

a. How would you describe Sek-Lung's relationship with his grandmother?

b. Why did the rest of Sek-Lung's family feel embarrassed by his grandmother's actions?

c. How does finding the jade peony at the end of the story help Sek-Lung with his grief?

d. How does this story reflect the theme *All That I Am*?

e. If you were to interview Wayson Choy, what three questions would you like to ask him about this story or how it was written?

2. WRITING DESCRIPTIVE PARAGRAPHS

Think about a family member who has had an impact on your life. What memories stand out in your mind? Jot down words or phrases that describe the person. Consider character traits and physical appearance, as well as memories you have of the person. Write a descriptive paragraph using these details. Will your readers be able to picture the person you describe? Use concrete nouns, verbs, adjectives, and adverbs to create your description.

3. LANGUAGE CONVENTIONS EFFECTIVE ADJECTIVES

Adjectives are words that describe, limit, or identify a noun or pronoun. There are two types of adjectives—descriptive and limiting. Both types can make your writing more realistic and interesting.

Descriptive adjectives add details and answer the question, *What is it like*? For example:

The *red* apple fell from the tree.

Limiting adjectives make nouns and pronouns more concrete and specific, and answer the questions *Which one?*, *How many?*, and *How much?* For example:

I saw *two* movies last week.

SELF-ASSESSMENT: Examine a story or poem that you've written, and analyse how you've used adjectives. Are they the best words you could have chosen? Are they specific enough? Have they made the sentences stronger? Do they give an accurate, clear description of what you are describing?

Four Voices

Who Am I?

Poem by Felice Holman

The trees ask me,
And the sky,
And the sea asks me
    Who am I?

The grass asks me,
And the sand,
And the rocks ask me
    Who am I?

The wind tells me
At nightfall,
And the rain tells me
    Someone small.

Someone small
Someone small
    But a piece
        of
          it
           all.

GOALS AT A GLANCE

- Use imagery to create meaning and description.
- Experiment with metaphor.

And I Remember

Poem by Afua Cooper

And I remember
standing
in the churchyard on Wesleyan Hill
standing and looking down on the plains
that stretch before me
like a wide green carpet
the plains full with sugar cane and rice
the plains that lead to the sea

And I remember
walking
as a little girl to school
on the savannahs of Westmoreland
walking from our hillbound village
walking along steep hillsides
walking carefully so as not to trip and plunge
walking into the valley

And I remember
running
to school on the road that cuts into the green carpet
running past laughing waters
running to school that rose like a concrete castle
out of my carpet of green
running with a golden Westmoreland breeze

And I remember
breathing
the smell of the earth plowed by rain and tractors
breathing the scent of freshly cut cane
breathing the scent of rice plants as they send
their roots into the soft mud

Yes, and I remember
thinking
this is mine this is mine
this sweetness of mountains
valleys
rivers
and plains
is mine
mine
mine

Some mornings
I get up real early before work
and head on up
to the lake.
The slam of the car door
echoes out on the water,
and then
it's like something starts
settling down inside me.
It's settling down into the
open spaces between
my skin and my bones
as I look at that lake
all covered in fog
and gray like rabbit skin.
Sometimes a heron comes
in for a landing,
and it's just me and him,
and all of a sudden
I feel like a heron.

I stand there
and I am feeling like it's me
floating out on that water.
It's me
picking through those reeds.
It's me flapping my wings and
it's my feet
hanging down uninterested
while the rest of my body works
to fly up off that lake.
Then the heron is gone,
and the jerk is back,
chewing on the styrofoam cup in his hand and
wishing for things
he can't even put a name to.
Quarter to eight
I get back in the car,
and eight on the dot
I am walking into Maywell's.
I am there.
Crossing the floor
with heron feet,
pouring coffee
with heron hands.
Working the day like
I'm flying.

Wanted: Someone Who Cares

Poem by Shawna Lynne Danielle Panipekeesick

Who cares enough to accept me as I am,
Who does not condemn me for my shortcomings,
Who helps me to learn from my mistakes.

Who cares enough to respect me as an individual
with the right to learn and grow at my own pace
and in my own unique fashion.

Who will stand by to help when I need it,
but will release me from my own guilt,
and help me find constructive ways to deal with reality.

Who will encourage me to explore the world about me,
Who will open my eyes to beauty and my ears to music,
Who will listen to my questions and help me find answers.

Who cares enough to help me achieve my full potential,
and who has faith in my ability to develop into a worthwhile person.
Could this someone be me?

1. RESPONDING TO THE POEMS

a. Which poem appeals to you the most? Explain.

b. What are the themes of the four poems?

c. Why do you think the poems have been grouped together?

d. What emotion is expressed in each of the poems?

e. Do you identify with any of the people in these poems? Explain.

2. WRITING CREATE A POEM

Think about a special place that you like to visit. Maybe it is a place you find beautiful or a place where you go to think. Write a poem about your special place. Use one of the poems in the selection as a model, if you wish.

- To help you remember and explore the ideas, emotions, and images connected with your topic, you could brainstorm a list, create a web, or make sketches.

- What **metaphors**, or comparisons, could you use to describe your special place? Metaphors can help to create atmosphere and to paint pictures for your reader. For example, in the poem from *Soda Jerk*, the poet uses a metaphor in the lines, "Crossing the floor/with heron feet."

> A **metaphor** is a literary device that helps the reader to picture what the author means because it compares one thing to something else. For example, "With heron hands" makes the reader think the hands are long and skinny.

- Think about the structure of your poem. What events do you want at the beginning, the middle, and the end?

- Consider the pace and rhythm of your poem. The way you arrange or break the lines in your poem can emphasize certain words. Having one or two words per line can slow readers down and make them take note of important words or ideas.

SELF-ASSESSMENT: Give yourself a mark out of ten for your poem. How do you think you could improve this mark?

3. VISUAL COMMUNICATION CREATE AN ILLUSTRATION

What did you think of when you read the words "running to school that rose like a concrete castle/out of my carpet of green" or "pouring coffee/with heron hands"? Choose one of the poems, and draw an illustration that you feel captures its emotion or spirit. You could also create a collage of images that you feel interprets the poem well. When you illustrate your poem

- think about the poem's message or theme
- brainstorm visual ideas related to the message or theme
- make rough sketches to experiment with ideas

Share your illustration with a classmate, explaining what you've done and why. Ask for feedback. What suggestions does he or she have to improve the poem?

STRATEGIES

4. POET'S CRAFT USE IMAGERY

How would you use words to paint a picture for your reader? In "Who Am I?" Felice Holman uses *personification* (describing a thing, idea, object, or animal as if it were a person); in the poem from *Soda Jerk* Cynthia Rylant uses metaphors and *simile* (comparisons using *like* or *as*); and in "And I Remember" and "Wanted: Someone Who Cares," the poets create vivid images through description. With a partner, discuss these techniques and the images used in the poems. Which images are effective? Why? An image can reveal character, create a mood, or explain an idea. Images, above all, appeal to the senses—touch, sight, taste, smell, or hearing.

When writing your own poems, remember to

- use description that helps your reader to experience what you are describing
- choose adjectives, adverbs, nouns, and verbs that are concrete

> **Imagery** is a technique poets and writers use to describe and appeal to the senses. There are many types of imagery including simile, metaphor, and personification.

Going Back Home

Art Essay by Toyomi Igus • Paintings by Michele Wood

WHEN I WAS A LITTLE GIRL, I HEARD MANY STORIES ABOUT MY FAMILY—where they came from, what life was like before I was born. I grew up in a big city in Indiana, but I tried to imagine what kind of house my ancestors lived in when they were enslaved in the South.

I was fascinated by my family's stories. I was the one who would listen to the grown-ups' tales. As I grew older, I tried to piece together my family's history from the scraps of memories they would share with me.

Have you ever had the opportunity to discover your family's history and heritage? Join artist Michele Wood on her journey into her past.

When you look at my art, you'll see that I often create quiltlike backgrounds. This is my way of showing how pieces of lives can fit together.

Because I'm an artist, I express my thoughts and feelings visually, through pictures. As I learned my family's history and all that they endured, I realized I come from a very strong people. I never tried to create a self-portrait before, but after going back home, an image of myself started to form in my mind.

Here it is. When I was little, I tried to take a picture of myself, and I put the camera too close in front of my face. The flash bulb made a square-shaped burn on my forehead. The mark is gone now, but I remembered it in this picture.

The house and fence represent the foundations of my past. The boards are my life's lessons—the crooked ones are the tragedies and hardships. I am holding a hen, which is the link to my rural southern heritage. After going back home, I know more about who I am and I can picture the person I want to be—a seeker of knowledge, a creator of visions, and a keeper of my family's history.

GOALS AT A GLANCE

- Analyse artwork.
- Create a self-portrait.

Michele Wood's self-portrait.

Wood's grandparents stand inside their house to show the opportunity they now had to make a new home. The pinwheels on the woman's skirt represent good luck and the changing cycles of life.

Music has always played an important role in African American culture.
In this painting, Wood depicts a blues musician.

1. RESPONDING TO THE ART ESSAY

a. How did Michele Wood find out about her ancestry?

b. How has Wood's quest to find out about her family history helped her with her own identity? What makes you think this?

c. Have you ever moved? What memories do you have of the other places where you've lived?

2. VISUAL COMMUNICATION VIEWING THE ART ESSAY

Look at Wood's paintings and discuss them with a partner. In what ways are they similar and different? What are the main colours used by Wood and what are their effects? What details in her paintings are most striking? How does she reveal her ancestry in the paintings? What images can you detect in the backgrounds? Why does she use a quiltlike background in her paintings? What do the different elements in her self-portrait symbolize?

3. MEDIA MAKER CREATE A SELF-PORTRAIT

Choose one of the following methods to create a self-portrait. Use a collection of photographs of different stages of your life.

- If you like to paint, you can use watercolours or oils. You can also draw and colour using pastels, charcoal, or pencil. Begin by looking in the mirror or at a good photograph of yourself.

- You could also create a digital self-portrait. Scan a photograph into your computer, then manipulate the image on screen.

- A self-portrait collage is another alternative. Choose a photograph. Then make a collage of the things, places, and objects that represent who you are.

- Share your work with others, explaining how you have achieved it.

How important do you think it is to fit in? Some people would do anything to gain…

Acceptance

Short, Short Story

by Vidhya Sridharan

"Nerd, Geek!"

Sandy was tired of not fitting in.

Monday morning. Dressed in black, belly button exposed, and wearing a sneer, she approached the cool kids. Her body tensed. Her steps faltered.

"Hey man," she said uncertainly. "What's up?"

They turned and smiled. Acceptance! She's in.

Then she realized how ridiculous she felt. Taking another look, Sandy knew she wasn't one of them. She turned and made her way to the library. ◆

GOALS AT A GLANCE

■ Respond critically to the story.
■ Design a poster.

33

1. RESPONDING TO THE STORY

a. How does Sandy try to fit in?

b. What changed Sandy's mind about wanting to fit in with the "cool" kids?

c. Do you find Sandy's actions believable? Why or why not?

d. Have you ever felt left out or excluded from things? Explain.

e. Think about the different "groups" in your school. What are the things that separate one group from another?

STRATEGIES

2. MEDIA MAKER CREATE A POSTER

Design a poster emphasizing the importance of being true to yourself. As you design your poster, consider the following:

- Think about your audience. What kinds of images will appeal to your target audience?
- Decide on the **tone** that would best suit your subject. Will it be informal, funny, or dramatic?
- Draw a rough sketch before finishing your final poster. It will help you decide the best placement for the visuals and text.
- Create a *slogan* (a short, catchy phrase that is used to attract the reader's attention).
- Choose a visual for your topic.

SELF-ASSESSMENT: Examine your poster. Does it present the message you are trying to convey? How could you improve it?

> The **tone** is the atmosphere or mood of a piece. It expresses the author's attitude or feeling about the subject of a piece of writing.

The choices we make can drastically affect our lives. One young man finds out just how important choices can be.

On the Sidewalk Bleeding

Short Story by Evan Hunter

The boy lay bleeding in the rain. He was sixteen years old, and he wore a bright purple silk jacket, and the lettering across the back of the jacket read THE ROYALS. The boy's name was Andy, and the name was delicately scripted in black thread on the front of the jacket, just over the heart. *Andy*.

He had been stabbed ten minutes ago. The knife had entered just below his rib cage and had been drawn across his body violently, tearing a wide gap in his flesh. He lay on the sidewalk with the March rain drilling his jacket and drilling his body and washing away the blood that poured from his open wound. He had known excruciating pain when the knife had torn across his body and then sudden comparative relief when the blade was pulled away. He had heard the voice saying, "That's for you, Royal!" and then the sound of foot-steps hurrying into the rain, and then he had fallen to the sidewalk, clutching his stomach, trying to stop the flow of blood.

He tried to yell for help, but he had no voice. He did not know why his voice had deserted him, or why the rain had become so suddenly fierce, or why there was an open hole in his body from which his life ran redly, steadily. It was 11:30 p.m., but he did not know the time.

There was another thing he did not know.

He did not know he was dying. He lay on the sidewalk, bleeding, and he thought only: *That was a fierce rumble. They got me good that time*, but he did not know he was dying. He would have been frightened had he known. In

■ Adapt a story into a media form.
■ Examine the features of a newspaper article.

his ignorance, he lay bleeding and wishing he could cry out for help, but there was no voice in his throat. There was only the bubbling of blood from between his lips whenever he opened his mouth to speak. He lay silent in his pain, waiting, waiting for someone to find him.

He could hear the sound of automobile tires hushed on the muzzle of rainswept streets, far away at the other end of the long alley. He lay with his face pressed to the sidewalk, and he could see the splash of neon far away at the other end of the alley, tinting the pavement red and green, slickly brilliant in the rain.

He wondered if Laura would be angry.

He had left the dance to get a package of cigarettes. He had told her he would be back in a few minutes, and then he had gone downstairs and found the candy store closed. He knew that Alfredo's on the next block would be open until at least two, and he had started through the alley, and that was when he'd been ambushed. He could hear the faint sound of music now, coming from a long, long way off, and he wondered if Laura was dancing, wondered if she had missed him yet. Maybe she thought he wasn't coming back. Maybe she thought he'd cut out for good. Maybe she'd already left the dance and gone home. He thought of her face, the brown eyes and the jet-black hair, and thinking of her he forgot his pain a little, forgot that blood was rushing from his body. Someday he would marry Laura. Someday he would marry her, and they would have a lot of kids, and then they would get out of the neighborhood. They would move to a clean project in the Bronx, or maybe they would move to Staten Island. When they were married, when they had kids…

He heard footsteps at the other end of the alley, and he lifted his cheek from the sidewalk and looked into the darkness and tried to cry out, but again there was only a soft hissing bubble of blood on his mouth.

The man came down the alley. He had not seen Andy yet. He walked, and then stopped to lean against the brick of the building, and then walked again. He saw Andy then and came toward him, and he stood over him for a long time, the minutes ticking, ticking, watching him and not speaking.

Then he said, "What's a matter, buddy?"

Andy could not speak, and he could barely move. He lifted his face slightly and looked up at the man, and in the rainswept alley he smelled the sickening odor of alcohol and realized the man was drunk. He did not feel any particular panic. He did not know he was dying, and so he felt only mild disappointment that the man who had found him was drunk.

The man was smiling.

"Did you fall down, buddy?" he asked.

"You mus' be as drunk as I am." He grinned, seemed to remember why he had entered the alley in the first place, and said, "Don't go way. I'll be ri' back."

The man lurched away. Andy heard his footsteps, and then the sound of the man colliding with a garbage can, and some mild swearing, lost in the steady wash of the rain. He waited for the man to come back.

It was 11:39.

When the man returned, he squatted alongside Andy. He studied him with drunken dignity.

"You gonna catch cold here," he said. "What's a matter? You like layin' in the wet?"

Andy could not answer. The man tried to focus his eyes on Andy's face. The rain spattered around them.

"You like a drink?"

Andy shook his head.

"I gotta bottle. Here," the man said. He pulled a pint bottle from his inside jacket pocket. He uncapped it and extended it to Andy. Andy tried to move, but pain wrenched him back flat against the sidewalk.

"Take it," the man said. He kept watching Andy. "Take it." When Andy did not move, he said, "Nev' mind, I'll have one m'self." He tilted the bottle to his lips and then wiped the back of his hand across his mouth. "You too young to be drinkin', anyway. Should be 'shamed of yourself, drunk an' layin' in a alley, all wet. Shame on you. I gotta good minda calla cop."

Andy nodded. Yes, he tried to say. Yes, call a cop. Please. Call one.

"Oh, you don' like that, huh?" the drunk said. "You don' wanna cop to fin' you all drunk an' wet in a alley, huh? Okay, buddy. This time you get off easy." He got to his feet. "This time you lucky," he said. He waved broadly at Andy, and then almost lost his footing. "S'long, buddy," he said.

Wait, Andy thought. *Wait, please, I'm bleeding.*

"S'long," the drunk said again. "I see you aroun'," and then he staggered off up the alley.

Andy lay and thought: *Laura, Laura. Are you dancing?*

The couple came into the alley suddenly. They ran into the alley together, running from the rain, the boy holding the girl's elbow, the girl spreading a newspaper over her head to protect her hair. Andy lay crumpled against the pavement, and he watched them run into the alley laughing, and then duck into the doorway not ten feet from him.

"Man, what rain!" the boy said. "You could drown out there."

"I have to get home," the girl said. "It's late, Freddie. I have to get home."

"We got time," Freddie said. "Your people won't raise a fuss if you're a little late. Not with this kind of weather."

"It's dark," the girl said, and she giggled.

"Yeah," the boy answered, his voice very low.

"Freddie...?"

"Um?"

"You're...you're standing very close to me."

"Um."

There was a long silence. Then the girl said, "Oh," only that single word, and Andy knew she'd been kissed, and he suddenly hungered for Laura's mouth. It was then that he wondered if he would ever kiss Laura again. It was then that he wondered if he was dying.

No, he thought, *I can't be dying, not from a little street rumble, not from just getting cut. Guys get cut all the time in rumbles. I can't be dying. No, that's stupid. That don't make any sense at all.*

"You shouldn't," the girl said.

"Why not?"

"I don't know."

"I love you, Angela," the boy said.

"I love you, too, Freddie," the girl said, and Andy listened and thought: *I love you, Laura. Laura, I think maybe I'm dying. Laura, this is stupid but I think maybe I'm dying. Laura, I think I'm dying!*

He tried to speak. He tried to move. He tried to crawl toward the doorway where he could see the two figures in embrace. He tried to make a noise, a sound, and a grunt came from his lips, and then he tried again, and another grunt came, a low animal grunt of pain.

"What was that?" the girl said, suddenly alarmed, breaking away from the boy.

"I don't know," he answered.

"Go look, Freddie."

"No. Wait."

Andy moved his lips again. Again the sound came from him.

"Freddie!"

"What?"

"I'm scared."

"I'll go see," the boy said.

He stepped into the alley. He walked over to where Andy lay on the ground. He stood over him, watching him.

"You all right?" he asked.

"What is it?" Angela said from the doorway.

"Somebody's hurt," Freddie said.

"Let's get out of here," Angela said.

"No. Wait a minute." He knelt down beside Andy. "You cut?" he asked.

Andy nodded. The boy kept looking at him. He saw the lettering on the jacket then. THE ROYALS. He turned to Angela.

"He's a Royal," he said.

"Let's...what...what do you want to do, Freddie?"

"I don't know. I don't want to get mixed up in this. He's a Royal. We help him, and the Guardians'll be down our necks. I don't want to get mixed up in this, Angela."

"Is he...is he hurt bad?"

"Yeah, it looks that way."

"What shall we do?"

"I don't know."

"We can't leave him here in the rain." Angela hesitated. "Can we?"

"If we get a cop, the Guardians'll find out who," Freddie said. "I don't know, Angela. I don't know."

Angela hesitated a long time before answering. Then she said, "I have to get home, Freddie. My people will begin to worry."

"Yeah." Freddie said. He looked at Andy again. "You all right?" he asked. Andy lifted his face from the sidewalk, and his eyes said: *Please, please help me*, and maybe Freddie read what his eyes were saying, and maybe he didn't.

Behind him, Angela said, "Freddie, let's get out of here! Please!" There was urgency in her voice, urgency bordering on the edge of panic. Freddie stood up. He looked at Andy again, and then mumbled, "I'm sorry," and then he took Angela's arm and together they ran toward the neon splash at the other end of the alley.

Why, they're afraid of the Guardians, Andy thought in amazement. *But why should they be? I wasn't afraid of the Guardians. I never turkeyed out of a rumble with the Guardians. I got heart. But I'm bleeding.*

The rain was soothing somehow. It was a cold rain, but his body was hot all over, and the rain helped to cool him. He had always liked rain. He could remember sitting in Laura's house one time, the rain running down the windows, and just looking out over the street, watching the people running from the rain. That was when he'd first joined the Royals. He could remember how happy he was the Royals had taken him. The Royals and the Guardians, two of the biggest. He was a Royal. There had been meaning to the title.

Now, in the alley, with the cold rain washing his hot body, he wondered about the meaning. If he died, he was Andy. He was not a Royal. He was simply Andy, and he was dead. And he wondered suddenly if the Guardians who had ambushed him and knifed him had ever once realized he was Andy.

Had they known that he was Andy, or had they simply known that he was a Royal wearing a purple silk jacket? Had they stabbed *him*, Andy, or had they only stabbed the jacket and the title, and what good was the title if you were dying?

I'm Andy, he screamed wordlessly. *I'm Andy!*

An old lady stopped at the other end of the alley. The garbage cans were stacked there, beating noisily in the rain. The old lady carried an umbrella with broken ribs, carried it with all the dignity of a queen. She stepped into the mouth of the alley, a shopping bag over one arm. She lifted the lids of the garbage cans delicately, and she did not hear Andy grunt because she was a little deaf and because the rain was beating a steady relentless tattoo on the cans. She had been searching and foraging for the better part of the night. She collected her string and her newspapers, and an old hat with a feather on it from one of the garbage cans, and a broken footstool from another of the cans. And then she delicately replaced the lids and lifted her umbrella high and walked out of the alley mouth with queenly dignity. She had worked swiftly and soundlessly, and now she was gone.

The alley looked very long now. He could see people passing at the other end of it, and he wondered who the people were, and he wondered if he would ever get to know them, wondered who it was on the Guardians who had stabbed him, who had plunged the knife into his body.

"That's for you, Royal!" the voice had said, and then the footsteps, his arms being released by the others, the fall to the pavement. "That's for you, Royal!" Even in his pain, even as he collapsed, there had been some sort of pride in knowing he was a Royal. Now there was no pride at all. With the rain beginning to chill him, with the blood pouring steadily between his fingers, he knew only a sort of dizziness, and within the giddy dizziness, he could only think: *I want to be Andy.*

It was not very much to ask of the world.

He watched the world passing at the other end of the alley. The world didn't know he was Andy. The world didn't know he was alive. He wanted to say, "Hey, I'm alive! Hey, look at me! I'm alive! Don't you know I'm alive? Don't you know I exist?"

He felt weak and very tired. He felt alone and wet and feverish and chilled, and he knew he was going to die now, and the knowledge made him suddenly sad. He was not frightened. For some reason, he was not frightened. He was only filled with an overwhelming sadness that his life would be over at sixteen. He felt all at once as if he had never done anything, never seen anything, never been anywhere. There were so many things to do, and he wondered why he'd never thought of them before, wondered why the rumbles and the dances and the purple jacket had always seemed so important to him before, and now they seemed like such small things in a world he was missing, a world that was rushing past at the other end of the alley.

I don't want to die, he thought. *I haven't lived yet.*

It seemed very important to him that he take off the purple jacket. He was very close to dying, and when they found him, he did not want them to say, "Oh, it's a Royal." With great effort, he rolled over onto his back. He felt the pain tearing at his stomach when he moved, a pain he did not think was possible. But he wanted to take off the jacket. If he never did another thing, he wanted to take off the jacket. The jacket had only one meaning now, and that was a very simple meaning.

If he had not been wearing the jacket, he would not have been stabbed. The knife had not been plunged in hatred of Andy. The knife hated only the purple jacket. The jacket was a stupid meaningless thing that was robbing him of his life. He wanted the jacket off his back. With an enormous loathing, he wanted the jacket off his back.

He lay struggling with the shiny wet material. His arms were heavy, and pain ripped fire across his body whenever he moved. But he squirmed and fought and twisted until one arm was free and then the other, and then he rolled away from the jacket and lay quite still, breathing heavily, listening to the sound of his breathing and the sound of the rain and thinking: *Rain is sweet, I'm Andy.*

She found him in the alleyway a minute past midnight. She left the dance to look for him, and when she found him she knelt beside him and said, "Andy, it's me, Laura."

He did not answer her. She backed away from him, tears springing into her eyes, and then she ran from the alley hysterically and did not stop running until she found the cop.

And now, standing with the cop, she looked down at him, and the cop rose and said, "He's dead," and all the crying was out of her now. She stood in the rain and said nothing, looking at the dead boy on the pavement, and looking at the purple jacket that rested a foot away from his body.

The cop picked up the jacket and turned it over in his hands.

"A Royal, huh?" he said.

The rain seemed to beat more steadily now, more fiercely.

She looked at the cop and, very quietly, she said, "His name is Andy."

The cop slung the jacket over his arm. He took out his black pad, and he flipped it open to a blank page.

"A Royal," he said.

Then he began writing.

1. RESPONDING TO THE STORY

a. Why don't any of the people who find Andy help him?

b. Why did Andy join a gang? With a partner, discuss Andy's reasons and whether or not they make sense to you.

c. Why does Andy take off his jacket?

d. What conclusions can you draw from the police officer's comment at the end of the story?

STRATEGIES

2. WRITING CREATE A NEWSPAPER ARTICLE

Write a short newspaper article reporting on the events surrounding Andy's death. Write quotes for the characters who came into contact with Andy. What do you think they will say about why they didn't help Andy?

Remember that newspaper articles are usually short, factual reports about people and events. Most articles are written in the inverted pyramid style. This means that each paragraph arranges information in order of significance. It also stands on its own and does not depend on the next paragraph to explain it. You could read newspaper articles to help you become familiar with styles. Here are a few suggestions to help you with your article:

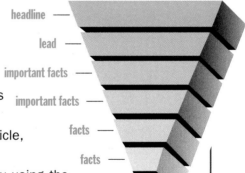

- Begin with the most interesting and important details. This is called the lead, and it should answer the questions *who, what, when,* and *where.*
- Put other important facts next in the article, and answer the *why* and *how* questions.
- Bring the article to life for the reader by using the dialogue from the story to develop your quotations.
- Write a catchy, short headline that suits the article.

SELF-ASSESSMENT: Read over your article and ask yourself these questions. Is the lead clear? Have I included the important facts? Will the reader understand my article?

The Road Not Taken
Poem by Robert Frost

Two roads diverged in a yellow wood,
And sorry I could not travel both
And be one traveller, long I stood
And looked down one as far as I could
To where it bent in the undergrowth;

Then took the other, as just as fair,
And having perhaps the better claim,
Because it was grassy and wanted wear;
Though as for that the passing there
Had worn them really about the same,

And both that morning equally lay
In leaves no step had trodden black.
Oh, I kept the first for another day!
Yet knowing how way leads on to way,
I doubted if I should ever come back.

I shall be telling this with a sigh
Somewhere ages and ages hence:
Two roads diverged in a wood, and I —
I took the one less travelled by,
And that has made all the difference.

GOALS AT A GLANCE

- Use a symbol to create meaning.
- Analyse a poem.

1. RESPONDING TO THE POEM

a. Does the speaker feel that he has made the wrong choice in taking the road "less travelled by"? If not, why does he sigh?

b. Why does the choice between two roads that seem so alike make such a big difference many years later?

c. What do the two roads in the poem represent?

2. LITERATURE STUDIES ANALYSING SYMBOLISM

Read the definition of **symbol** on this page. With a partner, discuss the symbol the author has used in the poem to create meaning. Was the symbol effective? Was its meaning clear? Discuss other symbols from poems or stories you have read recently.

> A **symbol** is a place, person, thing, or event that is used to represent something else. For example, a rainbow is often used as a symbol of hope.

Borders

Have you ever stood up for something you believe in? A brave and proud woman takes a different path at the…

Short Story by Thomas King

When I was maybe thirteen, my mother announced that we were going to go to Salt Lake City to visit my sister who had left the reserve, moved across the line, and found a job. Laetitia had not left home with my mother's blessing, but over time my mother had come to be proud of the fact that Laetitia had done all of this on her own.

"She did really good," my mother would say.

Then there were the fine points to Laetitia's going. She had not, as my mother liked to tell Mrs. Manyfingers, gone floating after some man like a balloon on a string. She hadn't snuck out of the house, either, and gone to Vancouver or Edmonton or Toronto to chase rainbows down alleys.

"She did real good."

I was seven or eight when Laetitia left home. She was seventeen. Our father was from Rocky Boy on the American side.

"Dad's American," Laetitia told my mother, "so I can go and come as I please."

"Send us a postcard."

Laetitia packed her things, and we headed for the border. Just outside of Milk River, Laetitia told us to watch for the water tower.

"Over the next rise. It's the first thing you see."

"We got a water tower on the reserve," my mother said. "There's a big one in Lethbridge, too."

"You'll be able to see the tops of the flagpoles, too. That's where the border is."

When we got to Coutts, my mother stopped at the convenience store and bought her and Laetitia a cup of coffee. I got an Orange Crush.

◆ ◆ ◆

"This is real lousy coffee."

"You're just angry because I want to see the world."

"It's the water. From here on down, they got lousy water."

"I can catch the bus from Sweetgrass. You don't have to lift a finger."

"You're going to have to buy your water in bottles if you want good coffee."

There was an old wooden building about a block away, with a tall sign in the yard that said "Museum." Most of the roof had been blown away. Mom told me to go and see when the place was open. There were boards over the windows and doors. You could tell that the place was closed, and I told Mom so, but she said to go and check anyway. Mom and Laetitia stayed by the car. Neither one of them moved. I sat down on the steps of the museum and watched them, and I don't know that they ever said anything to each other. Finally, Laetitia got her bag out of the trunk and gave Mom a hug.

I wandered back to the car. The wind had come up, and it blew Laetitia's hair across her face. Mom reached out and pulled the strands out of Laetitia's eyes, and Laetitia let her.

"You can still see the mountain from here," my mother told Laetitia in Blackfoot.

"Lots of mountains in Salt Lake," Laetitia told her in English.

"The place is closed," I said. "Just like I told you."

Laetitia tucked her hair into her jacket and dragged her bag down the road to the brick building with the American flag flapping on a pole. When she got to where the guards were waiting, she turned, put the bag down, and waved to us. We waved back. Then my mother turned the car around, and we came home.

We got postcards from Laetitia regular, and, if she wasn't spreading jelly on the truth, she was happy. She found a good job and rented an apartment with a pool.

"And she can't even swim," my mother told Mrs. Manyfingers.

◆ ◆ ◆

Most of the postcards said we should come down and see the city, but whenever I mentioned this, my mother would stiffen up.

So I was surprised when she bought two new tires for the car and put on her blue dress with the green and yellow flowers. I had to dress up, too, for my mother did not want us crossing the border looking like slobs. We made sandwiches and put them in a big box with pop and potato chips and some apples and bananas and a big jar of water.

"But we can stop at one of those restaurants, too, right?"

"We maybe should take some blankets in case you get sleepy."

"But we can stop at one of those restaurants, too, right?"

The border was actually two towns, though neither one was big enough to amount to anything. Coutts was on the Canadian side and consisted of the convenience store and gas station, the museum that was closed and boarded up, and a motel. Sweetgrass was on the American side, but all you could see was an overpass that arched across the highway and disappeared into the prairies. Just hearing the names of these towns, you would expect that Sweetgrass, which is a nice name and sounds like it is related to other places such as Medicine Hat and Moose Jaw and Kicking Horse Pass, would be on the Canadian side, and that Coutts, which sounds abrupt and rude, would be on the American side. But this was not the case.

Between the two borders was a duty-free shop where you could buy cigarettes and liquor and flags. Stuff like that.

We left the reserve in the morning and drove until we got to Coutts.

"Last time we stopped here," my mother said, "you had an Orange Crush. You remember that?"

"Sure," I said. "That was when Laetitia took off."

"You want another Orange Crush?"

"That means we're not going to stop at a restaurant, right?"

◆ ◆ ◆

My mother got a coffee at the convenience store, and we stood around and watched the prairies move in the sunlight. Then we climbed back in the car. My mother straightened the dress across her thighs, leaned against the wheel, and drove all the way to the border in first gear, slowly, as if she were trying to see through a bad storm or riding high on black ice.

The border guard was an old guy. As he walked to the car, he swayed from side to side, his feet set wide apart, the holster on his hip pitching up and down. He leaned into the window, looked into the back seat, and looked at my mother and me.

"Morning, ma'am."

"Good morning."

"Where you heading?"

"Salt Lake City."

"Purpose of your visit?"

"Visit my daughter."

"Citizenship?"

"Blackfoot," my mother told him.

"Ma'am?"

"Blackfoot," my mother repeated.

"Canadian?"

"Blackfoot."

It would have been easier if my mother had just said "Canadian" and been done with it, but I could see she wasn't going to do that. The guard wasn't angry or anything. He smiled and looked towards the building. Then he turned back and nodded.

"Morning, ma'am."

"Good morning."

"Any firearms or tobacco?"

"No."

"Citizenship?"

"Blackfoot."

He told us to sit in the car and wait, and we did. In about five minutes, another guard came out with the first man. They were talking as they came, both men swaying back and forth like two cowhands headed for a bar or a gunfight.

"Morning, ma'am."

"Good morning."

"Cecil tells me you and the boy are Blackfoot."

"That's right."

"Now, I know that we got Blackfeet on the American side and the

Canadians got Blackfeet on their side. Just so we can keep our records straight, what side do you come from?"

I knew exactly what my mother was going to say, and I could have told them if they had asked me.

"Canadian side or American side?" asked the guard.

"Blackfoot side," she said.

It didn't take them long to lose their sense of humour, I can tell you that. The one guard stopped smiling altogether and told us to park our car at the side of the building and come in.

We sat on a wood bench for about an hour before anyone came over to talk to us. This time it was a woman. She had a gun, too.

"Hi," she said. "I'm Inspector Pratt. I understand there is a little misunderstanding."

"I'm going to visit my daughter in Salt Lake City," my mother told her. "We don't have any guns or beer."

"It's a legal technicality, that's all."

"My daughter's Blackfoot, too."

The woman opened a briefcase and took out a couple of forms and began to write on one of them. "Everyone who crosses our border has to declare their citizenship. Even Americans. It helps us keep track of the visitors we get from the various countries."

She went on like that for maybe fifteen minutes, and a lot of the stuff she told us was interesting.

"I can understand how you feel about having to tell us your citizenship, and here's what I'll do. You tell me, and I won't put it down on the form. No one will know but you and me."

Her gun was silver. There were several chips in the wood handle and the name "Stella" was scratched into the metal butt.

We were in the border office for about four hours, and we talked to almost everyone there. One of the men bought me a Coke. My mother brought a couple of sandwiches in from the car. I offered part of mine to Stella, but she said she wasn't hungry.

I told Stella that we were Blackfoot and Canadian, but she said that didn't count because I was a minor. In the end, she told us that if my mother didn't declare her citizenship, we would have to go back to where we came from. My mother stood up and thanked Stella for her time. Then we got back in the car and drove to the Canadian border, which was only about ninety metres away.

I was disappointed. I hadn't seen Laetitia for a long time, and I had never been to Salt Lake City.

◆ ◆ ◆

When she was still at home, Laetitia would go on and on about Salt Lake City. She had never been there, but her boyfriend Lester Tallbull had spent a year in Salt Lake at a technical school.

"It's a great place," Lester would say. "Nothing but blondes in the whole state."

Whenever he said that, Laetitia would slug him on his shoulder hard enough to make him flinch. He had some brochures on Salt Lake and some maps, and every so often the two of them would spread them out on the table.

"That's the temple. It's right downtown. You got to have a pass to get in."

"Charlotte says anyone can go in and look around."

"When was Charlotte in Salt Lake? Just when was Charlotte in Salt Lake?"

"Last year."

"This is Liberty Park. It's got a zoo. There's good skiing in the mountains."

"Got all the skiing we can use," my mother would say. "People come from all over the world to ski at Banff. Cardston's got a temple, if you like those kinds of things."

"Oh, this one is real big," Lester would say. "They got armed guards and everything."

"Not what Charlotte says."

"What does she know?"

Lester and Laetitia broke up, but I guess the idea of Salt Lake stuck in her mind.

◆ ◆ ◆

The Canadian border guard was a young woman, and she seemed happy to see us. "Hi," she said. "You folks sure have a great day for a trip. Where are you coming from?"

"Stand-off."

"Is that in Montana?"

"No."

"Where are you going?"

"Stand-off."

The woman's name was Carol and I don't guess she was any older than Laetitia. "Wow, you both Canadians?"

"Blackfoot."

"Really? I have a friend I went to school with who is Blackfoot. Do you know Mike Harley?"

ALL THAT I AM • 51

"No."

"He went to school in Lethbridge, but he's really from Browning."

It was a nice conversation and there were no cars behind us, so there was no rush.

"You're not bringing any liquor back, are you?"

"No."

"Any cigarettes or plants or stuff like that?"

"No."

"Citizenship?"

"Blackfoot."

"I know," said the woman, "and I'd be proud of being Blackfoot if I were Blackfoot. But you have to be American or Canadian."

◆ ◆ ◆

When Laetitia and Lester broke up, Lester took his brochures and maps with him, so Laetitia wrote to someone in Salt Lake City, and, about a month later, she got a big envelope of stuff. We sat at the table and opened up all the brochures, and Laetitia read each one out loud.

"Salt Lake City is the gateway to some of the world's most magnificent skiing.

"Salt Lake City is the home of one of the newest professional basketball franchises, the Utah Jazz.

"The Great Salt Lake is one of the natural wonders of the world."

It was kind of exciting seeing all those colour brochures on the table and listening to Laetitia read all about how Salt Lake City was one of the best places in the entire world.

"That Salt Lake City place sounds too good to be true," my mother told her.

"It has everything."

"We got everything right here."

"It's boring here."

"People in Salt Lake City are probably sending away for brochures of Calgary and Lethbridge and Pincher Creek right now."

In the end, my mother would say that maybe Laetitia should go to Salt Lake City, and Laetitia would say that maybe she would.

◆ ◆ ◆

We parked the car to the side of the building and Carol led us into a small room on the second floor. I found a comfortable spot on the couch and flipped through some back issues of *Saturday Night* and *Alberta Report*.

When I woke up, my mother was just coming out of another office. She didn't say a word to me. I followed her down the stairs and out to the car.

I thought we were going home, but she turned the car around and drove back towards the American border, which made me think we were going to visit Laetitia in Salt Lake City after all. Instead she pulled into the parking lot of the duty-free store and stopped.

"We going to see Laetitia?"

"No."

"We going home?"

Pride is a good thing to have, you know. Laetitia had a lot of pride, and so did my mother. I figured that someday, I'd have it, too.

"So where are we going?"

Most of that day, we wandered around the duty-free store, which wasn't very large. The manager had a name tag with a tiny American flag on one side and a tiny Canadian flag on the other. His name was Mel. Toward evening, he began suggesting that we should be on our way. I told him we had nowhere to go, that neither the Americans nor the Canadians would let us in. He laughed at that and told us that we should buy something or leave.

The car was not very comfortable, but we did have all that food and it was April, so even if it did snow as it sometimes does on the prairies, we wouldn't freeze. The next morning my mother drove to the American border.

It was a different guard this time, but the questions were the same. We didn't spend as much time in the office as we had the day before. By noon, we were back at the Canadian border. By two we were back in the duty-free shop parking lot.

The second night in the car was not as much fun as the first, but my mother seemed in good spirits, and, all in all, it was as much an adventure as an inconvenience. There wasn't much food left and that was a problem, but we had lots of water as there was a faucet in the side of the duty-free shop.

◆ ◆ ◆

One Sunday, Laetitia and I were watching television. Mom was over at Mrs. Manyfingers's. Right in the middle of the program, Laetitia turned off the set and said she was going to Salt Lake City, that life around here was too boring. I had wanted to see the rest of the program and really didn't care if Laetitia went to Salt Lake City or not. When Mom got home, I told her what Laetitia had said.

What surprised me was how angry Laetitia got when she found out that I had told Mom.

"You got a big mouth."

"That's what you said."

"What I said is none of your business."

"I didn't say anything."

"Well, I'm going for sure, now."

That weekend, Laetitia packed her bags, and we drove her to the border.

◆ ◆ ◆

Mel turned out to be friendly. When he closed up for the night and found us still parked in the lot, he came over and asked us if our car was broken down or something. My mother thanked him for his concern and told him that we were fine, that things would get straightened out in the morning.

"You're kidding," said Mel. "You'd think they could handle the simple things."

"We got some apples and a banana," I said, "but we're all out of ham sandwiches."

"You know, you read about these things, but you just don't believe it. You just don't believe it."

"Hamburgers would be even better because they got more stuff for energy."

My mother slept in the back seat. I slept in the front because I was smaller and could lie under the steering wheel. Late that night, I heard my mother open the car door. I found her sitting on her blanket leaning against the bumper of the car.

"You see all those stars," she said. "When I was a little girl, my grandmother used to take me and my sisters out on the prairies and tell us stories about all the stars."

"Do you think Mel is going to bring us any hamburgers?"

"Every one of those stars has a story. You see that bunch of stars over there that look like a fish?"

"He didn't say no."

"Coyote went fishing, one day. That's how it all started." We sat out under the stars that night, and my mother told me all sorts of stories. She was serious about it, too. She'd tell them slow, repeating parts as she went, as if she expected me to remember each one.

Early the next morning, the television vans began to arrive, and guys in suits and women in dresses came trotting over to us, dragging microphones and cameras and lights behind them. One of the vans had a table set up with orange juice and sandwiches and fruit. It was for the crew, but when I told them we hadn't eaten for a while, a really skinny blonde woman told us we could eat as much as we wanted.

They mostly talked to my mother. Every so often one of the reporters would come over and ask me questions about how it felt to be without a country. I told them we had a nice house on the reserve and that my cousins had a couple of horses we rode when we went fishing. Some of the television people went over to the American border, and then they went to the Canadian border.

Around noon, a good-looking guy in a dark blue suit and an orange tie with little ducks on it drove up in a fancy car. He talked to my mother for a while, and, after they were done talking, my mother called me over, and we got into our car. Just as my mother started the engine, Mel came over and gave us a bag of peanut brittle and told us that justice was a hard thing to get, but that we shouldn't give up.

I would have preferred lemon drops, but it was nice of Mel anyway.

"Where are we going now?"

"Going to visit Laetitia."

The guard who came out to our car was all smiles. The television lights were so bright they hurt my eyes, and, if you tried to look through the windshield in certain directions, you couldn't see a thing.

"Morning, ma'am."

"Good morning."

"Where you heading?"

"Salt Lake City."

"Purpose of your visit?"

"Visit my daughter."

"Any tobacco, liquor, or firearms?"

"Don't smoke."

"Any plants or fruit?"

"Not any more."

"Citizenship?"

"Blackfoot."

The guard rocked back on his heels and jammed his thumbs into his gun belt. "Thank you," he said, his fingers patting the butt of the revolver. "Have a pleasant trip."

My mother rolled the car forward, and the television people had to scramble out of the way. They ran alongside the car as we pulled away from the border, and, when they couldn't run any farther, they stood in the middle of the highway and waved and waved and waved.

We got to Salt Lake City the next day. Laetitia was happy to see us, and, that first night, she took us out to a restaurant that made really good soups. The list of pies took up a whole page. I had cherry. Mom had chocolate. Laetitia said that she saw us on television the night before and, during the meal, she had us tell her the story over and over again.

Laetitia took us everywhere. We went to a fancy ski resort. We went to the temple. We got to go shopping in a couple of large malls, but they weren't as large as the one in Edmonton, and Mom said so.

After a week or so, I got bored and wasn't at all sad when my mother said we should be heading back home. Laetitia wanted us to stay longer, but Mom said no, that she had things to do back home and that, next time, Laetitia should come up and visit. Laetitia said she was thinking about moving back, and Mom told her to do as she pleased, and Laetitia said that she would.

On the way home, we stopped at the duty-free shop, and my mother gave Mel a green hat that said "Salt Lake" across the front. Mel was a funny guy. He took the hat and blew his nose and told my mother that she was an inspiration to us all. He gave us some more peanut brittle and came out into the parking lot and waved at us all the way to the Canadian border.

◆ ◆ ◆

It was almost evening when we left Coutts. I watched the border through the rear window until all you could see were the tops of the flagpoles and the blue water tower, and then they rolled over a hill and disappeared.

----

1. RESPONDING TO THE STORY

a. Why is not stating her nationality such an important issue for Laetitia's mother?

b. Do you think the mother did the right thing in not telling the border guards what they wanted to hear? Explain fully.

2. ORAL LANGUAGE RETELL THE STORY

Thomas King tells part of the story in **flashback**. Flashbacks can help explain the plot to the reader. Discuss the events, and make notes about the flashbacks. Retell the story in chronological order. What difference do you think that makes to the story?

> A **flashback** describes an earlier event in a story.

3. WRITING DEVELOP CHARACTERS

Characterization is the way the author describes the characters. The mother in "Borders" could be described as a multidimensional character. King has presented her in a realistic way and there are many different aspects to her character. By the end of the story, readers may feel that they really know and understand her. Flat characters are much simpler. The author presents the character with only one or two traits.

- Develop a character sketch for the mother in the story. For each trait, provide at least one detail from the story that illustrates it. You might begin by thinking of adjectives that you feel describe her.
- Identify and describe at least one flat character in this story. What is the author's purpose in showing these characters in this way?

STRATEGIES

4. EDITOR'S DESK COMPLEX SENTENCES

In "Borders," Thomas King uses a variety of simple sentences and complex sentences. A story that is full of simple sentences tends to be choppy and annoying to read. Using different types of sentences helps to create variety and keeps the reader interested. For example:

> They ran alongside the car as we pulled away from the border, and, when they couldn't run any farther, they stood in the middle of the highway and waved and waved and waved.

When you edit your next written work, add variety by turning simple sentences into complex sentences so that you have a balance.

*People find comic strips interesting because they reflect real life in humorous ways. Do you identify with the character in **Zits?***

Comic Strip by **Jerry Scott** and **Jim Borgman**

GOALS AT A GLANCE

- Analyse the features of comic strips.
- Create a comic strip.

1. Responding to the Comic Strip

a. Comic strips, like any good joke, often have a punch line—something that makes us laugh. Which frames in the three comic strips contain the punch lines?

b. Which comic strip is your favourite? Explain.

✳ 2. Oral Language Discuss Comic Strips

Newspaper cartoon strips often deal with serious issues in a humorous way. Look in a newspaper or in a collection of comic strips to find examples of such cartoons. With a partner or in a small group, discuss how the cartoonists have created humour.

3. Visual Communication Create a Comic Strip

Create your own four-frame comic strip. Invent two or three characters. Give them a problem or situation to resolve, and then create a humorous solution. You might use a humorous event or situation from your own life.

- Practise drawing the characters in different situations.
- Try different bits of dialogue between the characters.
- Once you've developed your ideas, divide a piece of paper into four squares, draw your characters, and include your dialogue in dialogue balloons.

Peer-Assessment: Ask a classmate to review your final draft and give you feedback on what is and isn't working. How can you improve your comic strip?

HOW TO BOOST YOUR
STUDY SKILLS

Goals at a Glance
• Create work plans. • Use study strategies.

The study skills below can help take the stress out of schoolwork.

Manage Your Time
When a teacher announces an assignment or a test, what is your response?

1. Do you leap to work right away?
2. Do you wait until the last possible minute?

It might surprise you to learn that the first approach isn't necessarily better than the second. That's because working feverishly without a plan can be just as dangerous as putting work off until later.

Time management is one of the most useful study skills you can acquire. Planning how to use your time will make it easier to juggle schoolwork, extracurricular activities, and personal commitments.

Plan Your Assignments
So, what's the secret to making a plan? The first and most important step is to know what you're trying to achieve.

Ask yourself these questions:
• What is the assignment?
• Do I understand what I'm supposed to do?
• Who can help me if I don't?

Now you're ready to draft your plan. Here are the steps you might follow:

1. Mark the due date on a calendar, such as a school planner or agenda.
2. Break down the assignment into a series of smaller tasks.
3. Based on your experience, estimate how long each task will take. Record the key dates for completing each one.
4. Make a list of the resources you will need. Consider where you will find them and whether any special arrangements are necessary.
5. Create a checklist of tasks and key dates to keep you focussed.
6. Give yourself lots of time for each task, especially if you have to share resources with others. Build in some time for relaxation, too!

PROCESS

Note Taking

One of the most important parts of developing good study skills is the ability to take useful, complete notes. You should take notes, both in class and when you are reading textbooks and other sources. Here are a number of useful strategies to help you.

1. When taking information from other resources, record the title and author of the source and the page numbers of the information you find. You may find that you need to refer to the source later if you don't understand a piece of information in your notes.

2. Decide what is the main point the author is making, and summarize the information in your own words. Being able to summarize the information will help you to understand it.

3. Keep your notes short, clear, neat, and concise. This will make studying them at a later date much easier.

4. If you're taking notes from a teacher's lecture, use your own short forms, abbreviations, contractions, and symbols to help you write quickly. Make sure the shortcuts you use in your writing make sense and are clear.

5. Review your notes within a day or two of writing them. Reading your notes aloud to yourself is a very effective way of learning new information. It will also give you a chance to decide if your notes are complete.

NOTE TAKING

from "Undersea Science" by Thomas Potts, YES Mag (Spring 1998, Issue 9) pp. 8-10.

Summary

A magazine article about aquanauts and exploring the ocean floor using technology.

Aquarius-underwater laboratory
-sits on the ocean floor
-houses four scientists & two technicians
-only underwater lab from which scientists can live up to 10 days at time.

When a test is near, review your notes carefully. Use a highlighter to mark the most important parts, and don't be afraid to write notes on your notes.

Self-Assessment

Assessing whether you're on track is a valuable study skill. Ask yourself these questions:

❏ Am I following my plan?
❏ Do I need to change my plan in any way?
❏ Am I taking too long to do this? How much time is left?
❏ Will this help me complete the task at hand?
❏ Am I satisfied with my work?

PROCESS

Do you recall a time that it took courage to be yourself? It's hard when someone close to you plays one of the cruelest of games.

Kath and Mouse

Short Story by Janet McNaughton

Her name was Helen, but Kath called her Mouse from her very first day at our school. "What is that Mouse doing at our table?" Kath said loudly, so Helen would know she had already broken one of the most important rules. No one sat at Kath's table without an invitation. I expected her to skitter away, like anyone else would, but instead she looked up and smiled. She did look like a mouse, with mouse-brown hair and small, sharp features but that smile said, maybe you could like me. So I ignored Kath, slid past the others, and sat down.

"Hi," I said, "My name's Kevin."

Then everyone else sat down. Even Kath. I didn't look at her, but I could feel the anger steaming off her. That winter, I seemed to be the only one who knew how to do things Kath didn't want. I had a secret weapon though, I'm her twin brother. And that winter, it seemed to be my job to prove you didn't get vaporized or turned into a frog if you did something that made Kath angry.

"Ready for the big concert?" I asked Renee across from me. I was trying to make things normal. Renee rolled her eyes and the conversation took off. She played percussion in the school band. I played trumpet, but I wasn't serious about it. Piano is really my instrument. Kath played oboe. It's a hard instrument and even I had to admit she was starting to get good. It wasn't just natural talent either. She really worked at it, forty-five minutes every day. Not that anyone else knew. If anyone phoned while she was practising, we were supposed to say she was out.

Renee and I talked about the concert until things seemed pretty normal. I was just beginning to relax when Kath spoke.

"So, Helen, do you play an instrument?" She put such a sneer in her voice that everyone at the table fell silent, waiting to see how this new kid would react.

When Helen spoke, her voice was very quiet. "No," she said, "No instrument. I just sing."

Kath snorted. "Sing! No choir in this school. Guess you're out of luck." Kath stood up then, to signal that the eating part of lunch was over. Everyone else at the table picked up their trays, following her like robots. Everyone except me and Helen, who now reminded me of a mouse I'd had to take away from our cat once, wounded.

"You could probably play in band if you wanted," I said, "Even this late. Mrs. Cromwell is really nice."

Helen shook her head. "No. I talked it over with Mom after Dad left. Voice is good for someone who moves a lot. I guess we won't move much now that we're in Torbay. The instrument is free and it isn't hard to move." She smiled, as if this were an old joke. Then she lifted her chin. "Besides, I'm a very good singer." The pride in her voice made her sound completely different. I was so surprised, I just nodded.

I hoped Kath would leave Helen alone, but I was dreaming. She started on Helen's backpack in the school bus on the way home. It was pretty odd looking, made of heavy, faded cloth, like denim, only pink. A name, "Robyn," was written on the flap in ballpoint pen. Kath leaned over the seat to stare at it. I was sitting across the aisle from Helen.

"Who's Robyn, Mouse?" Kath asked.

Helen ducked her head like she'd been hit. "I don't know."

"Where'd you get the backpack then?"

Helen kept her head down. "At a garage sale," she said. "I like it," she added.

"Right," Kath said, "It's so...unique." Everyone laughed.

By the time we got off the bus, I was so mad I could hardly see straight. "Who made you the queen of the world?" I yelled at Kath in the driveway.

She didn't even bother to get angry. She just gave me a look that made me feel cold all over and said, "It doesn't matter, does it? I just am, so you better get used to it," and walked away.

I knew something was up in gym the next day the way Kath and her friends came out of the change room, giggling. Then Amanda asked Ms. Saro to help her find some goal gloves in the storage room. As soon as they disappeared, Kath shot a soccer ball at Helen, hard. Helen dodged as Jen opened the gym door behind her. The ball flew out. "Oops," Jen said. "I think I'll help look for those goal gloves."

Helen stood near the open door.

"Go get the ball, you klutz," Kath ordered. "It's getting cold in here." I was standing across the gym, by the boys' change room. Helen hesitated, then did what Kath said. As soon as she stepped outside, another of Kath's friends closed the door. It was about ten below zero. Everyone else saw what happened. Nobody did anything. It only took half a minute for me to jog across the gym and open the door, but Helen was already shivering. I took the ball from her and hurried her inside.

I slammed the soccer ball down and kicked it so hard it flew all the way across the gym. "One more trick like that," I yelled at Kath, "And I tell. I mean it."

"Kevin, you're such a baby," Kath said. "We're just having fun." But I thought she looked worried.

After that, Kath was more careful. She had classes with Helen that I wasn't in. She knew she could do what she wanted, and no one would tell me. And it occurred to me that Kath might be mean to Helen just to bother me, so I backed off. I couldn't spend my life keeping track of Kath. Anyway, I had a piano conservatory exam coming up. It was nice to be able to just sit and play. The music was hard, but it was never mean.

Maybe Kath thought she could be queen of the school forever, but she made a mistake. Kath made fun of a girl named Christine, just once. More specifically, her ears. Christine was a good athlete, and popular. She started having parties. Sleepovers, horror movie parties, even dances. Kath was never invited. Christine wasn't mean, she just acted like Kath didn't exist. Kath tried to pretend it didn't matter, but it did. I knew when she came to me one Saturday night and said, "Dad will drive us into St. John's. Do you want to see a movie?"

"Aren't you afraid someone will see us together?" I teased.

She shrugged. "Everyone else was invited to Christine's."

That was truer than she knew. I'd been invited myself. But I didn't go and I didn't tell Kath. She was still my sister. "Let's go," I said, "But I pick the movie."

The next week, posters went up for a talent show to raise money for new library books. Overnight, our school changed. Suddenly, the halls were full of step dancers, clumsy jugglers, bad magic acts—everyone had a hidden talent, mostly ones they should have kept hidden. I thought about playing something from the conservatory exam, but it wasn't going to be that sort of night. I was pretty surprised when Helen came to me. I'd almost forgotten about her by then.

"You play piano, right?" she asked.

"Yeah, I do."

"Could you play this?" she showed me sheet music for "My Heart Will Go On," from *Titanic*. I almost told her nobody wanted to hear an old song like that, but then I thought, sheet music is expensive. So I opened it up instead. It looked medium hard.

"You want to sing at the talent show?" Helen bit her lip, but she nodded.

"Give me a week to practise. Then we'll try it together, okay?"

Her smile changed her face completely. "Thank you," she said, "That would be great," and she was gone.

I'd never really listened to the song, but the more I played the music, the more I liked it.

"That's a switch," Kath said when she heard me one night. "I thought that piano only played Bach."

"Ha ha," I said. "If you'll excuse me," and I started to play again, loudly, so she couldn't ask questions.

Helen found a church basement where we could practise without anybody knowing. The piano was badly out of tune. Helen's voice was thin and nervous. We sounded awful.

"It's pretty good," I told her.

Her look told me she knew how bad we were. "Maybe I should sit down," she said. "My knees are knocking."

She sounded better, but the piano was still awful. "We should practise at my place," I told her.

She laughed. "Right, and afterwards, your sister could have me for supper. As the main course."

"I don't know why she's like that," I said.

Helen shook her head. "I don't either. I used to think maybe the girls picking on me were secretly miserable or something, but lately, I'm not so sure."

"You don't have to prove yourself, you know," I said.

"But maybe I want to. Let's try one more time."

That night after supper, Kath made an announcement. "I've decided to audition for the talent show," she said.

"Ladies and gentlemen, Kathryn Morris and her magic oboe."

"Funny Kevin, but I'm not playing the oboe. I'm going to sing."

She watched me carefully while she said this, so I willed myself not to react.

"Aren't you going to offer to accompany me?" she asked.

"No. I'm not."

"I thought I might try that song you've been playing."

"It's not available."

"Kevin, that's mean." Kath looked like she might cry. She wasn't used to hearing no. I felt bad, but I couldn't explain. I was afraid of what Kath might do to Helen.

When she finally realized I was serious, she turned away. "Be that way then. It's not as if I need you."

At the audition, everyone was edgy. Girls in strange costumes giggled while they worked through bad dance moves, guys with decks of cards walked around muttering to themselves. Helen looked pale. "Want to give it a run-through?" I nodded towards the piano.

She shook her head. "I'd rather wait."

I don't know when Kath slipped into the room. She was dressed in hippie clothes and carried our father's battered old acoustic guitar. When she saw me with Helen, she waved me over. "This is why you wouldn't play for me?"

I nodded.

"I thought you were just being mean."

"No, Kath," I said. "I wasn't being mean. Truce?"

"Okay, truce."

Then people started disappearing towards the stage. After an act was auditioned, kids could stay in the audience if they were quiet. Three acts waited in the wings ahead of time. Kath was three acts ahead of us, so I got to see her. She sang an old Bob Dylan song, "Blowing in the Wind," and played three-chord guitar. It wasn't very good. When she finished, the applause was limp. A few months before, Kath would have brought the house down with the exact same song.

Two acts later, it was our turn. Helen didn't look pale anymore. She looked green. As I put the music on the piano, she rushed off-stage. For a minute, I thought she'd bolted, but she came back with a stool to sit on. Out in the audience, I saw Kath. When she smiled, she looked like the sister I'd always wanted.

What happened next was magic. With the piano in tune, Helen didn't have to struggle. Her voice blended and soared with the music, and for the first time, I understood what a terrific singer she was. She did too. Halfway through the song, she stood up, walked to the edge of the stage and sang to the audience like she'd been there every day of her life. When the final chords died, there was a deep silence then long applause. "My goodness," Mrs. Cromwell said. "That was lovely."

When we came off-stage, Christine came over to slap Helen on the back. "You've got to sing at my party Saturday! Say you'll come."

Helen nodded shyly.

I had a feeling no one would ever call her Mouse again. I looked at Kath, sitting alone. Queen of nothing now. So I went and sat beside her.

---

1. RESPONDING TO THE STORY

a. What does it mean to play "cat and mouse"? Give an example from a personal experience or from a movie, book, or TV show you have seen.

b. In what way does Kath play a "cat and mouse" game with Helen?

c. What pun has the author used in the title? Why is it appropriate?

d. Explain the significance of the character Christine. Why did the author bring her into the story?

2. READING USING CONFLICT

Read the definition of **conflict** on this page.
Discuss how the author has used the conflict
between characters to create tension. Why is
conflict an important part of a story? How does
conflict create a tense, fast-paced story?
Discuss the types of conflict that exist in other
stories you have read recently.

> **Conflict** is created in a story
> in four classic ways: human
> against self; human against
> human; human against nature;
> human against society.

STRATEGIES

3. WRITER'S DESK CREATE A SEQUEL

What happens to Kath, Helen, and Kevin after the story ends? Continue the
story. Be sure that the details and events you relate are consistent with the
original story. Here are a few suggestions to help you write your own short
story sequel.

Developing an Idea

- Think about "Kath and Mouse." What do you think the characters have
  learned in the story? Try to predict what they will do next.
- Develop a plot idea. Does Kath continue to bully others around her?
- List the characters that you want to include.

Drafting

- Write an outline that describes the plot, setting, point of view,
  and the main conflict. Will you tell the story from Kath's or Helen's
  point of view, or as an outsider looking in on the situation?
- Using your outline as a guide, write your story. Think about an
  exciting way to start. Grab your reader's interest right at the start.
- What will the mood or tone of your story be—funny, serious, or realistic?
- Use dialogue between characters to move the plot along and to reveal
  character.

Revising

Read your story, and ask yourself the following questions:

- Does the plot make sense? Is it interesting to the reader?
- Have I remained true to the original story?
- Are the characters' actions believable?

4. STORY CRAFT NARRATIVE POINT OF VIEW

Point of view refers to who is telling a story. The point of view is often one of the most important elements in a story. Stories can either be told from the first or third person points of view. In first person point of view, *I* or *we* are used. In third person point of view, the pronouns *he, she,* and *they* are used throughout.

Discuss the point of view of "Kath and Mouse." Who is the narrator? Is this character the best choice to tell the story? How would the story be different if it were told from the point of view of one of the other characters? What's the purpose of telling the story through this particular point of view?

SELF-ASSESSMENT: In your notebook, jot down observations about how you participated in the discussion. Did you express your views clearly? Did you consider everyone else's view?

REFLECTING ON THE UNIT

SELF-ASSESSMENT: WRITING

As you worked on the activities in this unit, what did you learn about
- descriptive paragraphs?
- developing characters?
- using imagery?
- symbols?

What else would you like to learn about writing? Develop a list of three goals that you feel could help you improve your writing. Revisit the writing activities in the unit. Can they help you to achieve your goals?

VISUAL COMMUNICATION

The stories, poems, and essay in this unit all have something to say about the factors that help to shape who and what we are. Create a poster that illustrates the factors that have formed your identity.

WRITING AND ORAL LANGUAGE

Select a poem or story you have recently written. Edit and revise it. Record a reading of your revision. Make a cassette of your reading and give it to a friend or family member.

SHORT STORIES

"We did not
change as
we grew older;
we just became
more clearly
ourselves."
Lynn Hall

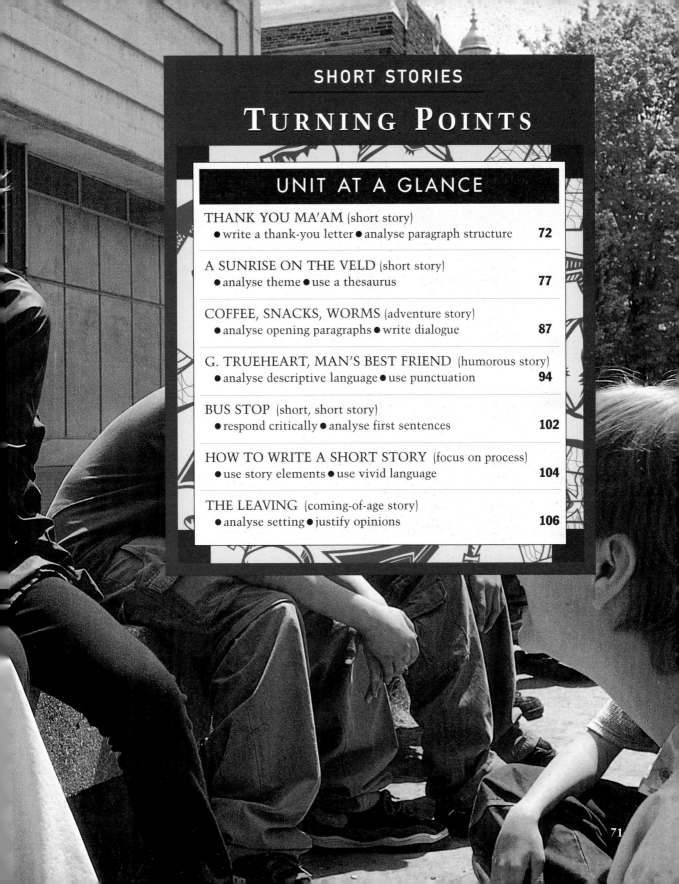

SHORT STORIES

TURNING POINTS

UNIT AT A GLANCE

When someone you don't know does a kind thing that ends up changing your life, perhaps it's enough to just say...

Thank You Ma'am

Short Story by Langston Hughes

S he was a large woman with a large purse that had everything in it but a hammer and nails. It had a long strap, and she carried it slung across her shoulder. It was about eleven o'clock at night, dark, and she was walking alone, when a boy ran up behind her and tried to snatch her purse. The strap broke with the sudden single tug the boy gave it from behind. But the boy's weight and the weight of the purse combined caused him to lose his balance. Instead of taking off full blast as he had hoped, the boy fell on his back on the sidewalk and his legs flew up. The large woman simply turned around and kicked him right square in his blue-jeaned sitter. Then she reached down, picked the boy up by his shirt front, and shook him until his teeth rattled.

After that the woman said, "Pick up my pocketbook, boy, and give it here."

She still held him tightly. But she bent down enough to permit him to stoop and pick up her purse. Then she said, "Now ain't you ashamed of yourself?"

Firmly gripped by his shirt front, the boy said, "Yes'm."

The woman said, "What did you want to do it for?"

The boy said, "I didn't aim to."

She said, "You a lie!"

By that time two or three people passed, stopped, turned to look, and some stood watching.

GOALS AT A GLANCE

- Write a thank-you letter.
- Analyse paragraph structure.

"If I turn you loose, will you run?" asked the woman.

"Yes'm," said the boy.

"Then I won't turn you loose," said the woman. She did not release him.

"Lady, I'm sorry," whispered the boy.

"Um-hmm! Your face is dirty. I got a great mind to wash your face for you. Ain't you got nobody home to tell you to wash your face?"

"No'm," said the boy.

"Then it will get washed this evening," said the large woman, starting up the street, dragging the frightened boy behind her.

He looked as if he were fourteen or fifteen, frail and willow-wild, in tennis shoes and blue jeans.

The woman said, "You ought to be my son. I would teach you right from wrong. Least I can do right now is to wash your face. Are you hungry?"

"No'm," said the being-dragged boy. "I just want you to turn me loose."

"Was I bothering you when I turned that corner?" asked the woman.

"No'm."

"But you put yourself in contact with *me,*" said the woman. "If you think that that contact is not going to last awhile, you got another thought coming. When I get through with you, sir, you are going to remember Mrs. Luella Bates Washington Jones."

Sweat popped out on the boy's face and he began to struggle. Mrs. Jones stopped, jerked him around in front of her, put a half nelson about his neck, and continued to drag him up the street. When she got to her door, she dragged the boy inside, down a hall, and into a large kitchenette-furnished room at the rear of the house. She switched on the light and left the door open. The boy could hear other roomers laughing and talking in the large house. Some of their doors were open, too, so he knew he and the woman were not alone. The woman still had him by the neck in the middle of her room.

She said, "What is your name?"

"Roger," answered the boy.

"Then, Roger, you go to that sink and wash your face," said the woman, whereupon she turned him loose—at last. Roger looked at the door—looked at the woman—looked at the door—*and went to the sink.*

"Let the water run until it gets warm," she said. "Here's a clean towel."

"You gonna take me to jail?" asked the boy, bending over the sink.

"Not with that face, I would not take you nowhere," said the woman. "Here I am trying to get home to cook me a bite to eat, and you snatch my pocketbook! Maybe you ain't been to your supper either, late as it be. Have you?"

"There's nobody home at my house," said the boy.

"Then we'll eat," said the woman. "I believe you're hungry—or been hungry—to try to snatch my pocketbook!"

"I want a pair of blue suede shoes," said the boy.

"Well, you didn't have to snatch *my* pocketbook to get some suede shoes," said Mrs. Luella Bates Washington Jones. "You could of asked me."

"Ma'am?"

The water dripping from his face, the boy looked at her. There was a long pause. A very long pause. After he had dried his face, and not knowing what else to do, dried it again, the boy turned around, wondering what next. The door was open. He could make a dash for it down the hall. He could run, run, run, *run!*

The woman was sitting on the daybed. After a while she said, "I were young once and I wanted things I could not get."

There was another long pause. The boy's mouth opened. Then he frowned, not knowing he frowned.

The woman said, "Um-hum! You thought I was going to say *but,* didn't you? You thought I was going to say, *but I didn't snatch people's pocketbooks.* Well, I wasn't going to say that." Pause. Silence. "I have done things, too, which I would not tell you, son—neither tell God, if He didn't already know. Everybody's got something in common. So you set down while I fix us something to eat. You might run that comb through your hair so you will look presentable."

In another corner of the room behind a screen was a gas plate and an icebox. Mrs. Jones got up and went behind the screen. The woman did not watch the boy to see if he was going to run now, nor did she watch her purse, which she left behind her on the daybed. But the boy took care to sit on the far side of the room, away from the purse, where he thought she could easily see him out of the corner of her eye if she wanted to. He did not trust the woman *not* to trust him. And he did not want to be mistrusted now.

"Do you need somebody to go to the store," asked the boy, "maybe to get some milk or something?"

"Don't believe I do," said the woman, "unless you just want sweet milk yourself. I was going to make cocoa out of this canned milk I got here."

"That will be fine," said the boy.

She heated some lima beans and ham she had in the icebox, made the cocoa, and set the table. The woman did not ask the boy anything about where he lived, or his folks, or anything else that would embarrass him. Instead, as they ate, she told him about her job in a hotel beauty shop that stayed open late, what the work was like, and how all kinds of women came in and out, blondes, redheads, and Spanish. Then she cut him a half of her ten-cent cake.

"Eat some more, son," she said.

When they were finished eating, she got up and said, "Now here, take this ten dollars and buy yourself some blue suede shoes. And next time, do not make the mistake of latching onto *my* pocketbook *nor nobody else's*— because shoes got by devilish ways will burn your feet. I got to get my rest now. But from here on in, son, I hope you will behave yourself."

She led him down the hall to the front door and opened it. "Good night! Behave yourself, boy!" she said, looking out into the street as he went down the steps.

The boy wanted to say something other than "Thank you, ma'am," to Mrs. Luella Bates Washington Jones, but although his lips moved, he couldn't even say that as he turned at the foot of the barren stoop and looked at the large woman in the door. Then she shut the door. ◆

1. RESPONDING TO THE STORY

a. The first sentence of the story suggests that the tone will be humorous. What other details in the story add to the humorous effect?

b. Despite the light tone, the story also deals with a serious subject. Which details in the story tell you that the purpose of the story is more serious?

c. Do you think that meeting Mrs. Jones will turn out to be a turning point in Roger's life? Explain.

d. What is the kindest thing that a stranger has ever done for you or someone you know?

2. WRITING CREATE A THANK-YOU LETTER

Write a thank-you letter to Mrs. Jones using the point of view or voice of Roger after several years have passed. In the letter, you should review the events and the effect her kindness had on Roger. Tell her about what has happened since. Remember that the focus of this unit is "turning points." Try to include some comments about how Mrs. Jones changed Roger's life.

3. LANGUAGE CONVENTIONS PARAGRAPH STRUCTURE

A paragraph is one or more related sentences about one main idea. A paragraph can also be *dialogue* (conversation between characters in a story). Story writers use a combination of narrative and dialogue paragraphs to tell the story. Reread "Thank You Ma'am" and examine the author's use of paragraphs. How are the narrative paragraphs used? How are the dialogue paragraphs used? Are they effective in helping you understand the story or keeping you interested? Do the dialogue paragraphs reveal information about the characters?

SELF-ASSESSMENT: Choose a piece of writing from your writing portfolio and analyse your use of paragraphs. How can you revise the paragraphs to make them more effective?

A Sunrise on the Veld

Short Story by Doris Lessing

Every night that winter he said aloud into the dark of the pillow: Half past four! Half past four! till he felt his brain had gripped the words and held them fast. Then he fell asleep at once, as if a shutter had fallen, and lay with his face turned to the clock so that he could see it first thing when he woke.

GOALS AT A GLANCE

■ Analyse theme.
■ Use a thesaurus.

77

It was half past four to the minute, every morning. Triumphantly pressing down the alarm knob of the clock, which the dark half of his mind had outwitted, remaining vigilant all night and counting the hours as he lay relaxed in sleep, he huddled down for a last warm moment under the clothes, playing with the idea of lying abed for this once only. But he played with it for the fun of knowing that it was a weakness he could defeat without effort; just as he set the alarm each night for the delight of the moment when he woke and stretched his limbs, feeling the muscles tighten, and thought: Even my brain—even that! I can control every part of myself.

Luxury of warm rested body, with the arms and legs and fingers waiting like soldiers for a word of command! Joy of knowing that the precious hours were given to sleep voluntarily!—for he had once stayed awake three nights running, to prove that he could, and then worked all day, refusing even to admit that he was tired; and now sleep seemed to him a servant to be commanded and refused.

The boy stretched his frame full-length, touching the wall at his head with his hands, and the bed foot with his toes; then he sprung out, like a fish leaping from water. And it was cold, cold.

He always dressed rapidly, so as to try and conserve his night-warmth till the sun rose two hours later; but by the time he had on his clothes his hands were numbed and he could scarcely hold his shoes. These he could not put on for fear of waking his parents, who never came to know how early he rose.

As soon as he stepped over the lintel, the flesh of his soles contracted on the chilled earth, and his legs began to ache with cold. It was night: the stars were glittering, the trees standing black and still. He looked for signs of day, for the greying of the edge of a stone, or a lightening in the sky where the sun would rise, but there was nothing yet. Alert as an animal he crept past the dangerous window, standing poised with his hand on the sill for one proudly fastidious moment, looking in at the stuffy blackness of the room where his parents lay.

Feeling for the grass-edge of the path with his toes, he reached inside another window further along the wall, where his gun had been set in readiness the night before. The steel was icy, and numbed fingers slipped along it, so that he had to hold it in the crook of his arm for safety. Then he tiptoed to the room where the dogs slept, and was fearful that they might have been tempted to go before him; but they were waiting, their haunches crouched in reluctance at the cold, but ears and swinging tails greeting the gun ecstatically. His warning undertone kept them secret and silent till the house was ninety metres back; then they bolted off into the bush, yelping excitedly. The boy imagined his parents turning in their beds and muttering: Those dogs again! before they were dragged back in sleep; and he smiled scornfully. He always looked back over his shoulder at the house before he passed a wall of trees that shut it from sight. It looked so low and small, crouching there under a tall and brilliant sky. Then he turned his back on it, and on the frowsting sleepers,* and forgot them.

He would have to hurry. Before the light grew strong he must be six kilometres away; and already a tint of green stood in the hollow of a leaf, and the air smelled of morning and the stars were dimming.

He slung the shoes over his shoulder, veld *skoen* that were crinkled and hard with the dews of a hundred mornings. They would be necessary when the ground became too hot to bear. Now he felt the chilled dust push up between his toes, and he let the muscles of his feet spread and settle into the shapes of the earth; and he thought: I could walk a hundred kilometres on feet like these! I could walk all day, and never tire!

He was walking swiftly through the dark tunnel of foliage that in daytime was a road. The dogs were invisibly ranging the lower travelways of the bush, and he heard them panting. Sometimes he felt a cold muzzle on his leg before they were off again, scouting for a trail to follow. They were not trained, but free-running companions of the hunt, who often tired of the long stalk before the final shots, and went off on their own pleasure. Soon he could see them, small and wild-looking in a wild strange light, now that the bush stood trembling on the verge of colour, waiting for the sun to paint earth and grass afresh.

The grass stood to his shoulders; and the trees were showering a faint silvery rain. He was soaked; his whole body was clenched in a steady shiver.

Once he bent to the road that was newly scored with animal trails, and regretfully straightened, reminding himself that the pleasure of tracking must wait till another day.

He began to run along the edge of a field, noting jerkily how it was filmed over with fresh spider web, so that the long reaches of great black clods seemed nettled in glistening grey. He was using the steady lope he had learned by watching the natives, the run that is a dropping of the weight of the body from one foot to the next in a slow balancing movement that never tires, nor shortens the breath; and he felt the blood pulsing down his legs and along his arms, and the exultation and pride of body mounted in him till he was shutting his teeth hard against a violent desire to shout his triumph.

Soon he had left the cultivated part of the farm. Behind him the bush

---

* **frowsting sleepers:** people sleeping in a stuffy room.

was low and black. In front was a long *vlei*, hectares of long pale grass that sent back a hollowing gleam of light to a satiny sky. Near him thick swathes of grass were bent with the weight of water, and diamond drops sparkled on each frond.

The first bird woke at his feet and at once a flock of them sprang into the air, calling shrilly that day had come; and suddenly, behind him, the bush woke into song, and he could hear the guinea fowl calling far ahead of him. That meant they would now be sailing down from their trees into thick grass, and it was for them he had come: he was too late. But he did not mind. He forgot he had come to shoot. He set his legs wide, and balanced from foot to foot, and swung his gun up and down in both hands horizontally, in a kind of improvised exercise, and let his head sink back till it was pillowed in his neck muscles, and watched how above him small rosy clouds floated in a lake of gold.

Suddenly it all rose in him; it was unbearable. He leapt up into the air, shouting and yelling wild, unrecognizable noises. Then he began to run, not carefully, as he had before, but madly, like a wild thing. He was clean crazy, yelling mad with the joy of living and a superfluity of youth. He rushed down the vlei under a tumult of crimson and gold, while all the birds of the world sang about him. He ran in great leaping strides, and shouted as he ran, feeling his body rise into the crisp rushing air and fall back surely onto sure feet; and thought briefly, not believing that such a thing could happen to him, that he could break his ankle any moment, in this thick tangled grass. He cleared bushes like a duiker,* leapt over rocks, and finally came to a dead stop at a place where the ground fell abruptly away below him to the river. It had been a three-kilometre-long dash through waist-high growth, and he was breathing hoarsely and could no longer sing. But he poised on a rock and looked down at stretches of water that gleamed through stooping trees, and thought suddenly: I am fifteen! Fifteen! The words came new to him, so that he kept repeating them wonderingly, with swelling excitement; and he felt the years of his life with his hands, as if he were counting marbles, each one hard and separate and compact, each one a wonderful shining thing. That was what he was: fifteen years of this rich soil, and this slow-moving water, and air that smelt like a challenge whether it was warm and sultry at noon, or as brisk as cold water, like it was now.

There was nothing he couldn't do, nothing! A vision came to him, as he stood there, like when a child hears the word *eternity* and tries to understand

---

* **duiker (dy-ker):** a kind of African antelope.

it, and time takes possession of the mind. He felt his life ahead of him as a great and wonderful thing, something that was his; and he said aloud, with the blood rising to his head: All the great people of the world have been as I am now, and there is nothing I can't become, nothing I can't do; there is no country in the world I cannot make part of myself, if I choose. I contain the world. I can make of it what I want. If I choose, I can change everything that is going to happen: it depends on me, and what I decide now.

The urgency and the truth and the courage of what his voice was saying exulted him so that he began to sing again, at the top of his voice, and the sound went echoing down the river gorge. He stopped for the echo, and sang again; stopped and shouted. That was what he was!—he sang, if he chose; and the world had to answer him.

And for minutes he stood there, shouting and singing and waiting for the lovely eddying sound of the echo; so that his own new strong thoughts came back and washed round his head, as if someone were answering him and encouraging him; till the gorge was full of soft voices clashing back and forth from rock to rock over the river. And then it seemed as if there was a new voice. He listened, puzzled, for it was not his own. Soon he was leaning forward, all his nerves alert, quite still: somewhere close to him there was a noise that was no joyful bird, nor tinkle of falling water, nor ponderous movement of cattle.

There it was again. In the deep morning hush that held his future and his past, was a sound of pain, and repeated over and over; it was a kind of shortened scream, as if someone, something, had no breath to scream. He came to himself, looked about him, and called for the dogs. They did not appear; they had gone off on their own business, and he was alone. Now he was clean sober, all the madness gone. His heart beating fast, because of that frightened screaming, he stepped carefully off the rock and went toward a belt of trees. He was moving cautiously, for not so long ago he had seen a leopard in just this spot.

At the edge of the trees he stopped and peered, holding his gun ready; he advanced, looking steadily about him, his eyes narrowed. Then, all at once, in the middle of a step, he faltered, and his face was puzzled. He shook his head impatiently, as if he doubted his own sight.

There, between two trees, against a background of gaunt black rocks, was a figure from a dream, a strange beast that was horned and drunken-legged, but like something he had never even imagined. It seemed to be ragged. It looked like a small buck that had black ragged tufts of fur standing up irregularly all over it, with patches of raw flesh beneath...but the patches of rawness were disappearing under moving black and came again elsewhere; and all the time the creature screamed, in small gasping screams, and leaped drunkenly from side to side, as if it were blind.

Then the boy understood: it *was* a buck. He ran closer, and again stood still, stopped by a new fear. Around him the grass was whispering and alive. He looked wildly about, and then down. The ground was black with ants, great energetic ants that took no notice of him, but hurried and scurried toward the fighting shape, like glistening black water flowing through the grass.

And, as he drew in his breath and pity and terror seized him, the beast fell and the screaming stopped. Now he could hear nothing but one bird singing, and the sound of the rustling, whispering ants.

He peered over at the writhing blackness that jerked convulsively with the jerking nerves. It grew quieter. There were small twitches from the mass that still looked vaguely like the shape of a small animal.

It came into his mind that he should shoot it and end its pain; and he raised the gun. Then he lowered it again. The buck could no longer feel; its fighting was a mechanical protest of the nerves. But it was not that which made him put down the gun. It was a swelling feeling of rage and misery and protest that expressed itself in the thought: If I had not come it would have died like this; so why should I interfere? All over the bush things like this happen; they happen all the time; this is how life goes on, by living things dying in anguish. He gripped the gun between his knees and felt in his own limbs the myriad swarming pain of the twitching animal that could no longer feel, and set his teeth, and said over and over again under his breath: I can't stop it. I can't stop it. There is nothing I can do.

He was glad that the buck was unconscious and had gone past suffering, so that he did not have to make a decision to kill it even when he was feeling with his whole body: This is what happens, this is how things work.

It was right—that was what he was feeling. *It was right and nothing could alter it.*

The knowledge of fatality, of what has to be, had gripped him for the first time in his life; and he was left unable to make any movement of brain or body, except to say: "Yes, yes. That is what living is." It had entered his flesh and his bones and grown into the furthest corners of his brain and would never leave him. And at that moment he could not have performed the smallest action of mercy, knowing as he did, having lived on it all his life, the vast, unalterable, cruel veld, where at any moment one might stumble over a skull or crush the skeleton of some small creature.

Suffering, sick, and angry, but also grimly satisfied with his new stoicism, he stood there leaning on his rifle, and watched the seething black mound grow smaller. At his feet, now, were ants trickling back with pink fragments in their mouths, and there was a fresh acid smell in his nostrils. He sternly controlled the uselessly convulsing muscles of his empty stomach, and reminded himself: The ants must eat too! At the same time he found that the tears were streaming down his face, and his clothes were soaked with the sweat of that other creature's pain.

The shape had grown small. Now it looked like nothing recognizable. He did not know how long it was before he saw the blackness thin, and bits of white showed through, shining in the sun—yes, there was the sun, just up, glowing over the rocks. Why, the whole thing could not have taken longer than a few minutes.

He began to swear, as if the shortness of the time was in itself unbearable, using the words he had heard his father say. He strode forward, crushing ants with each step, and brushing them off his clothes, till he stood above the skeleton, which lay sprawled under a small bush. It was clean-picked. It might have been lying there years, save that on the white bone were pink fragments of gristle. About the bones ants were ebbing away, their pincers full of meat.

The boy looked at them, big black ugly insects. A few were standing and gazing up at him with small glittering eyes.

"Go away!" he said to the ants, very coldly. "I am not for you—not just yet, at any rate. Go away." And he fancied that the aunts turned and went away.

He bent over the bones and touched the sockets in the skull; that was where his eyes were, he thought incredulously, remembering the liquid dark eyes of a buck. And then he bent the slim foreleg bone, swinging it horizontally in his palm.

That morning, perhaps an hour ago, this small creature had been stepping proud and free through the bush, feeling the chill on its hide even as he himself had done, exhilarated by it. Proudly stepping the earth, tossing its horns, frisking a pretty white tail, it had sniffed the cold morning air. Walking like kings and conquerors it had moved through this free-held bush, where each blade of grass grew for it alone, and where the river ran pure sparkling water for its slaking.

And then—what had happened? Such a swift, sure-footed thing could surely not be trapped by a swarm of ants?

The boy bent curiously to the skeleton. Then he saw that the back leg that lay uppermost and strained out in the tension of death, was snapped midway in the thigh, so that broken bones jutted over each other uselessly.

So that was it! Limping into the ant-masses it could not escape, once it had sensed the danger. Yes, but how had the leg been broken? Had it fallen, perhaps? Impossible, a buck was too light and graceful. Had some jealous rival horned it?

What could possibly have happened? Perhaps some Africans had thrown stones at it, as they do, trying to kill it for meat, and had broken its leg. Yes, that must be it.

Even as he imagined the crowd of running, shouting natives, and the flying stones, and the leaping buck, another picture came into his mind. He saw himself, on any one of these bright ringing mornings, drunk with excitement, taking a snapshot at some half-seen buck. He saw himself with the gun lowered, wondering whether he had missed or not, and thinking at

last that it was late, and he wanted his breakfast, and it was not worthwhile to track kilometres after an animal that would very likely get away from him in any case.

For a moment he would not face it. He was a small boy again, kicking sulkily at the skeleton, hanging his head, refusing to accept the responsibility.

Then he straightened up, and looked down at the bones with an odd expression of dismay, all the anger gone out of him. His mind went quite empty; all around him he could see trickles of ants disappearing into the grass. The whispering noise was faint and dry, like the rustling of a cast snakeskin.

At last he picked up his gun and walked homeward. He was telling himself half defiantly that he wanted his breakfast. He was telling himself that it was getting very hot, much too hot to be out roaming the bush.

Really, he was tired. He walked heavily, not looking where he put his feet. When he came within sight of his home he stopped, knitting his brows. There was something he had to think out. The death of that small animal was a thing that concerned him, and he was by no means finished with it. It lay at the back of his mind uncomfortably.

Soon, the very next morning, he would get clear of everybody and go to the bush and think about it.

1. RESPONDING TO THE STORY

a. Describe the boy's feelings and state of mind before he comes upon the buck. Describe a time in your life when you experienced a similar emotion.

b. Why does the boy not shoot the buck?

c. How does the boy feel at the end of the story? What has caused his mood to change so dramatically?

2. STORY CRAFT ANALYSE THE THEME

The *theme* of a story can be many things. It can be the central idea that unifies the story. It could be the purpose for which the story was written. It can also be what the narrator, **protagonist,** or reader discovers about life or about people by the end of the story. Discuss the theme of the story. What is the author's purpose? What is the author trying to communicate to the reader? What does the main character learn or discover at the end of the story? The next time you write a story, think about the theme, and ask yourself these questions:

> The **protagonist** is the main character in the story.

- What do I want the reader to know or learn?
- What is my purpose?
- How will I reveal the theme?

3. LITERATURE STUDIES POETIC LANGUAGE

The author expresses the boy's thoughts and feelings very poetically in the two paragraphs before the boy hears the buck's cries. With a partner, discuss some of these phrases and the images they create. What emotions do the images raise? Is the use of poetic language effective? What types of writing techniques are used?

Using phrases from these two paragraphs, write a poem that expresses the character's joy at being young and alive. You could draw or find an illustration that captures the spirit of your poem.

4. WRITING JOURNAL RESPONSE

The main character in "A Sunrise on the Veld" reaches a turning point and changes after his experience in the veld. In your journal, write about an event that in some way raised your awareness of some aspect of life. What was this event? How did it change you? Explain.

5. WORD CRAFT UNCOMMON WORDS

Reread the story and choose five words that are not commonly used. Try to figure out the meaning of each word from the other words surrounding it. Write a definition for each word, then check a dictionary to see if your definition is correct.

STRATEGIES

6. WRITER'S DESK USING THE THESAURUS

The author of "A Sunrise on the Veld" has a particular talent for description and poetic language. Relating colourful details using the perfect word helps create a special connection with your reader. Using a thesaurus can help you to find just the right word in your own writing.

Remember, however, that a thesaurus is not a book of *synonyms* (words with almost the same meaning), but rather a book on related concepts. Be very careful about the words you choose. Double-check the word in the dictionary to make sure it really means what you think it does.

SELF-ASSESSMENT: When you revise, re-evaluate your choice of word. Does the word really paint the best picture, or would a simpler word be more effective?

Coffee, Snacks, Worms

What would you do if you were threatened? One young woman turns the tables on a would-be thief.

Short Story by

Karleen Bradford

Stephanie took a step backwards, then stopped. She looked behind her and gasped in terror. The cliff edge crumbled beneath her feet, and far below her the sea crashed against the jagged, pointed rocks in an insane fury.

"No!" she cried.

But the terrible form of her pursuer advanced remorselessly. His hands reached out for her throat... She could feel his hot breath burning her cheeks... There was no escape...!

"Kate, you dodo! It's your stop. You're home!"

Kate came back to reality with a jolt and grabbed for her books. Flushing, she clambered over her seatmate and struggled along the aisle toward the bus door.

"Bye, Kate!"

"See you tomorrow, Kate!"

The cries followed her.

"Call me with the answers when you've finished the math homework!"

Kate gave Jeff Hodges a withering glance. The top math student in the class, he never missed an opportunity to embarrass Kate or put her down. Only that day he had made a fool of her by deliberately drawing the teacher's attention to her when he knew she wasn't listening.

"Daydreaming again, Kate?" Mrs. Richards had asked impatiently.

Daydreaming! She hadn't been daydreaming. She'd been plotting out a fabulous story. For some reason that seemed to annoy Jeff Hodges intensely.

Without bothering to answer him she fought her way through the bus and stepped off onto the road.

She stopped for a moment and looked at the buildings in front of her. Home. A crummy little garage and snack bar, sitting all alone like an unwelcome wart on the side of a dusty Ontario highway. Painted in broad, garish, vertical orange and white stripes. As if it didn't stick out enough already. A stack of useless-looking tires leaned against a drooping air hose that had stopped working months ago. A peeling, creaking sign in front of the snack bar read:

COFFEE

SNACKS

WORMS

Coffee, snacks, worms! That was her whole life? Her whole life had *been* coffee, snacks, worms. Her whole life was *going* to be coffee, snacks, worms. It was the most boring life in the whole world. This was the most boring place in the whole world. Nothing ever happened here. She hated it. With every fibre of her whole being, she hated every single orange and white stripe!

Heaving a sigh of anger and frustration, Kate slouched around the horrible building and slammed through the back door into her family's living quarters.

"Kate, I have to take Jimmy to the dentist and Jesse hasn't shown up." Her mother was waiting for her with an even more worried expression than usual on her face. "Could you take care of the snack bar for an hour or so by yourself? I hate to leave you alone. Your dad's not here, but he's shut the gas station down so you don't have to worry about that. Can you manage? It shouldn't be for long... Do you mind...?"

What difference did it make if she did. There was no one else. She'd have to take over.

"Sure, Mom," she muttered. Throwing her books down on the couch, she went on through into the snack bar.

There were only two customers there, both almost finished. Kate took their money, shrugged when neither one left a tip, and set to wiping up the tables after them. A trucker came in and asked for coffee. She gave it to him, hardly noticing what she was doing. A scruffy kid came in and asked for worms. Not bothering to hide the disgust on her face she went over to the worm refrigerator and took out a styrofoam tub containing dirt and fifteen guaranteed-fat worms. He and the trucker both left. She was alone again. Absentmindedly, she took up the dishcloth and began wiping the counter...

Stephanie pressed herself against the wall, straining against the ropes that tied her fast. The tunnel was pitch dark, but already she could feel the vibrations of the approaching train, hear its lonesome, wailing whistle. But, strain as she might, she knew that it was hopeless. There wasn't enough clearance between the wall and the train for a living, breathing body! Frantically, she twisted her hands, feeling the coarse rope cut into her flesh. She reached down to her shoulder and grabbed the rope that bound her there between her teeth. She ground her jaws together desperately...

"I've got a knife! Give me all the money in the cash register!"

Kate hadn't even heard the door open. She looked up incredulously. A thin, sick-looking boy was leaning on the counter, staring at her. A knife? He had a knife? It suddenly occurred to her that Stephanie had never been threatened with a knife. The time might come when she would be, and Kate didn't know anything about knives.

"What kind of a knife?" she asked.

"What do you mean, 'What kind of a knife?'" the boy echoed. "A big knife! With a very long, sharp blade! And I'm going to cut you with it if you don't give me all the money in that cash register right now!"

With a shock, Kate realized that he meant it. Then she took a closer look at him.

He doesn't look any older than I am, she thought. And he looks scared silly. I'll bet he doesn't have a knife. No way does he have a knife.

"Why?" she asked.

"Why what? Look—are you going to get that money, or am I going to have to cut you?" He still didn't make any move towards any knife.

"Why do you want the money?"

"Why?" he echoed again. "Because I'm starving, that's why. I haven't eaten in two days."

"Well, that's not very smart," Kate said, throwing the dishcloth back into the sink. The boy's mouth dropped open and he stared at her. "What I mean is… If you're really starving and you steal money from here that's not going to help you much. Like, you're hardly going to steal the money here, then order a sandwich or something and pay me for it, are you?"

The boy didn't seem able to answer.

"I mean. If you steal the money here, you're going to have to light out fast, right?" Then I'll call the police. Then, as far as I can see it, they'll either catch up with you and drag you into the police station—and you can be sure they won't feed you there—or if you do get away you'll have to hitchhike or something and get as far away from here as you can, as fast as you can. Either way, you're not going to get anything to eat, and you're still going to be hungry." As she spoke, Kate turned to the back counter and began slapping margarine onto slices of bread.

"What… What are you doing?"

"Making you a sandwich, turkey. You said you were starving, didn't you?" She tossed the sandwich onto a plate and pushed it over to him.

The boy stared at her.

"Go ahead. Eat it. It's not made of worms or anything." Kate stared back at him belligerently. "It's ham. Worms are for fish. Ham is for people."

The boy hesitated for a moment. He was standing, poised, as if ready for flight or attack but even he didn't know which. Then, as if of its own accord, his hand reached for the sandwich. Within seconds he was wolfing it down desperately.

"You weren't kidding about being hungry, were you?" Kate asked. She started to make another sandwich. Cheese this time. She set this in front of him, then filled up a mug with milk.

The boy didn't say a word, just sat down and gulped the food so fast he didn't seem to be chewing at all. Kate cut off a large slice of apple pie and slid that in front of him as well.

When he finished, the boy pushed himself back from the counter and looked up at Kate with slightly glazed eyes.

"You work here all the time?" he asked.

"My parents own the place," she answered shortly.

"They let you give away food like this?"

"No."

Times were even harder than usual lately, and Kate knew that her mother had every bit of food counted and measured. She'd answer for this.

"Who'll pay, then?" the boy asked.

"I will." She gathered up his dishes and almost threw them in the sink.

"But… How…?"

"It's okay. I've got money. I work Saturdays at the mall."

The boy stared at her in silence. Kate was beginning to feel uncomfortable.

"Have you ever done anything like this before?" she asked finally, gesturing towards the cash register. "I mean, you know, tried to hold up a place?"

"No." He sounded sheepish.

"Just as well. You're not very good at it."

"I guess not."

There was another awkward silence.

"What were you planning on doing? After you got the food?" Kate concentrated hard on scrubbing the already clean glass and plates.

"Hitching a ride west. I'm gonna try and find a job out there."

"I don't think you will," Kate said. "My brother Jesse has a friend went out a few months ago—he couldn't get a job anyhow and had to hitch his way back. He got home a week ago, tired, broke, and sick as a dog."

"Well," the boy protested angrily. "What else is there? What am I supposed to do?"

Kate abandoned the dishes. "You know anything about boats?" she asked.

"Boats! I should think so. Been brought up around the stinkin' things all my life. Don't know nothin' but boats!"

"And motors?"

"Sure. If you know boats, you know motors."

"Seems to me," Kate went on, "that a person who doesn't know anything but boats shouldn't be heading out west to the Prairies, of all places."

The boy started to answer, but she interrupted him. "Old Jed, up in town, he's starting to get his boats all ready for the tourist season and he was in here just the other day, saying he needs someone to help him. His place is right on Main Street, just by the river. There's a big sign there: 'Jed's Boats for Hire.' You couldn't miss it." She picked up the dishcloth out of the sink and started to wipe the counter again with it furiously. "We need worms, too. The guy who supplies us left town last week. You know how to pick worms?"

"Sure. Who doesn't?"

Who doesn't, indeed, Kate thought, her nose wrinkling automatically.

"Anyway," she went on, "there's work around here if you want it, I guess." She wiped her way down to the other end of the counter, her back to him.

"What about…About what I said when I came in…"

"Oh, that." Kate turned to face him. "Forget it. I didn't believe you anyway."

"I *could* work then. At least until I got enough to pay you back…"

Kate shrugged again. "Seems to me you might just as well," she said.

"Yeah. I guess I might."

He pulled himself off the stool and headed for the door, then stopped to stare back at her for a moment. There was a strange, unreadable look on his face, but all he said was, "Thanks." At the entrance he paused, took something out of his pocket, and threw it in the trash barrel.

Kate took a step backwards and felt for a chair. Her legs suddenly felt as if they were made of melting lead. She sank onto the chair as the door slammed shut. She'd only had a glimpse of the object as the boy had tossed it into the garbage, but that was enough.

He *had* had a knife!

For a moment she felt sick at the thought of what could have happened, then like an old familiar car clicking slowly into gear, her mind began working again…

Stephanie looked up, startled, as the snack bar door burst open. There, in front of her, stood a dishevelled, disreputable, totally terrifying figure. He swayed slightly, as if weak from disease or hunger, as he walked menacingly towards her, but she only had eyes for the gleaming, evil-looking, long-bladed knife that he carried in his right hand. It was pointing straight at her heart…

1. RESPONDING TO THE STORY

a. What adjectives would you use to describe Kate? the boy?

b. What difference has Kate made in the young boy's life?

c. How is this story similar to "Thank You Ma'am"? How is it different?

2. LITERATURE STUDIES ANALYSE OPENING PARAGRAPHS

The author of "Coffee, Snacks, Worms" opens the story with an exciting twist. You think you are reading an adventure story, and then it switches to a more realistic narrative. Do you think the opening of the story is effective? Why or why not? What is the purpose of opening a story this way?

Reread and assess the effectiveness of the opening paragraphs in other short stories. What other techniques do writers use? Make a list of the techniques you discover, and place it in your writing portfolio. You could try one of these ideas in the next story you write.

STRATEGIES

3. EDITOR'S DESK DIALOGUE

Dialogue (a conversation between characters) is one of the most important tools of story writers. Dialogue can reveal things about characters, and most importantly, move the plot along. Reread the story and analyse how the author uses dialogue. Does she use dialogue to reveal character or move the plot along? Is the dialogue authentic?

SELF-ASSESSMENT: Choose a short story from your writing portfolio that you would like to revise. Analyse how you've used dialogue.

- Does the conversation sound natural?
- Have you used words and phrases that suit the character who is speaking?
- Have you included the correct punctuation and structure? For example, have you used quotation marks and included a new paragraph every time a different character speaks?
- Have you used interesting dialogue tags such as *he said, she remarked, he smirked, they groaned*?

What's your idea of a hero? In this story of a boy, a dog, and a cougar, the real hero will surprise you!

G. TRUEHEART,
Man's Best Friend

Short Story by James McNamee

Tom Hamilton liked his Aunt Prudence. She taught at the university. Tom's father said she was all brains. Her name was Doctor Prudence Hamilton. When she came to Tom's father's farm in the Cowichan Valley on Vancouver Island, she always brought presents. Tom liked her.

He didn't like her constant companion, Genevieve Trueheart, a dog.

Tom Hamilton was fond of other dogs. He had a dog, a bull terrier called Rusty, a fighter right from the word go. Rusty kept the pheasants out of the garden and the young grain. He worked for a living. Tom couldn't like Genevieve Trueheart. She was good for nothing. She never even looked like a dog. She was a great big soft wheezing lazy wagging monster, a great big useless lump.

Genevieve had been born a Golden Retriever of decent parents and Aunt Prudence had papers to prove it. But Genevieve had eaten so many chocolates and French pastries and frosted cakes that she was three times as wide as a Golden Retriever ought to be. She had the soft muscles of a jellyfish. She couldn't run. She couldn't walk. All she could do was waddle. She was a horrible example of what ten years of living with Aunt Prudence would do to any creature. She looked like a pigmy hippopotamus with hair.

Genevieve Trueheart gave Tom Hamilton a hard time. She followed him. She went wherever he went. She was starved for boys. She never had a chance to meet any in the city. Tom couldn't bend over to tie a boot but her big pink tongue would lick his face. She loved him.

At half past eight when he finished breakfast and started for school, there on the porch would be Genevieve Trueheart waiting for him.

She wants to go to school with you, Tommy, Aunt Prudence always said.

GOALS AT A GLANCE

- Analyse descriptive language.
- Use punctuation in dialogue.

I think she'd better stay home, Tom always said. It's almost two kilometres. That's too far for her.

Take poor Genevieve, Tommy, Aunt Prudence and his mother always said. You know how she likes being with you.

Tom could have said, Why should I take her? When I take her the kids at school laugh at me. They ask, Why don't you send her back to the zoo and get a dog. But he didn't say that. It would have hurt Aunt Prudence's feelings.

On this morning he thought of something else to say. He said, A friend of mine saw a bear on the road. She had two cubs. We'd better leave Genevieve at home. I'll take Rusty.

Rusty has to stay to chase pheasants, his mother said.

What if I meet a cougar? Tom said.

A fat dog like Genevieve would be a fine meal for a cougar.

Tommy, stop talking, his mother said.

A cougar can pick up a sheep and jump over a fence, Tommy said.

Tom Hamilton, his mother said, get to school!

So Tom Hamilton went down the woodland road with Genevieve Trueheart panting and puffing and snorting behind him. Twice he had to stop while Genevieve sat down and rested. He told her, Rusty doesn't think you're a dog. He thinks you're a big fat balloon that's got a tail and four legs. Tom said, Genevieve, I hope a car comes on the wrong side of the road and gets you, you big fat slob. He never meant it. He said, I hope we meet those bears. He was just talking. He said, Do you know what I'm going to do at lunchtime, Genevieve? I'm going to give the fried pork liver that I have for you to another dog, to any dog who looks like a dog and not like a stuffed mattress, and your chocolate, Genevieve, I'll eat it myself. This was a lie. Tom Hamilton was honest.

Every kid who went to that school came with a dog. Yellow dogs. Brown dogs. Black dogs. White dogs. Black and white dogs. Black, white, and yellow dogs. Black, white, yellow, and brown dogs. They were a happy collection of dogs, and had long agreed among themselves who could beat whom, who could run faster than whom, who had the most fleas. From nine o'clock in the morning until noon they scratched. From noon until one they looked after their owners. From one o'clock until school was out at three they scratched.

These dogs did not welcome Genevieve. They were not jealous because she was a Golden Retriever and had papers to prove it; they didn't believe an animal with a shape like Genevieve was a dog. A Mexican hairless dog, one of those small dogs you can slip into your pocket, put his nose against Genevieve's nose, and what did she do, she rolled over on her back with her feet in the air. After that, there wasn't a dog who would have anything to do with Genevieve Trueheart.

The kids asked Tom, What's she good for?

Tom knew the answer but he never told them. She was good for nothing.

Boy! she's a ball of grease, the kids said.

She's a city dog, Tom said.

Why don't you leave her at home? the kids said.

Because my aunt gives me a dollar a week to walk her to school, Tom said. A lie.

Boy, oh, boy! a kid said, I wouldn't be seen with her for two dollars a week.

After school, Tom waited until all the others had left. He couldn't stand any more unkind words. He took his time going home. He had to. If he hurried, Genevieve would sit down and yelp. They came to the woodland road. It was like a tunnel. The tall trees, the Douglas firs, the cedars, and the hemlocks, all stretched branches over Tom's head. The air seemed cold even in summer. Owls liked the woodland road, and so did tree frogs, and deer liked it when flies were after them, but Tom didn't like it much. He was always glad to get out of it and into the sunshine. Often when he walked along this road he had a feeling things were looking at him. He didn't mind Genevieve too much here. She was company.

This day, Tom knew that something was looking at him. He had the feeling. And there it was!

There it was, all two and a half metres of it, crouched on a rock, above him, a great golden cat, a cougar, a Vancouver Island panther! Its tail was twitching. Its eyes burned green, burned yellow, burned bright. Its ears were flat against its head.

Tom's feet stopped. His blood and all his other juices tinkled into ice, and for a moment the whole world seemed to disappear behind a white wall. A heavy animal brushed against him, and at the shock of that, Tom could see again. It was Genevieve. She had sat down and, to rest herself, was leaning on his leg.

The cougar's ears were still flat, its eyes burning as if lighted candles were in them. It was still crouched on the rock, still ready to spring.

Tom heard a thump, thump, thump, thump, thump, and he thought it was the sound of his heart, but it wasn't. It was Genevieve beating her tail against the gravel to show how happy she was to be sitting doing nothing. That made Tom mad. If she had been any kind of a dog she would have known about the cougar before Tom did. She should have smelled him. She should have been just out of reach of his claws and barking. She should

have been giving Tom a chance to run away. That's what Rusty would have done. But no, not Genevieve; all she could do was bump her fat tail and look happy.

The cougar had come closer. A centimetre at a time, still in a crouch, he had slid down on the rock. Tom could see the movement in his legs. He was like a cat after a robin.

Tom felt sick, and cold, but his brain was working. I can't run, he thought, if I run he'll be on me. He'll rip Genevieve with one paw and me with the other. Tom thought, too, that if he had a match he could rip pages from one of his school books and set them on fire for he knew that cougars and tigers and leopards and lions were afraid of anything burning. He had no match because supposing his father had ever caught him with matches in his pocket during the dry season, then wow and wow and wow! Maybe, he thought, if I had a big stone I could stun him. He looked. There were sharp, flat pieces of granite at the side of the road where somebody had blasted.

The cougar jumped. It was in the air like a huge yellow bird. Tom had no trouble leaving. He ran to the side of the road and picked up a piece of granite.

Of course, when he moved, Genevieve Trueheart, who had been leaning against his leg, fell over. She hadn't seen anything. She lay there. She was happy. She looked like a sack of potatoes.

The cougar walked around Genevieve twice as if he didn't believe it. He couldn't tell what she was. He paid no attention to Tom Hamilton. He had seen men before. He had never seen anything like Genevieve. He stretched his neck out and sniffed. She must have smelled pretty good because he sat down beside her and licked one of his paws. He was getting ready for dinner. He was thinking, Boy, oh, boy! this is a picnic.

Tom Hamilton could have run away, but he never. He picked up one of those sharp pieces of granite.

The cougar touched Genevieve with the paw he had been licking, friendly-like, just to know how soft the meat was. Genevieve stopped wagging her tail. She must have thought that the cougar's claws didn't feel much like Tom Hamilton's fingers. She lifted her head and looked behind her. There can be no doubt but that she was surprised.

Tom was ashamed of her. Get up and fight! he yelled. Any other dog would fight. Rusty would have put his nips in before the cougar got finished with the job. But not Genevieve. She rolled over on her back and put her four fat feet in the air. She made noises that never had been heard. She didn't use any of her old noises.

The cougar was disgusted with the fuss Genevieve was making. He snarled. His ears went back. Candles shone in his green-yellow eyes. He slapped Genevieve between his paws like a ball.

Tom saw smears of blood on the road and pieces of Genevieve's hide in the cougar's claws. He still had a chance to run away. He never. He threw the piece of granite. He hit the cougar in its middle. The cougar turned, eyes green, eyes yellow.

How long the cougar looked at Tom, Tom will never know.

The sweet smell of Genevieve's chocolate-flavoured blood was too much for the cougar. He batted her about like a ball again. Tom picked up another piece of granite that weighed almost five kilograms, and bang! he hit the cougar right in the face.

The cougar fell on top of Genevieve. The cougar stood up and shook its head. Then it walked backwards like a drunken sailor.

And at that moment a bus full of lumberjacks who were going into town rounded the curve. The tires screeched as the driver stopped it, and thirty big lumberjacks got out yelling—well, you never heard such yelling, and the cougar quit walking backwards and jumped out of sight between two cedars.

What did Genevieve Trueheart do? That crazy dog waggled on her stomach down the road in the same direction the cougar had gone. She was so scared she didn't know what she was doing.

Boy, oh, boy! that's some dog, the lumberjacks said. She just won't quit. She's a fighter.

Yah! Tom said.

She's bleeding, the lumberjacks said. She saved your life. We'd better get her to a doctor.

They put Genevieve Trueheart and Tom Hamilton in the bus.

Boy, oh, boy! the lumberjacks said, a fighting dog like that is man's best friend.

Yah! Tom said.

The bus went right into Tommy's yard and the thirty lumberjacks told Tommy's mother and father and Aunt Prudence how Genevieve Trueheart, man's best friend, had saved Tommy.

Yah! Tom said.

Then Aunt Prudence put an old blanket and old newspapers over the back seat of her car so the blood wouldn't drip into the fabric when she was taking Genevieve Trueheart to the horse, cow, and dog doctor.

Aunt Prudence said, Now you know how much she loves you, Tommy. She saved your life.

Yah! Tommy said. ◆

1. RESPONDING TO THE STORY

a. What is the "turning point" in this story? What makes you think so?

b. Do you think this story is funny? Why or why not?

c. On page 95, the author says, "This was a lie. Tom Hamilton was honest." Do you think this statement is true? Explain fully.

d. Why does Tom feel such deep scorn for the dog?

2. LITERATURE STUDIES SIMILE

In a small group, discuss the way the author describes the dog. Read some of these phrases and sentences out loud and discuss the images that come to mind. Which description is your favourite? Why? Which of these descriptions use **similes**? What effect do the similes and other descriptions have? What mood do they help to create?

> A **simile** is a comparison of two different things using *like* or *as*. For example, "The swarm of mosquitoes hovered in the sky like a dark cloud."

In your journal, record similes to describe the following:

- your feelings before a test
- how your favourite hobby makes you feel
- your best friend
- a pet (either your own, a neighbour's, or friend's)
- your favourite food

As you develop similes, remember that they often compare two dissimilar things to create a striking image. Use one of these similes the next time you write a short story.

3. LANGUAGE CONVENTIONS PUNCTUATE DIALOGUE

Reread the story and think about how James McNamee has written the dialogue without quotation marks. Do you think this works? Why might he have done this? How else does McNamee use punctuation or sentence structure in a way that might be considered incorrect? What effect does this usage have? With your classmates, discuss the "correct" way to punctuate dialogue.

In your notebook, rewrite the following sentences from the story including the correct punctuation:

> Aunt Prudence said, Now you know how much she loves you, Tommy. She saved your life.
>
> Boy, oh, boy! the lumberjacks said, a fighting dog like that is man's best friend.
>
> Tom Hamilton, his mother said, get to school!

If you wrote to this author, what would you tell him about his use of punctuation? his sentence structure? his use of slang?

4. MEDIA MESSAGES ANALYSE STEREOTYPES

With a partner, discuss how dogs are often portrayed on screen. Use specific examples from sitcoms, dramas, and movies. Make a list of famous TV dogs and their characteristics. What similar characteristics are there among the different dogs? What is the dog **stereotype** that the media seems to use? How do you think G. Trueheart fits this image or stereotype? How doesn't she fit?

   If you were going to produce a TV show that included a dog, would you like that dog to be like G. Trueheart? Why or why not? What type of TV show might a dog like this be best-suited for?

A **stereotype** is an oversimplified picture, usually of a group of people, giving them all a set of characteristics, without consideration for individual differences.

Benji and *Homeward Bound* are two movies that portray dogs as heroes.

Is there one moment in your life that you will never forget, that you can remember with startling clarity?

Bus Stop

Short, Short Story
by W. D. Valgardson

We were in the middle of algebra class when the siren started. One moment, we were pondering the mysteries of mathematics and the next we were listening to the siren rise and fall and looking out the window. Beyond the houses and the bare limbs of the maples, there was the lake. We couldn't see it, but we knew it by heart, the curve of frozen sand, the kilometres of ice. It was a dull day with solid cloud cover. White ice, white clouds with a narrow band of daylight between.

You could see everyone listening. Even the teacher had stopped in place, his chalk held between thumb and first two fingers. There aren't many sirens in a small town. At first I thought it was the firetruck, then I realized it was too far away and the sound was too big. Then everyone's eyes swung toward a column of smoke that rose out over the lake and then there was the roar of a low flying T-33.

There were more sirens now. Smaller ones. Coming toward town. Half a dozen kids in the class were from the air base. Their fathers trained new pilots. One of the kids began to cry.

The sirens got real close, then went past, faded and stopped. At lunch time, we heard that the rescue truck got stuck in a snowdrift. A couple of locals took a tractor but they were in a hurry and the front end dropped into a crack. All this time, the second jet was circling, passing over the school low enough to make our desks tremble. A local pilot flew over and saw a body beside the hole in the ice where the plane went through. When he tried to land, he crashed but he wasn't hurt.

◆◆◆

GOALS AT A GLANCE

■ Respond critically to the story.
■ Analyse the first sentence of a story.

102

Yesterday, standing at a bus stop in Victoria, I started talking to an elderly lady. She asked me where I was from and I said Gimli and she said yes, she knew where that was, her son had been killed there while training as a pilot, he was practising flying without instruments and got disoriented by the snowy lake and the clouds and dove straight into the ice, only nineteen and they'd missed him terribly, but she doubted if after all this time I'd remember it. I was, I said to her without thinking, sitting in the third seat in the row closest to the window and I was doing algebraic equations when it happened.

----

1. RESPONDING TO THE STORY

a. Why do you think the narrator responds in the way he does to the woman at the bus stop? How is his response significant?

b. Why can't the narrator forget what happened to him years earlier?

c. Is there anything in this story that you would like to change? Explain fully.

d. What would you like to ask W. D. Valgardson about this story?

e. What strong descriptions has the author used? How do they help the reader?

f. How does this story fit into a theme about turning points?

2. LITERATURE STUDIES FIRST LINES

Reread Valgardson's first line. How does it set up the story, and grab your attention? What startling image does it create in your mind? Do you think this first sentence is effective? Why or why not? Would you change it? How does this first line connect to the last line? Is this connection important? Does it make the story better?

Reread and assess the effectiveness of the first lines in some other short stories. What types of sentences are used? Which sentences do you think are the most successful? Why is it so important to get the first line of a story right?

SELF-ASSESSMENT: Look through your writing portfolio and choose a short story that you'd like to revise. Evaluate the opening line. Is it effective? How can you change the first sentence to grab your reader's attention, and set up the story?

HOW TO WRITE A SHORT STORY

Goals at a Glance
- Structure a narrative using story elements.   • Use vivid language.

Story writing can't be boiled down to a few steps you should follow in the same order every time. But you can use the suggestions below to guide your writing. They will remind you about some of the most important aspects of story writing.

Choose an Idea

Most short stories are built around a single idea, for example:
- an exciting event
- a sudden realization or a lesson learned
- a mystery to be solved or a goal to be achieved.

Here are a few strategies for developing ideas.

1. Draw from your own experience. Create a list of important events in your life—failures, successes, amusing incidents, and so on. Could any of these be expanded into a story?

2. Do you have strong beliefs? Write them as statements, for example, "I believe that teenagers should be allowed to drive when they turn fourteen." What kind of story could you write to communicate this message?

3. Write about a personal interest or hobby. The special knowledge you have will help make your story entertaining.

4. Start with a "what if" question, such as, "What if my best friend and I got lost at sea?" Your answer might turn into a story.

Develop the Elements

Once you've decided on a basic idea for your story, you can begin to develop it further. Plan your short story in terms of the elements described below.

Characters: who the story is about. Short stories usually deal with a small number of characters.

Plot: what happens. A good plot keeps the reader guessing about what will happen next.

Kinds of Short Stories
- mystery
- adventure
- fantasy
- science fiction
- slice-of-life
- horror
- coming-of-age

PROCESS

Setting: where and when the story occurs. The reader should be able to picture a specific time and place.

Conflict: a struggle or opposition.

Mood: the main feeling the story creates. A word or two, such as *suspenseful* or *amusing,* can often sum up the mood.

Theme: the story's message. Some stories say something about life, such as, "True friendship is precious."

Climax: the most exciting or decisive moment. The climax usually comes near the end of the story. The reader sees it coming but usually can't predict the outcome.

As you plan, you might jot notes about your ideas or create a point-form outline.

Writer's Desk

Now that you've decided who your story will be about, what will happen, where it will take place, and so on, you can move to your first draft. Here are some pointers to consider.

1. As with any writing task, it's important to keep your audience and purpose in mind. Ask yourself questions such as:
- What details does the reader need to know?
- How can I hold the reader's interest?
- How does this sentence/paragraph fulfil my purpose?
2. Your first draft doesn't have to be perfect! Just keep writing until your story is complete.
3. Though it's useful to plan your story in advance, don't ignore a sudden inspiration. Some of your best ideas will come unexpectedly in the middle of writing.

Add the Finishing Touches

At the revision stage you have a chance to transform ordinary sentences into extraordinary ones. What specific words could you change to
- describe the characters more vividly?
- make the plot more interesting or exciting?
- bring the setting to life for the readers?
- reveal the conflict?
- capture the intended mood?
- reinforce your theme?
- increase the effectiveness of the climax?

Then proofread the story to correct grammar, spelling, and punctuation.

Publish Your Story

When you've revised, edited, and proofread your story, it's time to share it with the world! Make sure your finished copy is neat and easy to read. Add visuals if you like, and design an appealing cover.

Self-Assessment

Use the checklist below to reflect on the process you followed to write your story.
- ❏ I built my story around a single idea.
- ❏ When I planned my story, I considered the characters, plot, setting, conflict, mood, theme, and climax.
- ❏ I kept my audience and purpose in mind when I drafted my story.
- ❏ I revised specific words to make my story more vivid.
- ❏ I proofread my story.
- ❏ I made an appealing finished copy.

PROCESS

The Leaving

Have you and your family undergone changes? The family in this story meets a serious challenge.

Short Story
by Budge Wilson

She took me with her the day she left. "Where y' goin', Ma?" I asked. She was standing beside my bed with her coat on.

"Away," said Ma. "And yer comin', too."

I didn't want to go anywhere. It was three o'clock in the morning, and I was warm in my bed.

"Why me?" I complained.

I was too sleepy to think of any more complicated questions. In any case, there were no choices and very few questions back then when we were kids. You went to school and you came home on the school bus. If your father wanted you to shovel snow or fetch eggs, he told you, and you did it. He didn't ask. He told. Same with Ma. I did the dishes and brought in the firewood when it was required. She just pointed to the sink or to the woodbox, and I would leave whatever I was doing and start work. But at 3:00 a.m., the situation seemed unusual enough to permit a question. Therefore I asked again, "Why me?"

"Because yer the smartest," she said. "And because yer a woman."

I was twelve years old that spring.

GOALS AT A GLANCE

- Analyse setting.
- Justify opinions.

106

Ken Danby

Ma was a tall, rangy woman. She had a strong handsome face, with high cheekbones and a good firm chin line. Her lips were full. Her teeth were her own, although she smiled so rarely that you seldom saw them; her mouth tended to be held in a set straight line. She did not exactly frown; it was more as though she were loosely clenching her teeth. Her eyes were veiled, as if she had shut herself off from her surroundings and was thinking either private thoughts or nothing at all. Oh, she was kind enough and gentle enough when we needed it, though perhaps we needed it more often than she knew. But when we had cut knees or tonsillectomies, or when friends broke our hearts, she would hold us and hug us. Her mouth would lose its hard tight shape, and her eyes would come alive with concern and love.

Her lovely crisp auburn hair was short and unshaped making her face look uncompromising and austere. She wore baggy slacks over her excellent legs, and she owned two shabby grey sweaters and two faded graceless blouses. I did not ask myself why my mother looked this way, or why she had retreated behind her frozen face. One accepts one's parents for a long time, without theory or question. Speculation comes later, with adolescence and all the uncertainty and confusion it brings.

But when she woke me that chilly May morning, I was still a child. I rose and dressed quickly, packing my school bag with my pyjamas and toothbrush, the book I was reading, a package of gum, the string of Woolworth pearls that my grandmother had given me on my tenth birthday, and some paper to write and draw on. I wore jeans, my favourite blue sweater, my winter jacket, and rubber boots. I forgot my hat.

My mother had told me to be quiet, so I slithered down the stairs without a single board creaking. She was waiting at the door, holding a black cardboard suitcase with a strap around it. A shopping bag held sandwiches and some of last fall's bruised apples. She wore a brown car coat over her black slacks, and her hair was hidden under a grey wool kerchief. Her mouth had its tense fixed look but her eyes were alive. Even at my age and at that hour, I could see that.

We stopped briefly before walking out into the cold night air. The stove in the kitchen was making chugging noises, and from different parts of the small house could be heard a variety of snores and heavy breathing. My four brothers and my father were not going to notice our departure.

For a moment, my mother seemed to hesitate. Her mouth softened, and a line deepened between her eyebrows. Then she straightened her shoulders and opened the door. "Move!" she whispered.

We stepped into the night and started walking down the mountain in the direction of town, ten kilometres away. I did not quarrel with the need for this strange nocturnal journey, but I did question the reason.

"Ma," I said.

She turned and looked at me.

"Ma. Why are we leavin'?"

She did answer right away. It crossed my mind that she might not be sure of the reason herself. This was a frightening thought. But apparently she knew.

"I plans t' do some thinkin'," she said.

We walked quickly through the night. North and South Mountains closed off the sky behind us and far ahead, but a full moon made it easy to see our way on the frosty road. The hill country was full of scrub growth, stubby spruce, and sprawling alders, unlike the tidy fields and orchards of the Valley. But the frost lent a silver magic to the bushes and the rough ground, and the moonlight gave a still dignity to the shabby houses. It was cold, and I shivered. "Fergot yer hat," said Ma. "Here." She took the warm wool kerchief from her head and gave it to me. I took it. Parents were invincible, and presumably would not feel the cold. My mother was not a complainer. She was an endurer. It was 1969, and she was forty-five years old.

When we reached Annapolis, we stopped at a small house on the edge of town, and Ma put down her suitcase and dug around in her purse. She took out a key and opened the door. Even my silent mother seemed to think that an explanation was required. "Lida Johnson's in Glace Bay, visitin' her daughter. Said I could use the house while she's gone. Normie's at a 4-H meetin' in Bridgetown. Joseph's truckin'. We'll wait here till th' train goes."

"Maw," I asked, "how long we gonna be gone?"

She bent her head down from its rigid position and looked at the floorboards of the front hall. She touched her mouth briefly with her fist. She closed her eyes for a second and took a deep breath.

"Dunno," she replied. "Till it's time."

◆ ◆ ◆

We slept in the parlour until we left for the station.

I guess that ten-kilometre walk had shunted me straight from childhood into adolescence, because I did an awful lot of thinking between Annapolis and Halifax. But at first I was too busy to think. I was on a train, and I had never been inside one before. There were things to investigate—the tiny washroom with its little sink, and the funny way to flush the toilet. In the main part of the Dayliner, the seats slid up and down so that people could sleep if they wanted to. I watched the world speed by the windows—men working on the roads; kids playing in the schoolyards; cows standing dumbly outside barns in the chilly air, all facing in the same direction; places and towns I had never seen till then. My ma looked over at me and placed a comic book and a bag of peanuts on my lap. "Fer th' trip," she said, and smiled, patting my knee in an unfamiliar gesture. "Mind missin' school?" she added.

"No," I said. But I did. I had a part in the class play, and there was a practice that afternoon. I was the chief fairy, and I had twenty-five lines, all of which I knew by heart already. But this trip was also a pretty special, if alarming, adventure. It had a beginning but no definite end, and we were still speeding toward the middle. What would Halifax be like? We never had enough money to have more than one ride on the Exhibition Ferris wheel at Lawrencetown; but here we were buying train tickets and reading comics and eating peanuts and travelling to heaven knows what expensive thrills.

"Maw," I asked, "where'd the money come from?"

She looked at me, troubled.

"Don't ask," she said. "I'll tell you when you're eighteen."

Eighteen! I might as well relax and enjoy myself. But I wondered.

Before long, she fell asleep, and I felt free to think. Until then, it was almost as though I were afraid she would read my thoughts.

Why had we left? How long would we be gone? How would Pa and my brothers cook their dinner? How would they make their beds? Who would they complain to after a hard day? Who would fetch the eggs, the mail, the water, the wood, the groceries? Who would wash their overalls, mend their socks, put bandages on their cuts? It was inconceivable to me that they could survive for long without us.

◆ ◆ ◆

When we reached Halifax, we went to what I now realize was a cheap and shabby hotel in the South End of the city. But to me it seemed the height of luxury. The bed was made of some kind of shiny yellow wood. The bedspread was an intense pink, with raised nubbles all over it. A stained spittoon sat in the corner. There was actually a sink in the room, with taps that offered both cold and hot water. A toilet that flushed was down the hall. I checked under the bed; there was no chamber pot. But who needed it? There were two pictures on the walls—one of a curly-headed blonde, displaying a lot of bare flesh, and another of three dead ducks hanging upside down from a nail. I spent a lot of time inspecting both of these pictures.

Halifax was a shock to me. How could the buildings be so huge and the stores so grand? Here I was in the province's capital city before I really understood what a capital city could be. I admired the old stone buildings with their carvings around the doors and windows. I stretched my neck to see the tops of the modern apartments, with their glass and concrete reaching up into the clouds. The buses and cars alarmed me as they rushed up and down the long streets, but they excited me, too. The weather changed; it was warm and comforting, and the wind was gentle and caressing. We went down the hill to the harbour, and saw the bridge; rooted in the ground and in the sea bottom, it lifted its enormous metal wings into the sky. I marvelled that a thing so strong could be so graceful, so beautiful. What a lovely way, I thought, to get from one place to another. We walked across the bridge to Dartmouth, and watched the ships, far below, headed for Europe, for Africa, for the distant North. My mother, who had started to talk, told me about all these things. It was as though she were trying to tell me something important, but didn't want to say things right out. "They're goin' somewheres," she said. Later on, she took me out to Dalhousie University, and we walked among the granite buildings and beside the playing fields. "If yer as smart as the teacher claims," she said, "maybe you'll come here some day t' learn." I thought this highly unlikely. If we couldn't afford running water, how could we afford such a thing as that? I said so.

"They's ways," she said.

Ken Danby

We walked up and down Spring Garden Road and gazed in the big windows. I looked at a candy store with at least five million kinds of candy, shops with dresses so fancy that I could scarcely believe it, shelves full of diamonds and gold and sparkling crystal. "Is there ways for all this, too?" I asked my mother. She hesitated.

"Don't need all that stuff," she concluded.

The weather was dazzling—a sunny Nova Scotia May day.

We walked through the huge iron gates into the Public Gardens and ate our sandwiches and apples beside the duck pond. I kicked off my rubber boots and wiggled my toes in the sun as I watched the swans and the yellow ducklings. The Gardens were immense, full of massive and intricate flowerbeds, winding paths, and strange exotic trees. There were statues, a splashing fountain, an elaborate round bandstand, and a little river with a curved bridge over it. Lovers strolled arm in arm, and children shrieked with laughter as they chased the pigeons. I asked Ma why everyone seemed so happy. "Dunno," she said. "Weather does things t' people." She looked around. "And maybe some of them's free," she added.

On the second day, we watched women racing to work in the morning, mini-skirts flipping, heels clicking, faces eager, faces tense. We looked on as shopping women pulled twenty-dollar bills out of their purses as though they were nickels. We visited the courthouse and looked at the pictures of the stern-faced judges as they watched us from the walls. "They fixes things what aren't right," said Ma. I wondered how. "But not always," she added.

We spent an hour in the public library, looking at the shelves and shelves of books, smelling their wonderful book smells, idly turning the pages. On a book dolly, she picked up a copy of *The Feminine Mystique*. She, who had not to my knowledge read a single book since I was born, said shyly, "I read this book." I was astonished.

"You!" I exclaimed. "How come? When?"

"I kin read!" she retorted, miffed. "Even if y' leaves school in Grade Five, y' kin read. Y' reads slow, but y' knows how."

"But where'd you get it?" I demanded, amazed.

"Y' remember that day the Salvation Army lady brought us that big box o' clothes?" she asked. "Yer pa was mad and said we didn't need no charity. But I hid the box, and after a time he forgot about it. Well, there was other things in there, too—an egg beater, some toys what I gave to Lizzie's kids, even a string o' yellow beads and a bracelet that I bin savin' fer you. And some books. There was comic books and that big colourin' book y' got fer Christmas, and them *Popular Mechanics* magazines the boys read, and a coupla others. And this." She placed the palm of her hand on the book.

"Seemed like it was for me, special. So I read it. She was real tough goin', but I read every word. Took me near a year. Finished it last Thursday."

I could hardly believe it. My ma didn't even read recipes. She kept them all in her head. I asked, "Was it good?"

She thought for a moment before answering. "She was a real troublin' book. But she was good."

I couldn't understand that. "If it was so troublin', why was it so good?"

She answered that one without hesitation. "Found I weren't alone," she said. She stroked its cover tenderly before putting it back on the dolly. I liked the library, with all the silent people bent over their books, and the librarians moving soundlessly to and fro. I wasn't used to quiet places.

In the afternoon, we climbed the Citadel and went into its museum, walking up and down among the sea things, old things, rich things. Later on, we went to what I thought was a very fancy restaurant. There were bright, shiny chrome tables with place mats of paper lace and green glass ashtrays. I ordered a hot dog and chips, because that was my favourite meal. My mother, her mouth now soft and cheerful, ordered something with a strange name.

"Ain't gonna come all this way and spend all th' hen money jest t' eat what I kin eat at home," she said.

The egg money! So that was it. I let on I didn't notice. But a thrill of fear ran through me. I wondered what Pa would do.

In the evening we returned early to the hotel, and I slept deeply, but with strange and troubled dreams.

◆ ◆ ◆

On the third day, Ma said, "It's time. T'day we go home." I asked why.

"Because," she said.

"Because why?" I insisted.

She was silent for a moment, and then said again, "It's time." I was pleased. It had been an interesting trip, but it frightened me a little because there were no explanations, no answers to my unspoken questions. Besides, I was afraid that someone else would get to be chief fairy in the school play. "Have you done yer thinkin'?" I asked. She looked at me strangely. There was hope in her look and an odd fierce dignity.

"I has," she said.

◆ ◆ ◆

We took the bus home instead of the train, and it was late afternoon when we arrived in Annapolis to start the ten-kilometre climb to our farm. The day was damp and cold, and I wore my mother's wool kerchief again. We were very quiet, and I knew she was nervous. Her mouth was back in its taut line, and her eyes were troubled. But even in the wind, her shoulders were straight and firm, and I could feel a difference in her. Fearful though her eyes were, she was fully alert, and you could sense a new dogged strength in the set of her face.

There was no such strength in me, except such as I derived from her. Home is home when you are twelve, and I did not want to live a tourist's life in Halifax forever. But I worried every step of the ten long kilometres.

As we turned the bend at Harrison's Corner, we could see the farm in the distance. It was as though I were seeing it for the first time. The house had been white once, but it had needed paint for almost nineteen years. Around the yard was a confusion of junk of all kinds: two discarded cars—lopsided and without wheels—an unpiled jumble of firewood, buckets, a broken hoe, rusty tools, an old oil drum for burning garbage. To the left were the few acres of untidy fields dotted with spruce trees and the grey skeletons of trees long dead of Dutch elm disease. To the right, close to the henhouse, was the barn—small and unpainted, grey and shabby in the dim afternoon light. We could hear the two cows complaining, waiting for milking time.

When we opened the kitchen door, they were all there. My four big brothers were playing cards at the table, and my father was sitting by the kitchen stove. I had forgotten how darkly handsome he was. But because it was not Sunday, he was unshaven, and his eyes glared out at us from beneath heavy black eyebrows.

Pa rose from his chair and faced us. He was very tall, and his head almost reached the low ceiling. He seemed to fill the entire room.

His voice was low and threatening. "Where you bin, woman?" he said.

She spoke, and I was amazed that she had the courage. Then I realized with a jolt that his words were little different in tone and substance from hundreds I had heard before: "How come my supper's not ready, woman?" "Move smart, woman! I'm pressed fer time!" "Shut up them kids, woman!" "Move them buckets, woman! They're in my way!" "This food ain't fit t' eat, woman. Take it away!"

She spoke quietly and with dignity. "You is right to be angry, Lester," she said. "I left a note fer y', but I shoulda tole y' before I left."

"Shut yer mouth, woman, and git my supper!" he shouted, slamming his hands down on the table.

She moved to the centre of the room and faced him. "My name," she began, and faltered. She cleared her throat and ran her tongue over her lower lip. "My name," she repeated, this time more steadily, "is Elizabeth."

He was dumbfounded. My brothers raised their heads from their card game and waited, cards poised in mid-air.

Pa looked at her. He looked at me. Then he looked at Jem and Daniel and Ira and Bernard, sitting there silent and still like four statues, waiting for his reaction.

Suddenly my father threw back his head and laughed. His ugly laughter filled the little kitchen, and we all listened, frozen, wishing for it to stop.

"'My name is Elizabeth!'" he mocked, between choking guffaws, slapping his thighs and holding his stomach, and then he repeated himself and her, mincingly, "'My…name…is…Elizabeth!'" Then his face changed, and there was silence. "Git over her 'n' make my supper, woman! I'm gonna milk them cows. But my belly is right empty, and y' better be ready when I gits back from th' chores!"

I watched my mother. During the laughter, I could see her retreat for a minute behind her eyes, expressionless, lifeless, beaten. Then she took a deep breath and looked at him directly, squarely, with no fear in her face. Pain, yes, but no fear. My brothers looked down and continued their card game.

"Act smart there, Sylvie," she said to me, as soon as he had left. "I need yer help bad. You clean up, 'n' I'll fix supper." She was already moving swiftly about the kitchen, fetching food, chopping onions, peeling potatoes.

In the sink was a mountainous pile of dirty dishes. Open cans, crusted with stale food, cluttered the counter. I surveyed the scene with distaste.

"Ma," I asked, complaining like the true adolescent that I had now become, "how come they couldna washed the dishes themselves? They goes huntin' and fishin' and has lotsa little vacations in th' winter. We always do their work for them when they're gone. How come we gotta clean up their mess?"

"Listen," she said, cutting the potatoes and dropping them into the hot fat, "the way I sees it is y' kin ask fer kindness or politeness from time t' time. But y' can't expect no miracles. It's my own fault fer raisin' four boys like they was little men. I shoulda put them in front of a dishpan fifteen years ago. Now it's too late. Yer pa's ma did the same thing. She aimed t' raise a boy who was strong and brave, with no soft edges." She wiped her forehead with the back of her hand. "All along I bin blamin' men fer bein' men. But now I see that oftentimes it's the women that makes them that way." It was a long, long speech for my ma. But she went on. "The boys is seventeen, eighteen, nineteen, and twenty years old. Y' can't start makin' 'em over now. They's set." Then she smiled wryly, with a rare show of humour. She bowed formally in the direction of the card game. "I apologizes," she said, "to your future wives."

Then she stopped, and looked from one son's face to the next, and so on, around the table. "I loves you all, regardless," she said softly, "and it's worth a try. Jem"—she spoke to the youngest—"I'd be right grateful if you'd fetch some water for Sylvie. She's real tired after the long walk."

Jem looked at his brothers, and then he looked at her. Water carrying was woman's work, and she knew she was asking a lot of him. He rose silently, took the bucket from her, and went outside to the well.

"And you," she said, addressing Daniel and Ira and Bernard, "One snigger out of you, and yer in bad trouble." I'm sure she knew she was taking an awful chance. You can say a thing like that to little boys, but these were grown men. But no one moved or so much as smiled when Jem returned. "I thank you right kindly," said Ma, thereby delivering a speech as unusual as her other one.

◆ ◆ ◆

You could say, I suppose, that our leaving made no large difference in my mother's life. She still worked without pay or praise, and was often spoken to as though she were without worth or attraction. Her days were long and thankless. She emptied chamber pots and spittoons, scrubbed overalls and sheets on her own mother's scrub board, and peeled the frozen clothes from the line in winter with aching fingers. But not all things remained the same. She now stood up to my father. Her old paralytic fear was gone, and she was able to speak with remarkable force and dignity. She did not nag. Nagging is like a constant blow with a small blunt instrument. It annoys, but it seldom makes more than a small dent. When she chose to object to Pa's cruel or unfair behaviour, her instrument was a shining steel knife with a polished cutting edge. A weapon like that seemed to make my father realize that if he went too far she would leave. After all, she had done it once before. And this time, she might not return.

So there were changes. One day, for no apparent reason, he started to call her Elizabeth. She did not let on that this was remarkable, but the tight line of her mouth relaxed, and she made him a lemon pie for supper. She fixed up the attic storeroom as a workroom for herself. The boys lugged up her treadle sewing machine, and she brought in an old wicker chair and a table from the barn. It was a hot room in summer and cold in winter, but it was her own place—her escape. She made curtains from material bought at Frenchy's, and hooked a little rug for the floor. No one was allowed to go there except her. She always emerged from this room softer, gentler, more still.

I never did hear a single word about the missing egg money. Maybe Pa didn't notice, or perhaps Ma attacked the subject with her sharp-edged knife. Possibly it was the egg money that sent me to Dalhousie—that and my scholarship and my summer jobs. I never asked. I didn't really want to know.

When I was home last February during the term break, I stole a look into Ma's attic room. There were library books on the table, material on the sewing machine, paper piled on the floor for her letters to me and to the boys. I respected her privacy and did not go in. But the room, even in that chilly winter attic, looked like an inviting place.

My ma is now fifty-five, and has a lot of life still to live. My pa is fifty-eight. He still shaves once a week, and he has not yet cleared up the yard. But he often speaks to my mother as though she were more of a person and less of a thing. Sometimes he says thank you. He still has a raging temper, but he is an old dog, and new tricks come hard. He loves my mother and she him, with a kind of love that is difficult for my generation to understand or define. In another time and in another place, the changes could have been more marked. But my mother is a tough and patient woman, and these differences seem to be enough for her. Her hair is worn less severely. Her mouth is not set so straight and cold and firm. She talks more. She has made a pretty yellow blouse to wear with her baggy slacks. She smiles often, and she is teaching her two grandsons how to wash dishes and make cookies.

◆ ◆ ◆

I often wonder about these things: but when my mind approaches the reasons for all that has happened, my thinking slides away and my vision blurs. Certainly the book and the leaving do not explain everything. Maybe my mother was ready to move into and out of herself anyway; and no one can know exactly what went on in her thoughts before and after she left. Perhaps she was as surprised as I was by the amount of light and warmth she let in when she opened the door to step into the dark and frosty morning. But of that strange three-day departure, I can say, as Ma did of her book, "She was a real troublin' trip. But she was good."

----

1. RESPONDING TO THE STORY

a. Were you surprised by anything that happened in the story? Explain.

b. How would you describe the main characters in the story—Sylvie, Elizabeth, Lester? Do you think they're realistic characters? Explain.

c. What is the main idea of the story? Why do you think so?

d. Have you ever read "a real troublin' book"? What do you think Elizabeth means by this?

e. What point of view is used in this story? Why does the author use this point of view?

2. LITERATURE STUDIES ANALYSE SETTING

In your notebook, write a paragraph describing the setting of this story. Include notes about how you know this. Why is the setting significant? How does understanding when and where this story takes place help you understand the characters? Do you think the events in this story could take place in a modern and urban setting? Explain.

3. ORAL LANGUAGE CLASS DISCUSSION

As a class, discuss what Elizabeth says about the roles and rights of men and women. Is there a statement in the story that you strongly agree or disagree with? Explain fully. What do you think Budge Wilson is trying to say about society in the 1960s? Do you think what she's saying has any connections to society today? Explain.

4. WRITING A FRIENDLY LETTER

What do you think would happen if Elizabeth left again? Do you think Elizabeth and Lester would write to each other? Choose one of these characters and write a letter to the other. What will the letter say? What emotions will be expressed? Remember to keep in character as you write. Exchange letters with someone who has chosen the other characters.

5. VISUAL COMMUNICATION RECREATE THE SETTING

If this story were a play, what do you think the stage in the last act (when Elizabeth and Sylvie return home) would look like? Draw some sketches, or use magazine visuals, and then write a descriptive paragraph that describes that setting. A descriptive paragraph describes and makes your reader see, hear, smell, and feel what you are describing. Use specific nouns, verbs, adjectives, and adverbs to create the description. Add details, and experiment with different writing techniques such as simile, metaphor, and personification. Share your sketches or paragraph with a partner and explain what you intended.

SELF-ASSESSMENT: WRITING

As you worked on the activities in this unit, what did you learn about

- paragraph structure?
- punctuation in dialogue?
- setting?
- opening sentences?
- publishing?
- short stories?

What else would you like to learn about writing?

VISUAL COMMUNICATION

Compile a collection of comic strips that illustrate the theme of this unit. Organize your collection into categories and develop a comic "essay." Accompany each comic strip with a commentary.

MEDIA MAKER

Create a movie poster. Assume that one of the stories in this unit is being made into a movie. You've been assigned the task of creating a promotional poster for it. How will you sum up what the movie is about?

LITERATURE STUDIES

Think about the types of short stories you've read throughout the unit. What different types of stories were there? How would you classify each story? Choose your favourite type and list its features.

EXPLORING

"There are things that are known,
and things that are unknown;
in between are doors."

Anonymous

EXPLORING

FINAL FRONTIERS

UNIT AT A GLANCE

What would you do if a Martian landed in your backyard? This tongue-in-cheek tale takes that what-if to absurd heights.

The Day the Martian Landed

Short Story by Pierre Berton

The flying saucer landed on Fred Foster's back lawn at three o'clock on a Saturday afternoon. Fred's oldest daughter, Mona, answered the door. There was a little green man standing there; he had a bald head, bulbous eyes, huge ears, and a pair of antennae protruding from his forehead. He was wearing a goldfish bowl on his head. She recognized him at once as a Martian.

"Take me to your leader," said the newcomer politely.

"Hey, Pop!" Mona called. "There's a Martian at the back door wants to see you."

Fred Foster was sitting in his undershirt in the television room, watching the football on Channel Two. "Tell him we don't want any!" he called back. "Whatever it is, we got plenty!"

"He ain't selling nothing, Pop," Mona called back. "He's a *Martian.*"

Fred Foster got up wearily. "They'll do anything to get into the house," he said. "Last week they told me I'd won a free health course."

He glared at the Martian, who was still standing politely in the doorway.

"Okay," said Foster, "come out with it. What are you selling? And don't try to tell me you're taking a survey or something. We had that one."

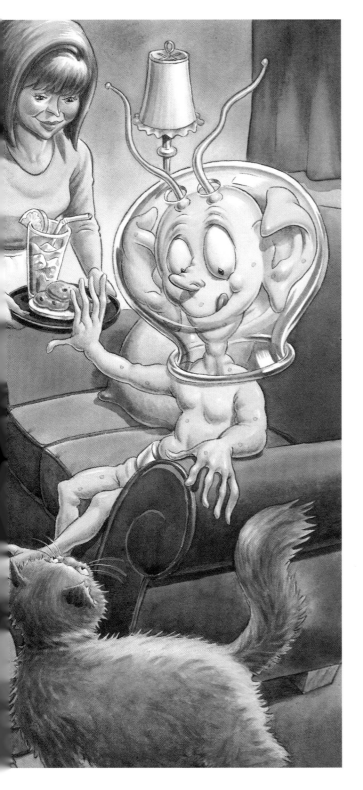

"Take me to your leader," said the Martian politely, just as he'd been taught in rocket school.

"I think he's got something to do with Atomic Appliances," said Mrs. Foster, coming to the door and wiping her hands on her apron. "They've always got some gimmick or other."

But Fred Foster had been feeling the Martian, pulling at its ears and fiddling with its antennae. "By George," he said. "I believe the fellow *is* a Martian!"

"Of course," said Mona. "I'd know him anywheres."

"Well for heaven's sake, invite the man in," said Mrs. Foster. "I'll just make some nice iced tea."

So they asked the Martian into the sitting room and they all sat down and looked at him while Mrs. Foster got the iced tea ready.

The Martian refused the iced tea politely and also the chocolate chip cookies. But when the Persian cat jumped up on his lap, he ate that instead, fur and all. The Fosters were a bit put out, but didn't like to say anything since the Martian was company.

"Take me to your leader," the Martian said, looking around wistfully for another cat.

"By George, he's right," said Fred Foster. "This is one of those diplomatic things."

"Who *is* our leader?" Mona asked him.

Well now, there was a poser. Mrs. Foster insisted that it was the mayor, but Fred held out for the premier.

"Now, hold on, Fred," said Mrs. Foster. "If you're going to go to the top, then you have to go right to the secretary of state or maybe even to the prime minister."

"You've hit it, Mother!" said Fred Foster. "The prime minister, of course. This Martian comes from another country, don't he? Well, then he has to meet the head of a *country*. I'll just go and call up the prime minister now."

So he put in a long-distance call to Ottawa and made it person-to-person just in case the prime minister should be away on a trip or something. But he did not get him, only a young man whose name sounded like Grlb and who assured Fred Foster that he could speak for his chief.

"Well, all right," said Fred Foster. "Look, we've got a Martian here. He's landed in our backyard in one of those saucer things that they've been seeing around and he wants to go up to Ottawa and meet the prime minister personally."

The young man wasn't in the least surprised. He said that Mr. Foster would get a letter about it, and two days later the letter came:

The Prime Minister has asked me to tell you how very interested he was in your experience Saturday last and how much he appreciates your taking the trouble to call him personally regarding it.

He has expressed the hope that should you ever be in Ottawa you will drop in to the visitors' gallery of the House of Commons and watch the democratic process of this great nation in action.

         Sincerely yours,
         REGINALD GLRB
         Assistant to the Prime Minister

This didn't seem very satisfactory.

"Maybe we ought to call the newspapers," said Mrs. Foster. The Martian was becoming a bit of a nuisance. He lived most of the time in his flying saucer, but periodically he would appear at the door and plaintively say, "Take me to your leader."

So Fred Foster got on the phone to a huge metropolitan daily, which I will not name here so that no one can say I am biassed. The newspaper reporter who answered was very interested in the flying-saucer story. Fred could hear him scribbling furiously.

"Come out and see for yourself," said Fred Foster, but the reporter said that wouldn't be necessary; they could get all the details by phone and thus catch the home edition.

That afternoon there was a hilarious story on the second front page about Fred Foster's Martian, illustrated by comic cartoons. The story was immediately copied by the other two huge metropolitan papers, and the following day, sparing no expense, one of them actually sent a reporter to see the Fosters. The Fosters invited him into the sitting room, where he photographed all of them and took down some more quotes for his paper.

"The Martian's out back in his saucer," said Fred Foster. "Come on now and I'll show him to you."

But the reporter looked at his watch and said he really didn't have time, if he was going to catch the early edition and beat the other papers with his pix. He said he had all he needed, anyway; they probably wouldn't use more than two folios of copy, or maybe even just captions under a three-column photo on page three. Which was the way it turned out.

"MARTIAN" SLEPT HERE, according to Mr. and Mrs. J. Forster (centre, left) of 224B Cecil St., and daughter Mona, fourteen (right), point to the spot on couch where they claim visitor from Mars sat and drank iced tea.

The following night the little Martian (who wasn't actually a Martian, but certainly an alien) took off in his flying saucer feeling a bit frustrated. He landed in a backyard in Poughkeepsie, New York, knocked on the door, and started all over again: "Take me to your leader," he said hopefully.

He had been doing it for six and a half years without getting anywhere. He was a very stubborn Martian.

----

1. RESPONDING TO THE STORY

a. What is Fred Foster's reaction when he meets the Martian? How would you have reacted?

b. Do you believe the prime minister's assistant took Foster's phone call seriously? Why or why not? Explain fully.

c. Discuss some of the stereotypes Berton has used. Who is stereotyped? Why might Berton have used stereotypes?

d. What parts of this story do you find amusing? Explain. How does Berton create humour?

2. STORY CRAFT CREATE DIALOGUE

Dialogue is a conversation between people. Writers create realistic dialogue in many ways.

- They copy normal speech. This may mean using short, broken sentences or sentence fragments.
- They use slang.
- They use an apostrophe to show missing letters and contractions.
- They use ellipsis points (…) or dashes (—) to show where words have been left out or where speech has been interrupted.

Reread the story and identify the dialogue techniques the author has used. Are they effective? Do they reflect normal speech? How does the dialogue add to the humour of the story?

3. MEDIA MAKER WRITE A NEWSPAPER ARTICLE

Reread "The Day the Martian Landed." Adapt the story into a newspaper article the reporter in the story should have written. Remember to answer the five W's: *who, what, when, where,* and *why.* Identify the events and dialogue you can use to write the article. For ideas on writing a newspaper article, see page 43.

Set up your newspaper article similar to other articles you've read. Include a headline, photo and caption, a by-line, and a subhead.

Compare your article with a partner's. What were the similarities and differences in your articles?

Martian Invades Canadian Suburb

MARTIAN CLAIMS TO HAVE SEEN *SOJOURNER* ON MARS

Article by Jensen Basanti

The flying saucer landed on Fred Foster's back lawn at three o'clock on a Saturday afternoon.

The Martian (above) came to earth on a peaceful mission.

A trip to the moon has always been Kate's goal.
Now that she's there, can she handle the pressure?
Could you?

Moon
MAIDEN

SCIENCE FICTION STORY
BY ALISON BAIRD

"You can't do it, sis," Matt had said. And he had looked down his nose at her in his maddening, superior way. Matt was no giant himself, but it was easy to look down at Kate.

"Oh, yeah?" She'd glared up at her brother, hands on hips. "Well, I don't care what you think, I'm going. What's the point of winning a lunar study scholarship if you don't use it?"

It had been a hot and smoggy day, she remembered, with an ultraviolet alert, so the two of them had been stuck indoors and Matt, as usual, had taken out his boredom and frustration on Kate.

"One: you're way too young—"

"I'm nearly fourteen!"

"Two: you're a nitwit," Matt had finished.

And that settled it. After that "nitwit," no power in the universe could have prevented Kate Iwasaki from embarking on the shuttle for Luna Base.

But Matt had had a parting shot. "You'll never spend half a year on the Moon! You'll end up going crazy, like all those loony Lunies."

GOALS AT A GLANCE

- Analyse descriptive paragraphs.
- Experiment with ellipsis points.

Kate had shivered at that; she'd heard about the moon-madness. It started with hallucinations. Then you began talking to imaginary people, even yelling and screaming at them, or sometimes recoiling from invisible horrors. That was when the security guards came and "escorted" you away. It was a fact of life on Luna Base; some people just could not take the claustrophobic atmosphere: the isolation was worse than on the most remote polar weather station or deep-sea lab on Earth.

But Kate firmly pushed her fears aside. "I'm going, and that's that," she had declared, lifting her chin.

Now she smiled with satisfaction as the small lunar shuttle carrying her and the other students planed low over the surface of the Mare Tranquillitatis. Through the window she could see flat plains of ash-coloured lunar soil—*regolith*, the instructor called it—strewn with modest-sized impact craters, some no more than a decimetre across. *Not too impressive,* Kate thought. She'd already been on much more spectacular trips, to the giant craters Tycho and Copernicus, and to the lunar mountain ranges, the Alps and Apennines. But this outing was always the most popular. The shuttle's interior was crammed to capacity with eager students.

The spacecraft slowed and hovered briefly before setting down gently on its four wide landing pods. The cabin ceased to thrum and vibrate as the engines were cut, and a flashing light came on over each air lock. The students all rose and shuffled down the aisle in their cumbersome space suits, pulling on their helmets.

"All right, to the air locks, just four at a time now," the instructor told them as he checked their helmet seals. "And don't stampede; form proper lines."

Kate managed to be one of the first in the air locks. She held her breath as the metal door slid open, and all sound ceased with the release of the air. When they climbed out, most of the kids bounced around like demented kangaroos the minute they reached the surface. Kate just stood looking up at the sunlit face of Earth, its blue-white glow fifty times brighter than the brightest moonlight. Poor polluted overcrowded Earth! No, she wasn't in any great hurry to go back there.

With some difficulty the instructor managed to herd them all together and direct them to their destination. At the sight of it, the students began to babble with excitement.

Tranquillity Base. The flagpole—bent out of shape by the blast of the *Eagle's* engines when it had escaped back into space—had been straightened to preserve the image of the site as it had appeared on the old footage. But everything else was as it had been left: the descent stage of the lunar module, the instruments, even the astronauts' footprints. It was all surrounded by a towering steel wire fence topped with surveillance cameras: no one must get too near, trample on the sacred footprints of Armstrong and Aldrin, or carve their initials on the plaque attached to the leg of the descent stage.

A hushed silence now fell as the words on the plaque were quoted solemnly by the instructor: "Here men from the planet Earth first set foot up on the Moon. July 1969 A.D. We came in peace for all mankind."

First set foot on the Moon. Kate wondered how those two men must have felt when they first climbed out onto the lunar soil. Above them had been the same jet-black sky and sunlit Earth, about them the same barren, crater-strewn plain. But for those pioneering space explorers there had been no emergency response teams, no Luna Base with its decorative greenery and mall full of brightly lit shops. No other living thing—not so much as a microbe—had shared the grey wasteland with them. The nearest human being had been the pilot in the orbiting command service module, high above. All the rest of humanity had been crowded into that cloud-swathed sphere nearly four hundred thousand kilometres away. Other explorers would follow over the years and feel that isolation in turn; but to be the *first...* Kate shivered. First to walk the grey solitudes, first to disturb the thick soft dust no wind had ever lifted... She realized suddenly that she had strayed somewhat and was now some distance away from the others. She turned hastily to rejoin them.

But there was a woman standing in the way.

Kate stared. It was not unusual for a stray tourist or maintenance worker to be out here on the lunar surface. But this woman was different.

She wasn't wearing a space suit.

She stood there as though the moon's airless surface were the most natural place for her to be: a slender woman, Asian-featured, wearing a kimono of some green silky material embroidered with flowers. There were real flowers in her hair—shell-pink blossoms nestling among ebony tresses piled neatly atop her head. About her neck there hung a string of lustrous, cream-coloured pearls. The gaze of her large brown eyes was cool, solemn, and direct.

There were no footprints behind her, nor were there any shadows on the grey ground at her feet.

Kate's breath boomed like thunder inside her helmet. Her mouth was dry as a bone. The gravity that allowed the other students to leap and bound around the steel fence seemed to be binding her to the ground. As she stared helplessly, the woman in the green kimono approached. There was no smile of welcome on the delicate features; her expression was sombre, her tread light but purposeful as she drew closer to Kate.

Kate longed desperately for something to break the spell. But fear and disbelief immobilized her. The pale woman was almost touching her; an arm in a long, flowing sleeve reached out towards Kate's faceplate. It stopped before actually making contact, the white hand raised in a gesture of...command? Entreaty? Kate could not take her eyes from the woman's; they were as deep as shadows, their gaze calm and compelling. She was willing Kate to do something. But what?

The hand gestured again. *Open your faceplate,* it said, as plain as speech.

Kate tried to swallow and couldn't.

Open it—let me touch you...

"No," Kate whispered. But it was only a croak.

The woman who was not—could not—really be there gazed at Kate steadily. The embroidered flowers upon her pale-green robe stood out in precise and minute detail, real as the harshly lit moon rocks, the granular patterns in the soil. Without speaking, the woman commanded her again. Her will reached out across the airless space like a lightning bolt arcing from cloud to cloud.

Raise your faceplate—now.

"Kate? KATE?"

At the sound of the voice, jarringly loud inside her helmet, Kate moved at last—straight upward, in a leap that would have cleared an Olympic high jump back on Earth. She spun, arms flailing, before falling slowly back to the lunar surface.

"Kate? Did I startle you? Sorry." It was the instructor; he was standing over her, peering out through his faceplate with a mixture of amusement and concern. Kate scrambled to her feet, grateful for his timely interruption—then she went rigid again, her heart hammering. The woman was still there, standing a few paces away.

The instructor couldn't see her.

Kate spoke with an effort. "I...I was just...daydreaming. And I..." Her voice faded away, for the woman was gliding silently toward her again, her eyes intent.

"We're heading back to the base now," the instructor told her.

She hastily joined him, springing along at his side. She wondered wildly for a moment if the ghostly woman would follow, join them in the shuttle's cramped interior, disembark with them, and wander about in the brightly lit mall...

But a glance over her shoulder showed her only the flat and empty plain. The green-robed figure had vanished as though it had never been there at all.

◆ ◆ ◆

"Want to come to the VR-cade with us, Kate?" one of the boys asked. "They've got some great new games."

Kate whirled, startled, to face the other students. "What? Oh...no, thanks. I think I'll just go to my quarters—I'm kind of tired."

"See you later then." The other kids moved away through the Lunar Mall in a noisy chattering group, gliding gracefully in the weak gravity. Kate was left alone.

She walked on through the mall in a daze. *It starts with hallucinations,* she thought. Matt had been right; she was going moon-mad. Only a crazy would come here to live, people on Earth said: social misfits, loners, eccentrics of all kinds—they ended up here, like a kind of flotsam cast up from Earth. Loony Lunies! But why should *she* suffer from moon-madness? She had only been here for three Earth months, and she'd been enjoying every minute of it. Now she recalled, with a pulse of horror, the woman in the strange robe with its intricate pattern of long-petalled flowers embroidered on the green material. They intruded on her vision, for a terrifying instant were clearer than the scene of shops and pedestrians around her.

No—go away!

She realized in alarm that she had almost said it out loud.

So much for sensible, scientific Kate Iwasaki, she thought bitterly. *I'll have to go to the counsellor now, and he'll ship me home on the next shuttle.* She looked fearfully at the other shoppers. Surely they must see how tense and obviously agitated she was. She thought one or two of them looked at her oddly as they passed, and she hastily turned toward a storefront, pretending to admire the wares on display.

It was Ramachandra's gift shop. She'd often paused to gaze at the items in its display case, all beyond her own modest price range. Most souvenirs here were tacky and cheap: plastic models of shuttles or moon rocks with "A gift from Luna Base" emblazoned on them in gold letters. But Mr. Ramachandra sold quality goods. Loveliest of all were the little sculptures which he made himself: graceful figures and animal shapes that seemed to quiver with life. Kate pretended to examine one now, an elegant figure of a woman with a hunting bow in her hands. The string was of gold wire, the arrow poised and ready for flight. A hound stood at the woman's side, eager, ready to spring.

"Artemis, Goddess of the Moon," said a voice in her ear.

She looked up, and to her embarrassment found herself staring into the face of Mr. Ramachandra himself: an elderly Indian man, with white hair wisping around a bald, nut-brown scalp. He was attired, as always, in an outrageous many-coloured robe adorned with bits of flashing mirror that glittered as he moved. His eyes were darkest brown, the colour of black coffee.

She realized to her dismay that she was on the verge of tears, and that Mr. Ramachandra knew it.

"Something is wrong," he said in an undertone, making it a statement of fact rather than a question.

Kate gulped a lungful of air, furious with herself. "It's nothing," she managed to say, but the answer rang false even in her own ears.

"Oh, dear. *That* kind of nothing." He waved to a door at the back of his shop. "I was just going to have a cup of tea. Will you join me? Tea can be an excellent restorative."

She didn't really want to join him, but it was either that, or risk bawling in public like an idiot. *If I'm going to have to leave Luna Base, at least let me do it with some dignity*, she thought, and followed Mr. Ramachandra into the back room. It was small and cluttered, with half-finished figurines of stone, wood, or clay sitting on the shelves.

"I'll just put the kettle on," said Mr. Ramachandra. "There. Now perhaps you'd like to tell me what's wrong?"

"Oh, nothing really. I'm just going crazy, is all," she replied, smiling wanly.

"If so, you're in the right place. Only a lunatic would go to the Moon. We are all a little bit odd, we Lunies, wouldn't you agree?"

"This is more than just being odd. I've got moon-madness." Tears welled in her eyes, and she blinked, hard. "Hallucinations and everything. They'll have to send me back home."

"What sort of hallucinations are you having?"

In a few short sentences she told him. It was easy to talk of it in here, with the kettle on the stove and the workroom all around her, small and cluttered and normal. Mr. Ramachandra raised his white eyebrows when she had finished.

"Curious," he said. He rose and went to the kettle, which was already shrieking for attention. He glanced at her thoughtfully over his shoulder. "You're Japanese, aren't you, Kate?" he added abruptly as he filled a teapot, waiting patiently as the water, slowed by the low gravity, slid down the kettle's spout like ketchup.

"Canadian, actually," she corrected.

"But you are Japanese by descent, am I right?"

"Yes," she admitted, wondering where this was leading.

"Curious," he said again. He settled in his chair as the tea steeped. "Are you familiar with Japanese folklore and legends?"

"Not really. I'm more into science."

"Then you'll not be familiar with the old tale of the maiden of the Moon?" She shook her head and he continued, a faraway look in his eyes, "There was once an old couple in long-ago Japan, who yearned for a child of their own. One day when the husband was cutting bamboo, he found a tiny human infant, a little girl, tucked away in one of the hollow stems. He and his wife raised this girl-child, and she grew into a beautiful maiden. But she would not marry any of the wealthy men who came to ask for her hand in marriage. She explained that she was a magical being, a child of the Moon, and one day she would have to return to her own people in the moon-world. And, indeed, there came a night when a company of glorious spirit people descended upon a moonbeam, and they bore the lovely moon-maiden away with them into the sky as her foster parents watched in sorrow." His coffee-coloured eyes looked deep into hers. "You're quite sure you've never heard this story?"

Kate hesitated. "Pretty sure." She had, in fact, no recollection of it whatsoever.

"And yet your hallucination, as you call it, seems strongly reminiscent of it. Moon-people. Elegant spirit beings in a lunar realm. It almost makes one wonder if there might not be a kind of ancestral memory, or..."

"Or what?"

"Or perhaps what you saw was—real."

She stared. *He's the crazy one, not me,* she thought.

"The Moon," Mr. Ramachandra continued as he poured the tea into two large mugs, "the Moon is many things. It is a home for us, and a provider of useful resources. But it is also a place of myth and fable—a repository of dreams, if you will." His own face took on a dreamy look. "A land about which myths have been woven is a haunted place. How haunted must the Moon be, which hangs in the sky for all to see, which all cultures have held in common since the dawn of time!

"Among these empty wastes dwells the Chinese goddess Chang'o, in the form of an immortal toad; and the Man in the Moon wanders about with his bundle of sticks on his back and his faithful dog at his side; and the Maori woman Rona, exiled here after cursing the moon-god, gazes longingly at the Earth to which she can never return. For us Hindus, the Moon is associated with Soma, god of the sacred plant that brings ecstasy to mortals. I have felt positively blissful ever since I first arrived here.

"Now perhaps Mr. Ramachandra's mind is only making him believe that he feels the presence of the god. Perhaps that is the explanation. And then again," he added, with an impish smile, "perhaps it isn't."

She stared at him over her steaming mug. "What are you saying—that all those things are real?"

He answered with a question of his own. "Why did you come to Luna Base?"

She shrugged. "I guess I just wanted to see the Moon. It's always interested me."

"How so?"

"Oh, I don't know," she said irritably. "Is it important?"

"It might be." Mr. Ramachandra sipped his tea and stared into space. "The original moon landings, now—why did those astronauts come here? It was quite pointless, from a scientific standpoint. It had already been demonstrated that automated machines could do the same thing more cheaply and with no risk to human life. But we are a romantic and impractical species, we humans."

Kate made a dismissive gesture. "My dad said it was all done for political reasons."

"The space race was, yes. But the desire to walk upon the Moon—that goes back further to the old myths and legends, to dreamers like Jules Verne.

That is why the world watched and held its breath in 1969. And that is why some of us come here—not the tourists, who only want to do what the neighbours haven't done, to take pictures, and jump higher than on Earth. No, it is the Moon of myth and magic that calls people like you and me."

"But if the woman I saw was…real, then everyone else should have seen her too," Kate argued.

"Maybe not, if it was a spirit you saw." He put down his mug and waved his arms about vaguely. "The spirit realm is everywhere, but it is not like our physical reality. It is different for each one of us, or so I believe."

Kate looked away. "I…would rather she wasn't real. You see, she wants me dead."

"Why do you say that?"

Kate rose and began to pace the little room. "She wanted me to open up my faceplate. To let all my air out, and die. She *wanted* that. I could see it, in her eyes."

"But you don't know why she would want such a thing?"

"No! That's just it. Why? What's it all about?" She was almost shouting now.

Mr. Ramachandra's voice and gaze remained calm. "Why don't you ask her?"

◆ ◆ ◆

Kate stood tensely inside the main air lock, listening to her own short, sharp breaths. She'd have to be quick: students weren't allowed out on their own. The metal door slid open; there was a hiss of expelled air; and dust grains danced briefly before settling again. Before her lay smooth grey ground surrounded by barren hills: the desolate grandeur of the Taurus-Littrow Valley.

Kate drew a deep breath and leaped out of the air lock.

She bounded down the length of the valley, halting only when the safe comforting glow of the base was far behind her. A huge, grey-white boulder sprawled up ahead, casting a long shadow under the harsh sun. Kate paused next to it, and waited.

"Come on," she whispered. "Where are you?"

Nothing stirred. The valley was empty, as it had been for billions of years. Kate turned slowly, scanning the hills, the drab grey ground.

And then, quite suddenly, she noticed the tree.

It was no more than a few moon-strides away on the valley's flat floor, growing where nothing should be able to grow: a slender sapling covered in sharp-pointed leaves. As she stared at it, leaves and branches stirred, as though bending to the whim of a wind. The little tree bowed and swayed before her, offering no explanation for itself, a green intrusion on the moon-scape.

Kate swallowed hard. *Hallucinations again*. She missed the Earth, with its green growing things, that was all. But the tree did not fade as she approached it. It looked so *real*. She must try to touch it, prove to herself that it wasn't actually there...

And then she halted in mid-stride, for the shapes of other trees were appearing all around her. Insubstantial at first, like smoke or shadow, their spindly forms solidified as she watched. The grey land around her bore a blush of green. Above her, blossoms hung amid the stars, clustering on the half-seen boughs of some flowering tree. She whirled. The great grey boulder was still there, but now its rugged sides were mottled with moss and lichen and surrounded by large-fronded ferns. The other rocks also remained where they had been, but they had changed. Random moon-rubble no longer, they formed part of a garden whose lush greenery they complemented, as if by design. A large ornamental pond spread before her, a mirror for black sky and blue Earth; beside it stood a squat stone lantern, its peaked roof sheltering a flame that danced as it fed upon some other, alien air.

Then Kate saw the woman.

She was walking along the far side of the pool. Her jet-black hair now streamed loosely upon her shoulders, teased by the same wind that played in the little tree, and her robe was white. Where she walked, grass sprang from the regolith; it did not so much sprout as suddenly appear, as though her presence called it into being. And there was a path beneath her feet, a path lit by stone lanterns that ran winding into the hills beyond—hills that were rocky and barren no longer. On one jade-green summit there rose pagoda-roofed towers, their windows glowing warmly against the black sky.

The white-clad woman was now close enough to touch. Kate's blood turned to ice, but she held her ground. The woman raised one hand, gesturing gracefully.

Suddenly Kate understood.

She was being invited to join the woman: to go with her up the winding curves of that lamplit path, up into the hills that were empty no more. Up to the palace with its shining towers. There would be music and warmth within, and light and laughter; and something more, more than any of these things, something for which her heart hungered...

Kate set a booted foot upon the path, mesmerized. She would go. She would enter that palace, that place of light where a welcome awaited her. All that came between her and that realm was this heavy, cumbersome suit that she wore. It held her back, anchored her to the dead realm of the airless waste. She could cast it off, set it aside, be freed forever from the need for it.

Freed...

Understanding came to Kate in a blinding flash, and she halted in the middle of her second step. The woman in white turned to her, eyes inquiring. Kate made herself meet those deep tranquil eyes, boldly and directly.

"No," she said.

The sound of her voice could not reach the woman. Or could it? The dark eyes widened, the hovering hand fell. The woman faced her, eyes steady and intense, imposing her will.

"*No,*" Kate said again, more forcefully. "I want to stay here. *Here.* Do you understand? I'm not going with you!"

The woman stared at her, first with gentle puzzlement, then with comprehension, which broke upon her face like a wave. For the first time her deep eyes smiled. She shook her head and laughed soundlessly. Then, in an instant, she was gone.

With her went all the life and colour of that other world. Trees and shrubbery wisped away to nothingness; the Earth-reflecting pool rippled away like a heat mirage, and there in its place was the dry, grey ground. The far hills were bare and lifeless once more, the lofty towers bowed and faded. Of the garden only the boulders remained, forlorn as bare bones. Kate was alone once more. Her eyes misted, but only briefly.

She drew a sharp, shuddering breath. And headed back through the silent valley to Luna Base.

◆ ◆ ◆

Mr. Ramachandra was modelling clay in his workshop. When he glanced up and saw Kate standing in the doorway, he smiled but said nothing, his fingers continuing to pinch and stroke the clay.

"I confronted her," she blurted.

He put the clay down. "Ah."

"You were right," said Kate. "Everything was all right. She didn't mean me any harm; she only wanted me to join her, in *her* world. I think she believed I wanted to. When I looked in her eyes, it was as though she understood. I don't think I'll ever see her again."

He titled his head to one side, considering. "No, I don't suppose you will."

"So, what happened out there? Was she real? Or did it all just happen inside my head? Was I moon-mad, and did going out there cure me?"

He looked thoughtful. "If I were making up a story, I would say that your spirit came from the Moon; that you inhabited this sphere long before you were born in a human body. And that is why you longed for the Moon, like the maiden in the folktale, why you came here as soon as you had the chance. It was a homecoming, if you will. But you realized that to return to your spirit life, you would have to leave your human, physical life behind, together with your family and friends down on Earth. And you couldn't make yourself do that."

He rose and went to a shelf, taking from it a small figurine, which he held out to her. Kate stared at it: a woman in a flowing kimono, standing upon a base that curved like the crescent moon. "It's beautiful," she said shyly.

"It is the moon maiden from the story."

She reached out, ran a finger over the exquisite folds of the robe, the flying hair. "How...how much are you asking for it?"

He pressed the little figurine into her hands. "Consider it a gift," he said. "I do not charge my friends."

She thanked him, stammering a little, then met his dark brown eyes again. "You know, that was really dangerous, sending me out onto the surface all by myself. I might've cracked...flipped open my faceplate, or something. What made you so sure I'd be all right?"

He said nothing, but continued to gaze at her, calmly and confidently, a smile at the corners of his mouth.

"Thanks," she said awkwardly.

Then she turned and walked away, the moon maiden clutched in her hands.

----

1. RESPONDING TO THE STORY

a. With a partner, discuss the sequence of events in the story and the characters' actions and reactions.

b. Do you think the author has created an effective story? Explain.

c. Do you think Kate was really hallucinating? Why or why not? Explain fully.

d. Why is Kate tempted by the Moon Maiden?

e. Why might people who dare the unknown be thought of as crazy?
   What do you think?

2. EDITOR'S DESK DESCRIPTIVE PARAGRAPHS

Reread the story and take note of the descriptive paragraphs. A descriptive paragraph describes a place, object, or idea with vivid words and imagery. A good descriptive paragraph creates a picture in the reader's mind. Analyse the use of descriptive paragraphs in the story. Are the paragraphs effective? Do they create a picture in your mind? What writing techniques, such as simile, metaphor, or personification, does the author use to create the images? Are these images effective?

SELF-ASSESSMENT: Choose a piece of writing from your writing portfolio that you would like to revise. Select a paragraph that could be improved by adding description. Rewrite the paragraph, adding descriptive details and vivid imagery. As you write other stories, or informational writing, consider using descriptive paragraphs.

3. LANGUAGE CONVENTIONS ELLIPSIS POINTS

Reread the "Moon Maiden" paying attention to the **ellipsis points** used in the story. Ellipsis points are most often used to show a thought has been left unfinished or to show a pause or break in speech. For example:

> I...I was just...daydreaming. And I...
> It looked so real. She must try to touch it, prove to herself that it wasn't actually there...

> **Ellipsis points** are a series of three dots used to show that something has been left out.

What is the effect of the above sentences? What do they show about how the character in the "Moon Maiden" is feeling and acting? Are the ellipsis points effective? What do they add to the story?

Jot down a few sentences from the story that use ellipsis points. Analyse the purpose of the punctuation. Does it help to reflect natural speech or the character's thought processes?

The next time you write dialogue for a story, experiment with ellipsis points.

4. WRITING A FRIENDLY LETTER

Take on the role of Kate and write a letter home to her brother, Matt, or to another family member. What would Kate tell her brother? What would Kate tell her parents? Be sure to stay true to the character. For example, Kate probably wouldn't tell her brother about the Moon Maiden but she might tell a friend or her parents. Share your letter with a classmate, asking them to write back.

WHO'S OUT THERE?

RADIO INTERVIEW

BY *Barbara Frum*

What is your view of UFOs? In this radio interview, Barbara Frum discovered evidence that technology could be the answer.

I was studying my research for an interview about remotely-controlled "ghost planes" with John Taylor, the editor of *All the World's Aircraft*, when all of a sudden it hit me. Mr. Taylor, describing these new weapons, could have been mistaken for one of our UFO "scientists." When I suggested to Taylor that his RPV (remotely-piloted vehicle) missiles seemed able to do a lot of things that flying saucers are famous for, he got as excited about the implications as I was. And so, instead of talking about the RPV, as we were scheduled to, we spent our time on what I still believe was the even hotter news angle—the true story of the UFO.

GOALS AT A GLANCE

■ Analyse the features of a radio interview.
■ Write a radio interview.

141

FRUM: Mr. Taylor, when I first read about the RPV it sounded remark-
          ably like a UFO. How many countries now have these and how
          many are developing them?

TAYLOR: Something like six or seven countries at the moment. The main
          operator, of course, is America. There are some in the United
          Kingdom, some in Canada, some in Italy, Germany, and Japan.
          The Soviet Union has some. We know very little about theirs at
          the moment but they certainly have some.

FRUM: Why aren't they vulnerable to being tracked and chronicled?

TAYLOR: Well, the little mini RPV that the Rand Company has produced,
          for example, doesn't have any straight lines anywhere. Every
          possible surface is curved, so if you pick it up by radar, you get
          what the radar people call "scatter." The signals don't bounce
          back towards your receiver. They go off into space. The RPV
          itself is made of plastic. If you were lucky enough to pick it up,
          it would look about the size of a very tiny bird.

          But let me tell you a little story. I spoke to a very senior officer
          of an air force in Europe and said to him, "Do you have any
          evidence of Soviet RPV missiles flying over your country?" And
          he said, "You've seen reports in the press about UFO sightings
          over our country, haven't you?" So I said, "Yes." He said, "Well,
          do you believe in flying saucers?" "Not really." "Well, what else
          could they be, then?" And so I said, "Well, they could be RPV
          missiles. If you shot down a Soviet RPV, would you tell the
          press?" And his reply was, "When we shoot down things, we
          don't tell the press."

FRUM: Not "if," but "when."

TAYLOR: Right.

FRUM: You're describing something with round sides, which can hover
          low. You haven't talked about sound. But you've written about
          laser beams and we're hearing about blue rays right now in
          Arizona. I just wonder if people are seeing the testing of the RPV
          when they sight a UFO.

TAYLOR: I think this is quite likely, yes. Some of these aircraft are very,
          very quiet.

FRUM: What about the low ones that hover, would they emit light?

TAYLOR: You'd have light from the engines. You'd see the engine exhaust,
          so they would appear to emit light. You see, if you get any

sort of light or any engine exhaust glowing through a damp atmosphere, you'll get a very peculiar sort of glow with a halo around it, very often.

FRUM: People always say that UFOs can turn suddenly, that they can move suddenly, drift, loiter, hover, and then zoom away.

TAYLOR: Well, not having a pilot on board, you can pull a very, very tight turn with an RPV. You can pull a much tighter turn and impose greater loads on it than you can on a piloted aircraft, because a man wouldn't survive. Therefore, they can turn remarkably quickly, yes.

FRUM: Isn't that fascinating. You may be really onto something, Mr. Taylor.

TAYLOR: Well, it could be, it's possible. Obviously, there are many things going on all the time in aviation that don't get highly publicized. The American reconnaissance aircraft, the SR-71, which is the fastest airplane ever to serve with any air force, was virtually unknown for years. The Secretary of State announced that it existed, but we didn't know it had already been tested and was in service by then. You can keep an aircraft like that very quiet if you want to.

FRUM: Could that explain why authorities always pooh-pooh these sightings? Maybe this could account, too, for why some of these sightings are seen zooming along power lines and roads.

TAYLOR: They could be test vehicles doing all sorts of jobs. Obviously, if you're going to test one of these aircraft, if you can get it to fly very accurately along one of your own power lines, you know how accurately you can control it over a long distance.

FRUM: So running it along power lines makes sense as a test?

TAYLOR: Oh, yes, along straight roads, just to test it, to test how stable it is, how well it will keep to a pre-programmed course, if it's going to be out of your control range. Already we have something like twenty or twenty-five variants of one design from the Rand Company. They were used extensively in Vietnam for reconnaissance and they brought back some very remarkable photographs.

FRUM: Mr. Taylor, I have a feeling that you may have accounted for something that's been mysterious for a long, long time. ◆

1. Responding to the Radio Interview

a. In two or three sentences write a summary of the article.

b. Who is John Taylor? Why is his testimony believable? What makes him a credible source?

c. What is Taylor's explanation for the possible sightings of UFOs?

d. Do you find this a believable explanation? Why or why not? Explain fully.

e. Was there any part of the interview you did not understand?

2. Literature Studies Features of a Radio Interview

With a partner, reread "Who's Out There?" and discuss the features of a radio interview. What is the purpose of a radio interview? How is information obtained? Listen to interviews on the radio and jot down the features. Compare your list of features to your classmates'.

STRATEGIES

3. Media Maker Develop a Radio Script

With a group of classmates, develop your own radio interview. Think of a subject or topic you would like to find out more information about. Interview an expert on the topic. Tape the interview, review the tape, and transcribe the interview into a radio script. With a group member, you could take on the roles of interviewer and interviewee, and perform the interview. Keep these suggestions in mind.

- Research the event, issue, or person until you have enough background information to develop some questions.
- Develop your list of questions.
- Contact the person you would like to interview and explain your purpose. Ask permission to tape the interview.
- Remember to listen carefully, and be ready to ask follow-up questions in response to what you hear.
- Take notes to remind you of what was discussed in the interview.

Scan this article's photos, captions, and headings, and predict what it will be about.

Radical Robots

Article from YES Mag with
John Garrett

A short, six-wheeled robot with a metallic claw opens an apartment door. It surveys the scene with its TV camera eye, transmitting images to police officers waiting outside the building. An officer gives the robot a command to direct its water cannon at the suspect hiding in a corner. Before the suspect can recover from the effects of the water blast, police move in and make an arrest.

Is this a scene from a futuristic movie or is it for real? While most of us will not see metallic "RoboCops" in our home town any time soon, this event actually took place.

Robots are no longer the imaginative creations of science fiction writers. There are hundreds of thousands of robots in the world today. These robots come in all shapes and sizes—from the micro to the mammoth. Some are little more than metal arms while others are bristling with sensors and cameras.

The tasks robots perform are practically endless: they run errands in hospitals, patrol buildings at night, spray-paint cars, perform surgical operations, shear sheep, and explore the ocean floor. Robots have been on the moon and, unlike humans, they have been to Mars.

GOALS AT A GLANCE

- Analyse point of view.
- Write a time line.

145

Robots are especially good at dull and dangerous jobs. They're not bothered by extreme heat or cold, loud noise, or toxic fumes—things which would make a human worker very uncomfortable, hearing impaired, or sick. Robots never ask for a bathroom break, they never get careless, and they never get bored of doing the same old job again and again and again.

While real robots may not have all the capabilities of some of Hollywood's fictional creations, roboticists are making advances every day. Who knows? Maybe one day roboticists will be creating robots more fantastic than anything yet proposed by movie producers and science fiction writers.

If It Only Had a Brain

Most robots have computer "brains." Responsible for receiving and transmitting information, decision making, and memory, a robot's computer brain carries instructions that tell the robot what to do and how to do it.

Today computers can carry out millions of instructions per second. Faster computers mean, for example, that a robot can respond more quickly. But speed isn't everything. Scientists are still not sure how the 100 billion neurons in our brains allow us to think and move, so designing a robot that can do many things that we take for granted—such as picking up a chocolate-filled pastry without crushing it or instantly telling the difference between a shadow and a hole in the floor—is still a big challenge.

In 1997, a small robotic vehicle, called *Sojourner*, explored the surface of Mars.

Robots at Work

International Submarine Engineering (ISE) of Port Coquitlam, BC builds robots to go boldly where humans can't: deep under the sea. ISE robot submarines lay and maintain submarine cables and pipelines, work on offshore oil platforms, collect samples and data for scientists, and help detect and remove ocean mines.

Some ISE robots work on their own, controlled by programs in computers they carry. One such robot submarine called *Theseus* has made journeys of 400 km in open water and 16 km under Arctic sea ice. *Theseus* is 10 m long, about the size of a small whale. Its battery powered electric motor pushes it along at 7.5 km/h. *Theseus* was designed to lay undersea cables connecting ocean sensors to shore.

Most ISE robots are controlled by human operators in ships or on oil platforms. Wires or optical fibres connect the operator and the robot, carrying commands and bringing back video images and sensor data

Theseus has made journeys of 400 km in open water.

from the work site. The operators use the submersible's manipulator arms and tools to turn valves, move pipes or cables, weld, plug in connectors, and collect samples, including live animals such as crabs.

In 1997, a four-wheeled robot called *Nomad* trundled over more than 215 km in Chile's rugged Atacama Desert. About the size of a small car, *Nomad* was designed to help researchers prepare for future missions to Antarctica, the moon, and Mars. *Nomad* was outfitted with a wide array of sensors including a laser range finder which helped it figure out how far away objects were. The laser range finder sent out invisible pulses of laser light then timed how long it took the light to bounce off objects and come back. This information along with images from its cameras helped *Nomad* locate cliffs and craters.

In 1994, the eight-legged *Dante II* robot descended into an active Alaskan volcano. Decked out with gas and temperature sensors, scanning laser range finder, colour zoom and leg view cameras, *Dante II* transmitted a steady flow of information via microwave and satellite to anxious scientists waiting 140 km away.

Nomad (above) was designed to help prepare for future missions to the moon and Mars.

Dante II, (right) an eight-legged robot, walked where no one can go—into an active volcano.

1. RESPONDING TO THE ARTICLE

a. What advancements have been made in robot technology? Give three examples from the article.

b. Discuss this article with a friend. Predict what the future of robots will be. How will robots such as these affect exploration?

2. LITERATURE STUDIES POINT OF VIEW

Reread the article, paying attention to the point of view. Is it first person, second person, or third person? Is the point of view used effective? In factual writing, such as magazine and newspaper articles, the third person point of view is often used. Sometimes in other types of writing, such as speeches or guides, the second person is used. It makes a more intimate connection with the reader because it feels like the author is talking directly to you.

Examine other informational articles in magazines and newspapers, concentrating on point of view. What point of view is used? How is the point of view different or similar to the point of views used in fiction pieces that you've read?

3. MEDIA MESSAGES PORTRAYAL OF ROBOTS

With a group of classmates, discuss the roles robots have played in television shows and in the movies such as *Lost in Space* and *Star Wars.* What are they like? What capabilities do the robots have? Are the robots the heroes or villains? Why have robots been effective villains? Why have they been effective heroes?

4. WRITING DEVELOP A TIME LINE

Develop a time line for a modern technology, such as the computer or the Internet. Add to the time line your belief about how the technology will change in the future. What fantastic events can you predict? Use the suggestions on the process page on conducting research on pages 160-161 to help you research.

Shooting the Sun

Poem by Amy Lowell

Four horizons cozen me
To distances I dimly see.

Four paths beckon me to stray,
Each a bold and separate way.

Monday morning shows the East
Satisfying as a feast.

Tuesday I will none of it,
West alone holds benefit.

Later in the week 'tis due
North that I would hurry to.

While on other days I find
To the South content of mind.

So I start, but never rest
North or South or East or West.

Each horizon has its claim
Solace to a different aim.

Four-souled like the wind am I,
Voyaging an endless sky,
Undergoing destiny.

GOALS AT A GLANCE

- Analyse rhyme scheme.
- Use punctuation in poetry.

1. RESPONDING TO THE POEM

a. Read the poem aloud and listen to it carefully. Tell a partner what you think.

b. What does the poet mean by "each horizon has its claim"?

c. How does the speaker feel at different points in the poem? Explain.

2. POET'S CRAFT RHYME SCHEME

Rhyme is the repetition of the same sound, usually at the end of words. In traditional poetry, the words at the end of each line in a **stanza** rhyme with each other. For example, "me" rhymes with "see" in the first stanza. This is called the rhyme scheme. "Shooting the Sun" has an *aa* **bb** <u>cc</u>... rhyme scheme. What is the effect of a regular rhyme scheme? Does it make the poem easier to read? Harder? Read the poem aloud concentrating on how the words sound.

Reread and assess the effectiveness of the rhyme scheme in other poems. Make a list of the different types of rhyme schemes you come across, for example, *a* **b** **b** *a*, *a* **b** *a* **b**, or *a* *a* **b** **b**. The next time you write a poem, use one of the rhyme schemes you have discovered.

> A **stanza** is a repeated unit with the same number of lines and the same rhyme scheme. Stanzas are used to organize a poem in much the same way paragraphs are used to organize prose. In free verse, a poem may be organized by stanzas, but will not have a regular rhyme scheme.

3. LANGUAGE CONVENTIONS PUNCTUATE POETRY

Poets sometimes adapt punctuation, line breaks, and capitalization to suit their needs. Traditional poems often begin each new line with a capital letter, whether or not it marks the beginning of a sentence. However, in modern poetry there are no set rules for punctuation. Reread "Shooting the Sun" and take note of the punctuation used. Is punctuation used in a traditional way? Or is there no punctuation? What was the author's purpose in the type of punctuation used?

Rewrite the poem in sentences and try adjusting the punctuation to fit normal sentence structure. What differences do you notice? Why do you think the poet chose to change the punctuation and break the lines in these particular places?

SELF-ASSESSMENT: Choose a poem from your writing portfolio and examine how you've used punctuation, line breaks, and capitalization. Try another way of punctuating. How does it change your poem?

In 1986, the space shuttle
Challenger *exploded after*
taking off. In this story, a boy
reacts to the tragic event.

A Major Malfunction

S h o r t   S t o r y
b y   M i k e   K i l p a t r i c k

Whew! Made it.

I finished the last question and put down my pen. Maybe even passed this one. Wouldn't *that* be nice? My fingers felt stiff from writing, and I clenched and opened my hand several times.

The room had that artificial hush to it, the hush of a class during a big test. I listened. Overhead—the low, eternal hum of the fluorescent lights. Behind me—a muted rustling sound as Andy shifted in his chair. Around me—breathing. Yeah, I could hear everybody breathing. Kind of comforting. Outside in the hall, a locker door slammed shut. Voices and laughter echoed, then disappeared.

"One minute," Mr. Kent warned, jolting me back to reality. He leaned back against the heating vent and scanned the room. Behind rimless glasses, his eyes looked as grey as the January sky.

"Oh, sirrrrr!" wailed Mary Sinclair.

I glanced at my paper and my answer to question three. I'd written: "'Out, out brief candle' is from the famous 'tomorrow and tomorrow and tomorrow' speech. This is when Macbeth learns that the queen, who got him into the whole mess, is dead. It's a metaphor expressing how short life is."

Why couldn't Shakespeare write in English? I thought.

"Make sure you sign your names on the upper right hand corner of each page," instructed Mr. Kent. He rubbed the back of his neck with his left hand.

The gesture reminded me of my grandfather, who used to do that when he got tired. Grandpa Pat had died of a heart attack just before Christmas, and I couldn't keep him out of my head. I pictured him now, sitting upstairs, looking out his bedroom window, listening to the radio. That's how I'll always picture him: eighty-five years old, a bantam rooster of a man, sitting waiting to die.

I sighed. Our family expected it of course, but his death really threw me. I missed him, you know.

Click, craaaaackle, the intercom sputtered to life.

"Your attention please!" said Mrs. Lacey, our principal, her tone unusually grim. "I have a rather sad announcement to make. The United States shuttle *Challenger* has blown up on takeoff. It appears that all seven astronauts, including teacher Christa McAuliffe, have been killed."

Our class was stunned. Everybody stopped writing, and we all looked at each other. Nobody seemed to know how to react. The quiet of exam-time deepened. Time seemed to elongate. Tilt, ding, whoops! Something shifted inside me. I felt suddenly off balance.

Honest to God, my first impulse was to laugh. No kidding, it almost slipped out. I couldn't help it. I mean, the news surprised me. It seemed impossible.

Andy, my best friend, *did* laugh, a snort, then an incredulous giggle cut short by an embarrassed cough.

"It's not funny," Brad Anderson said from the seat beside Andy. Fifteen, six feet tall, Brad played quarterback for the junior football team and he thought he was real tough.

A guy on my left, two aisles over, was almost crying. His knuckles dug into his eyes. His shoulders were bunched as if he didn't want to be seen. I mean, you don't cry at our school unless you want to be branded a wimp.

I turned around to say something to Andy. Brad was towering above him, his face twisted with rage. He drew back his fist and—whap! Andy's head snapped back. His eyes opened wide.

"Hey!" I said, frightened.

"Boys!" Mr. Kent called sharply.

"What're you laughin' at?" Brad snarled at Andy, his voice breaking.

Mr. Kent moved towards them. "Brad, sit down."

"I don't think it's funny something happened to the shuttle," Andy tried to explain. "That's not why I laughed."

"You better not laugh," Brad warned, retreating to his seat. "You shouldn't laugh."

"Off my back, doorknob!" Andy told him, holding his jaw.

"That's enough!" ordered Mr. Kent. He looked shaken up, as if he wasn't sure what to do. That scared me. Mr. Kent always seemed so sure of himself.

Andy spoke softly, addressing not only Brad but the rest of us as well. "I didn't think they could die, that's all. Not *them*." Andy's eyes stayed glued to the top of his desk. He didn't seem afraid or anything. Angry maybe. Confused. Hurt that people misunderstood his laughter.

The bell rang and we all filed out of the classroom. The hall buzzed with the news. I felt awful. I'd been going to laugh too. The announcement felt like a bad joke. I mean, people like that don't die. They're not supposed to. Heroes don't die. Sylvester Stallone never dies in his movies. Neither does Arnold Schwartzenegger. The thought of those astronauts dying was absurd, something you'd laugh at because you knew it couldn't be happening.

Andy and I went down to the student lounge. The place was crowded, all of us watching the TV perched up on a wall unit. "There they are," Andy whispered.

On the screen, the flickering figures of the crew walked out across the tarmac. Her hair a tangle of curls, Christa McAuliffe stepped out of the line for a second and said something into the camera. Her face crinkled with laughter, and in that moment she reminded me of a kid, like some of the girls I know, all excited when they're about to begin a wild roller coaster ride.

And then the countdown.

Liftoff.

The explosion.

And afterwards…on the ground, the faces of the onlookers: confusion, fear, knowledge. Up in the sky, the long, white vapour trail falling silently through the air like some disconnected umbilical cord.

The first time we watched, I somehow thought maybe it wouldn't happen, maybe they'd made a mistake. Maybe, maybe, maybe…but of course I was wrong. During the next few replays I kept hoping for a different ending.

"Beam me up, Scottie," Andy said, shaking his head in disbelief. "This ain't how it's s'posed to go. This never happens on *Star Trek*."

"Yeah," I agreed. "Where's Captain Picard?"

"Where's Data?"

Something held us there in the lounge. We skipped all our afternoon classes to watch the coverage; a lot of students did.

About two o'clock a bunch of kids came in, some Grade Twelvers. Leather jackets with studs. Spiked hair. They crowded up to the front and stood watching for a few minutes.

"So, like, how long's this stuff gonna be on?" a girl with orange hair and army boots asked.

"All afternoon," Andy said.

"Oh Gawd!" She rolled her eyes. "I can't stand it. We're gonna miss our soaps."

Her boyfriend scowled. He pulled at the safety pin stuck through his left earlobe. "They can't do that. We always watch 'General Hospital.'"

"C'mon, eh?" someone said. "Be quiet. We wanna see this."

"I bet you do," the punker hissed. "You're the kinda creep who slows up to slobber over a car accident."

"Ghouls!" the orange-haired girl yelled as her crowd pushed their way out of the room.

◆◆◆

That night they showed the disaster on the TV the whole evening. I kept switching channels to find the coverage...don't know why I was so fascinated. After all, what'd I care about that teacher? I never met her. Hey, I don't even *like* teachers. Maybe I *am* a ghoul. Still, without my wanting it to, her death really bothered me.

There they were again, the crew walking, arms swinging, Christa McAuliffe stepping excitedly out to say something, the ice-covered, glistening sheen of the bottom of the rockets, the countdown, the liftoff, and then...

I must've watched twenty reruns. What began to strike me as weird and particularly gruesome was the conversation between Mission Control and the pilot.

"*Challenger*, go at throttle up."

"Roger, go at throttle up."

Orange mushrooming fireball...what the..? Something obviously wrong. Vapour trail stopping mid-flight, then forking.

"We're at a minute fifteen seconds, velocity eight hundred and eighty-four metres per second."

Mission Control's voice didn't change. That's what was so awful. There was no horror in it, no surprise, no emotion. He did pause though, and there was a long hush. Then, still in that mechanical tone, still unchanged, the voice continued.

"Flight controllers are still looking very carefully at the situation. Obviously a major malfunction. We have no downlink."

I turned the television off around eleven. The picture collapsed inward and then the screen went blank. Time to hit the sack.

Upstairs, I got into bed and turned on the radio. A talk show had some experts discussing the cause of the tragedy: politicians and scientists connected to the project, an astronaut. I listened for a while and finally turned the radio off. I got up and padded into the hall. Grandpa Pat's room was across from mine. I opened his door.

A lingering whiff of pipe tobacco—his brand, Sir Walter Raleigh—hit me. Still around, after all these weeks. Towards the end, I used to come here every night. I'd wake up scared he was going to die, and I'd come in to check on Grandpa.

I'd stand in the doorway. Asleep, he'd be snoring. The snore came up slowly and rolled around in his throat. Sometimes it stopped.

I'd wait for it to continue but it had stopped right in the middle. I'd think, *heart attack!* and sneak closer.

He'd start to snore again.

Alert now, I'd watch him closely. Grandpa Pat slept on his back, his mouth grotesquely open. The snore would roll around in his throat again…and stop.

Oh man, he's dead! I'd think. He's stopped breathing for real.

I'd reach out to touch him, and his breath would catch like an engine starting up, and the snore would burst out again, making me jump with surprise.

Then I'd be scared to leave. As long as I was watching him, Grandpa would be safe. That's what I pretended, what I half-believed. All I had to do was concentrate and Grandpa Pat wouldn't die.

Now, here in the darkness, I looked at the empty bed. I felt like crying. He wasn't a hero or anything. He never fought in any war. He never went up in any rocket. I think Grandpa Pat had only been on a plane twice in his whole life.

I closed the door and went back to bed. I lay thinking, videos of Grandpa running through my mind: There he was, giving me a hug. White, soft, dandelion-fluff hair. As a kid, I used to love running my fingers through it. There he was again. We used to watch TV together—the late movie on Saturday nights. I remember Grandpa snorting with disgust at ol' Duke Wayne. "T'warn't true!" he told me. "Ain't no heroes and no villains like that. Just people, just us humans."

I remember the wood scimitar he made me one Halloween, and the colourful shield he built from an old garbage can lid.

I remember playing peewee hockey at six in the mornings and Grandpa Pat watching me from behind the boards, his breath a plume of white smoke in the freezing cold arena.

As I fell asleep, the last image I saw was that white, white vapour trail falling silently in the sky like some unattached umbilical cord.

THE *CHALLENGER* EXPLOSION

The space shuttle *Challenger* exploded just moments after takeoff in 1986. All seven astronauts on board were killed. Christa McAuliffe, a teacher, was the first civilian to go on a shuttle mission.

The shuttle disaster was brought home to North Americans in a way never experienced before. The launch was televised live, and many people watched the explosion occur.

It was the first major disaster in our quest to explore space.

1. RESPONDING TO THE STORY

a. Why does the main character feel like laughing when he hears about the *Challenger*? Do you think this is a natural reaction? Explain.

b. Why does the main character draw a parallel between the astronauts on the *Challenger* and his grandfather?

c. What is the main character's definition of a hero? Do you agree or disagree? What is your definition of a hero?

d. How does this story fit into a theme on exploration?

2. ORAL LANGUAGE GROUP DISCUSSION

With a group of classmates, discuss the following statement: "Exploring space is worth the dangers involved in exploring it." As you discuss the statement, refer to "A Major Malfunction." Do you think the astronauts on board the *Challenger* thought it was worth it to risk their lives? Would you risk your life to go into space?

After discussing the statement, write a diary entry as one of the astronauts on the *Challenger*. What would they have written in a diary entry the night before liftoff?

3. RESEARCHING RESEARCH REPORT

Research a major disaster that has happened in the 20th century, for example, the sinking of the *Titanic,* the Halifax Explosion, or the Manitoba Flood. What were the effects and how did the world, the country, or a particular community respond? See the process page on conducting research on pages 160-161 to help you with ideas on researching. You could present your report as a written paper or as an oral presentation.

4. LANGUAGE CONVENTIONS NOUNS AND VERBS

Nouns and verbs are the backbone of writing. Whenever possible, use strong, concrete, specific nouns and vivid, precise, energetic verbs in your writing. Whether you are writing a story or a research report, the nouns and verbs you use can make the difference between good writing and OK writing. For example:

	noun	verb

Weak   The nice *smell* of apple dumplings *was* in the air.
Strong   The *aroma* of apple dumplings *wafted* by.

Aroma is a stronger, more creative word than *smell,* and *wafted* is a far more striking verb than the weak, non-specific *was. Was* requires a whole phrase (in the air) to back it up. Reread the story and examine how the author uses nouns and verbs effectively.

SELF-ASSESSMENT: Flip through some of your own writing to find places where you could substitute a strong noun or verb.

Goals at a Glance

- Investigate research topics. • Locate, summarize, and organize information.

You'll find that strong research skills are useful in most of your classes, and in life outside of school as well. Almost any research project involves the following basic tasks.

Define Your Research Goal

Before you start researching, have a clear idea of what you're trying to learn. Even though you will usually be asked to conduct research on an assigned topic, you will probably have to narrow that topic to something more specific.

Activity #2 on page 159 asks you to research a 20th-century disaster. The first way to narrow the topic is to focus on one particular disaster—the Manitoba Flood of 1997, for example. Next you should define a research goal by drafting one or two specific questions that you will try to answer, such as:

- How did Manitobans respond to the flood?
- What damage did the flood cause?

It's useful to brainstorm a whole list of specific questions you *could* answer, then choose one that really interests you.

Locate the Information

Now that you've defined your goal, locate the resources that can best help you meet it. Probably your first stop will be the school library. Take some time to check out the *human* resources—teachers and librarians. They can help by suggesting the resources you should go to first. Here are the most important resources:

- **Catalogues and indexes** are categorized lists that can help you track down other resources relating to your specific topic or goal.
- **Reference works** such as encyclopedias give general information.
- **Periodicals** (magazines and newspapers) are best for gathering information on current events or specific interests.
- **Books** contain detailed information on a wide variety of topics.
- The **Internet** provides instant access to a vast amount of data.
- **Videos and other non-print media** provide information in audio and visual forms.

PROCESS

Select Information

Your next step is to select the resources and the information you are going to use. There are two things to keep in mind.

1. Select **reliable** information. Use the following questions to assess reliability:

- What is the copyright date of the resource? It will tell you whether the information is up-to-date. If you are checking a Web site on the Internet, the home page should say when the site was last updated.
- Who wrote/created the resource? Look for names of authors, institutions, or publishers that are well-known.
- Is the resource biassed? Ask yourself whether the information comes from a person or group that might be trying to persuade people to hold a certain point of view. Are all sides of the topic presented?

2. Select **relevant** information. Information is relevant when it helps you answer your research question. You should also consider how much detail the resource is providing. For example, a magazine article written for the general public is probably a more useful resource than a lengthy government report filled with technical terms.

Organize Your Findings

Keeping your research findings organized is important because eventually you will combine information from many sources into one presentation.

- Create a point-form outline showing the question you want to answer and possible subtopics. This will help you organize your notes. (You can revise your outline if your research gives you new ideas.)
- Use your note-making skills to summarize relevant information from the resources you have selected.
- Record your notes on index cards. Each card should contain
  - one important piece of information;
  - a heading that tells what subtopic the information belongs with;
  - full information about the source (title, author, publisher, place and date of publication, page number).

After you have gathered the information you think you need from all your sources, sort your notes into the subtopics you identified. Does your outline place your information in a logical, effective order?

Using your research notes and outline, write your paper or plan your presentation.

Self-Assessment

Use the checklist below to assess the strengths and weaknesses of the research you did.

- ❏ I defined my research topic as a question.
- ❏ I located the most appropriate resources.
- ❏ I selected reliable and relevant information.
- ❏ I organized my notes by topic.
- ❏ When I used other people's ideas, I acknowledged the source.

PROCESS

High Flight

Poem by John Gillespie Magee, Jr.

Oh! I have slipped the surly bonds of Earth
    And danced the skies on laughter-silvered wings;
Sunward I've climbed, and joined the tumbling mirth
    Of sun-split clouds—and done a hundred things
You have not dreamed of—wheeled and soared and swung
    High in the sunlit silence. Hov'ring there,
I've chased the shouting wind along, and flung
    My eager craft through footless halls of air. . . .

Up, up the long, delirious, burning blue
    I've topped the wind-swept heights with easy grace,
Where never lark, or even eagle flew—
And, while with silent, lifting mind I've trod
    The high untrespassed sanctity of space,
Put out my hand and touched the face of God.

Fueled

Poem by Marcie Hans

Fueled
by a million
man-made
wings of fire—
the rocket tore a tunnel through the sky—
and everybody cheered.
Fueled
only by a thought from God—
the seedling
urged its way
through the thickness of black—
and as it pierced
the heavy ceiling of the soil—
and launched itself
up into outer space—
no
one
even
clapped.

RESPONDING TO THE POEMS

a. What are the moods of the poems? How do the speakers feel?

b. What are the main ideas of the poems? Why do you think so?

c. What kind of craft do you think the speaker is flying in "High Flight"?

d. Which of the two actions in "Fueled" do you think is the most difficult to do? Explain.

e. What two things is the poet in "Fueled" comparing? Do you find the comparison effective? Why or why not?

f. How do these poems fit into a theme on exploration and technology?

FINAL FRONTIERS • 163

One of the last frontiers
humans have left
to explore is the sea.
Find out how technology
helps aquanauts
in their quest
to understand
the secrets
of the deep.

Undersea
Science

Magazine
Article

By Thomas Potts

If you saw the movie *Titanic*, you witnessed the awesome technology marine scientists use to explore the ocean floor. Submersibles and high-tech robots allow scientists to explore, take pictures and video, and recover small artifacts from deep inside ships that can sit 3000 m beneath the surface. But submersibles can only spend about six hours on the bottom before they need to return to the surface and recharge their batteries. What if scientists could actually live on the ocean bottom for over a week?

Scientists using the *Aquarius* undersea laboratory are able to do just that. Located in the Florida Keys, about 72 km south of Miami, the futuristic laboratory sits on the bottom of the ocean. Over 13 m long and 3 m wide, *Aquarius* can house four scientists and two technicians. In fact, it's the world's only underwater laboratory from which scientists can live

■ Write an informational article.
■ Analyse audience and purpose.

and work for up to ten days at a time! Operated by the National Undersea Research Center at the University of North Carolina at Wilmington, the laboratory is designed to make the inhabitants, known as aquanauts, as comfortable as possible while they study coral reef biology, geology, and chemistry.

The Underwater Landscape

Aquarius and its baseplate, a large stand with four adjustable legs filled with over 25 t of lead, sit in 19 m of water on a sand patch surrounded by living coral reefs. A giant buoy bobbing at the surface is connected to *Aquarius* by an array of hoses and cables.

Each science mission starts from the surface. Four scientists and two technicians put on heavy, one-half centimetre thick, rubber-like wet suits and twin scuba cylinders and dive off a boat. Although the water isn't much cooler than a typical bath, about 26°C, divers can become chilled after spending hours working out on the reef. After swimming through the crystal-clear blue water and large schools of violet-coloured fish feeding on microscopic plants and animals, the aquanauts finally make their way to *Aquarius.*

Welcome Aboard

Aquarius is divided into three compartments, or locks, each serving a specific function. The wet porch is the aquanaut's doorway from the ocean environment to the lab's dry interior. It works like an inverted bucket which is filled with air and then submerged underwater. The air pocket keeps water from filling the wet porch beyond a certain level in the opening, known as the moonpool. The aquanauts stow their dive gear here and have a chance to take a hot freshwater shower.

Two aquanauts relax in the bunkroom.

The middle lock, or entry lock, houses the lab's only toilet. It also serves as a separate decompression chamber in case the aquanauts need to decompress at different times. Thick iron doors close off the entry lock from the wet porch on one side and the main lock on the other.

While inside *Aquarius*, aquanauts spend most of their time in the main lock where they find many of the comforts of home: a microwave oven for cooking their lunch and dinner, a sink with hot running water, and a refrigerator stocked with milk, fruits, and vegetables. A curtain separates the main living area from the bunkroom. Three bunks stacked one on top of another line each wall of the bunkroom. A large porthole at the end of the lab gives aquanauts an unrivalled show of marine life as they wake up each morning.

Keeping in Touch

Even though the aquanauts may feel completely removed from civilization, *Aquarius* is connected to a life support buoy on the surface. The buoy looks like a 5.5 m wide doughnut with a tower sticking up in the middle. The simple design hides thousands of dollars worth of computers, generators, batteries, and communications equipment. This is what keeps the laboratory running. Fresh air, water, and electricity are continually pumped down to *Aquarius*.

A series of computers constantly transmits critical data through the microwave tower to shore, 14 km away. Here, the rest of *Aquarius*'s crew monitors carbon dioxide, temperature, and humidity levels inside the lab as well as the mechanical systems inside the buoy. Cellular telephone service and marine radios provide voice communication between the aquanauts and the surface. An Internet link will soon allow the aquanauts to talk with the entire world through cyberspace.

Living on the Bottom

Before *Aquarius* was launched, scientists who wanted to dive under the sea were limited by their equipment. Submersibles and scuba are great systems, but limited battery and air supplies mean that scientists must surface after spending just a few precious hours underwater. They only see a snapshot of what's happening in the water or on the sea floor. They often don't know what's going on while they're on the surface. It's like watching a two-hour movie in short, two-minute video clips. If you watch enough clips, you're likely to get an idea about the story. But some things just won't be clear, and you'll always wonder what happened during the parts you didn't see.

Aquarius Monitors the Environment

Marine scientists use *Aquarius* to help them answer some very important questions about coral reefs. Corals reefs are communities of simple colonial organisms called polyps. Most coral polyps deposit calcium around themselves; when the polyp dies, the calcium shell is left behind. Scientists estimate that coral reefs support one-third of all the world's fish species and up to one million total animal species.

Scientists have found that by looking at coral fossils, they may be able to determine how the climate has changed over millions of years. This is especially important when trying to predict future effects of global warming. Other scientists have looked at tissue damage of juvenile marine animals caused by increased levels of ultraviolet radiation.

How Can Aquanauts Stay Down So Long?

The concept of saturation diving explains how aquanauts can live inside *Aquarius* for extended time periods. Your body tissues, muscle and fat, are like a sponge. No matter how long a sponge stays in a bucket of water, it only absorbs a certain amount of liquid. The same goes for your body tissues. Saturation divers only absorb a certain amount of nitrogen and other inert, or slow dissolving, gases in their tissues no matter how long they stay submerged at a certain depth. That's why aquanauts only need to decompress at the end of their mission.

Decompression

Aquanauts are required to undergo a seventeen-hour decompression period after completing a ten-day mission in *Aquarius*. While the actual lab never leaves the bottom, the air pressure inside *Aquarius* is gradually adjusted until the lab's pressure is the same as air pressure at the surface. This allows the inert gas bubbles to dissolve out of body tissues without causing any problems. Think of it like this: if you have a balloon with a small leak in it, and you step on it, softly at first and then gradually harder, the air will seep out at a nice even pace. If you stomp on the balloon, however, you'll probably cause some serious physical damage.

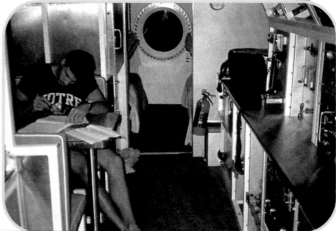

Aquanauts have to undergo a seventeen-hour decompression after a ten-day mission on board the *Aquarius*.

1. RESPONDING TO THE ARTICLE

a. What do you think the origin of the word *aquanaut* is?

b. Why would scientists want to explore the ocean?

c. In your notebook, list the pros and cons to being an aquanaut. Would you like to be an aquanaut? Explain fully.

2. ORAL LANGUAGE AUDIENCE AND PURPOSE

Discuss the audience and purpose of informational writing. Is informational writing used to inform or explain? Or is it used to entertain? Who is the audience for a piece such as "Undersea Science"?

As you discuss the audience, think about the source of the article. In what type of publication did it appear? Most informational articles appear in magazines that are targeted to particular audiences. A science magazine for example, targets people who have an interest in science.

STRATEGIES

3. WRITING AN INFORMATIONAL ARTICLE

With a partner, read the article and discuss the following questions. How is the article organized? How can you tell what is in each section of the article? Examine the pictures. What type of information do the pictures reveal? Are they informational or are they included to "dress up" the text?

Write an informational article about a subject that interests you. For example, the development of the Internet, computer animation, or collecting comic books. Think about how you will organize your article. Will you use headings to organize and attract the reader's eye? Will you include pictures or diagrams that complement the text and help you to explain the concepts? Remember that spelling and the use of correct vocabulary is very important in informational writing. One misspelled word or one wrong use of a word will cause the reader to question the rest of the article. Have you used words correctly? Have they been spelled right? Use a dictionary or a spell check at the editing and proofreading stages of your writing to help you.

Post your article on the school's Web site or share it with your classmates.

What would you do if you had the chance
to travel to the future?

THE CHOICE

Short, Short Story by W. Hilton-Young

Before Williams went into the future, she bought a camera and a tape recorder. She also learned shorthand. That night, when all was ready, we made coffee. She might want some—if and when she came back.

"Goodbye," I said. "Don't stay too long."

"I won't," she said.

I watched her carefully. She hardly seemed to move at all. She was back from her trip within the second she had left. It seemed that way, at least, by our sense of time.

We had not been sure how long she would be away. Maybe a minute. Maybe several years. But here she was, as if she had never left.

"Well?" I asked.

"Well," she said, "let's have some coffee."

I poured it out, waiting for her to say something. As I gave her a cup, I said again, "Well?"

"Well, the thing is, I can't remember."

"Can't remember? Not a thing?"

She thought for a moment. Then she said sadly, "Not a thing."

"But your notes? The camera? The tape recorder?"

The notebook was empty. The film was still at No. 1, where she had set it. The tape in the tape recorder had not been used.

"But why?" I asked. "How did it happen? Can't you remember anything at all?"

"I remember only one thing."

"What was that?"

"I was shown everything. Then I was given the choice of whether I should remember it or not, after I got back."

"And you chose not to? But what an odd thing to—"

"Isn't it?" she said. "I can't help wondering why."

GOALS AT A GLANCE

- Write alternate endings.
- Respond critically in a group.

1. RESPONDING TO THE STORY

a. Do you think Williams really travelled into the future? What evidence is there that she did or didn't?

b. In your notebook, write a paragraph to describe what Williams saw that she might want to forget.

c. Do you agree with the choice Williams made? Explain fully.

d. When is knowledge sometimes not a good thing?

2. WRITING ALTERNATE ENDING

Write a different ending to the story in a way that sustains the mood and suspense. What could Williams have learned in the future? Was the future so horrible? Or was she afraid that revealing the future would change the way things are to happen? Make a list of possible endings. Choose the best one and write your ending.

PEER-ASSESSMENT: Share your ending with a group of classmates, and ask for feedback. Is the ending believable? Has the ending maintained the mood of the original story? What do you think of your classmates' alternate endings?

REFLECTING ON THE UNIT

SELF-ASSESSMENT: LANGUAGE CONVENTIONS

As you worked on the activities in this unit what did you learn about
- nouns and verbs?
- creating dialogue?
- punctuating poetry?
- ellipsis points?

What else would you like to learn about language conventions?

WRITING AND MEDIA MAKER

With a classmate, develop a short script for a radio interview between two people from different selections.

LITERATURE STUDIES

In your notebook, develop a comparison chart for two selections—one of the stories and one of the informational selections. What categories will you use to compare them (for example, language, message, and interest level)? Or choose your favourite descriptive paragraph from any selection in the unit. Explain why you like it to a classmate.

MYTHS

THE MYTHOLOGY LIBRARY
CELTIC
MYTHOLOGY
THE MYTHS AND LEGENDS OF THE CELTIC WORLD

ARTHUR COTTERELL

FATHER
AND
DAUGHTER
TALES

Retold by Josephine Evetts-Secker
Illustrated by Helen Cann

ANN PILLI
REALMS OF GOLD
MYTHS & LEGENDS
From Around the World

Illustrated by
KADY MACDONALD DENTON

Viviane Koenig

FOUR
ANCESTORS
Stories, Songs, and Poems from Native North America

WATER
FIRE
AIR
EARTH

TOLD BY JOSEPH BRUCHAC

PICTURES BY
S.S. BURRUS · JEFFREY CHAPMAN · MURV JACOB · DUKE SINE

A WORLD OF TALES

"Such stories flow in our bloodstream,
run riot in our souls."

David Creighton

"Where do stories come from?" a character in this tale asks.
How would you answer this question?

THE GIFT of STORIES, THE GIFT of BREATH

Short Story by Joseph Bruchac

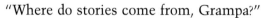

"Where do stories come from, Grampa?"

The little girl looked up at her grandfather. Her face was very serious.

"Well," Grampa Obomsawin said, his brown face opening into a smile, "the ones you hear from me, I tell them to you."

"That's not what I mean, Grampa," the little girl said, pulling hard on her braid.

"Now, what do you mean, Cecile?" Grampa Obomsawin said, leaning forward to show he was really listening.

"I mean before you knew them."

"Some people say that the stories come from the earth, from the stones themselves. A long, long time ago there were a few people who were patient enough to listen to the stones. Every time they heard a new story, they gave the stones a gift of some kind, maybe some beads or a nice arrow-head. And so the stones kept telling more stories to them. Those folks learned those stories and then told them to the other people. That might be so, but I don't think that's the whole story."

Grampa Obomsawin paused. Cecile knew it was her turn to say something, to show she'd been listening. "What is the whole story, Grampa?"

"The whole story is that the stories are all around us. They're inside us, too. They're like our breath. You know how you can see your breath when it is very cold?"

Cecile nodded. She remembered those winter mornings when her breath was like a white cloud of smoke around her face.

"That reminds us that the fire of life is inside us," Grampa Obomsawin continued. "Those stories are in there, keeping us warm, just as the fire does.

GOALS AT A GLANCE

■ Respond critically to the selection.
■ Respond personally by writing a story.

And our breath is moist, just like the clouds, which carry the rain. So there is water in the stories, too. The Earth and the Air, the Fire and the Water are our four ancestors, and they all come together to make the stories.

"Long ago, our Creator made the world, and He filled it with stories. Those stories are a gift to us, just like the gift of breath. They're everywhere, all around us. They're inside of us, too, just like that breath we usually can't see. But if we're quiet and we listen, sometimes we'll hear a story."

"So I have stories in me, too, Grampa?"

"You do, indeed. Just keep looking, and sometimes, like on those mornings when you can see your breath, you'll see them. Just keep listening, and you'll hear them, as you do that little wind that is blowing now."

"I'm listening, Grampa," Cecile said.

Grampa Obomsawin smiled. "I'm listening, too," he said.

Then they sat there for a long time, both of them listening for the stories in the wind.

----

1. RESPONDING TO THE TALE

a. What is the message of this tale?

b. Do you believe that you have stories inside? Explain.

c. What does the grandfather mean when he says, "These stories are a gift to us"?

2. WRITING "FREE-WRITE" A STORY

Write a story following the grandfather's directions, "But if we're quiet and we listen, sometimes we'll hear a story." Write any story that floats into your mind as you follow these directions. Write without worrying about spelling or grammar, or if the story makes sense. Allow your pen to just flow across the paper, following your thoughts. Once you've finished writing, read your story, and reflect on the results of this method of writing.

3. VISUAL COMMUNICATION ILLUSTRATE THE STORY

Reread the story and jot down notes about the images that come to mind as Joseph Bruchac speaks of the story stones, and the wind that carries stories. How would you illustrate this selection? What section or phrase brings strong images to mind? Write a description of the illustration you think this piece needs. Take a photo, or create a painting, to illustrate this story. Share your image with a classmate, explaining why you think it's suitable.

The White Stone CANOE

How far would you travel to seek someone you love? Read this tale to find out how far one young man will go.

Ojibwa/Chippewa Tale
by Henry Rowe Schoolcraft

There was once a very beautiful young woman, who died suddenly on the day she was to have been married to a handsome young man. He was also brave, but his heart was not strong enough to endure this loss. From the hour she was buried, there was no more joy or peace for him. He would often visit the spot where the women had buried her and sit there, dreaming.

Some of his friends thought he should try to forget his sorrow by hunting or by following the warpath. But war and hunting had lost their charms for him. His heart was already dead within him. He pushed aside both his war club and his bow and arrows.

He had heard the old people say there was a path that led to the land of souls, and he made up his mind to follow it. One morning, after having made his preparations for the journey, he picked up his bow and arrows, called to his dog, and started out. He hardly knew which way to go. He was only guided by the tradition that he must go south. As he walked along, he could see at first no change in the face of the country. Forests and hills and valleys and streams had the same look that they wore in his native place. There was snow on the ground, and sometimes it was even piled and matted on the thick trees and bushes. But after a long while it began to diminish, and finally disappeared. The forest took on a more cheerful appearance, the leaves put forth their buds, and before he was aware of the completeness of the change, he found himself surrounded by spring.

GOALS AT A GLANCE

- Demonstrate understanding by retelling the tale.
- Increase understanding by comparing two tales.

176

He had left behind him the land of snow and ice. The clouds of winter had rolled away from the sky. The air became mild. A pure field of blue was above him. As he went along he saw flowers beside his path and heard the songs of birds. By these signs he knew that he was going the right way, for they agreed with the traditions of his people.

At length he spied a path. It led him through a grove, then up a long, high ridge, on the very top of which there stood a lodge. At the door was an old man with white hair, whose eyes, though deeply sunken, had a fiery brilliance. He had a long robe of skins thrown loosely around his shoulders and a staff in his hands.

The young man began to tell his story. But the old chief stopped him before he had spoken ten words. "I have expected you," he said, "and had just risen to welcome you to my lodge. She whom you seek passed here only a few days ago, and being tired from her journey, rested herself here. Enter my lodge and be seated. I will then answer your questions and give you directions for the remainder of your journey."

When this was accomplished, the old chief brought the young man back out through the door of the lodge. "You see yonder lake," said he, "and the wide-stretching blue plains beyond. It is the land of souls. You now stand upon its borders, and my lodge is at the gate of entrance. But you cannot take your body along. Leave it here with your bow and arrows and your dog. You will find them safe on your return."

So saying, he went back into the lodge, and the traveller bounded forward, as if his feet had suddenly been given the power of wings. But all things retained their natural colours and shapes. The woods and leaves, the streams and lakes, were only brighter and more beautiful than before. Animals bounded across his path with a freedom and confidence that seemed to tell him there was no bloodshed here. Birds of beautiful plumage lived in the groves and sported in the waters.

There was one thing, however, that struck him as peculiar. He noticed that he was not stopped by trees or other objects. He seemed to walk directly through them. They were, in fact, merely the souls or shadows of real trees. He became aware that he was in a land of shadows.

When he had travelled half a day's journey, through a country that grew more and more attractive, he came to the banks of a broad lake, in the centre of which was a large and beautiful island. He found a canoe of shining white stone tied to the shore. He was now sure that he had followed the right path, for the aged man had told him of this. There were also shining paddles. He immediately got into the canoe and had just taken the paddles in his hands when, to his joy and surprise, he beheld the object of his search in another canoe, exactly like his own in every respect. She had exactly imitated his motions, and they were side by side.

At once they pushed out from the shore and began to cross the lake. Its waves seemed to be rising, and at a distance looked ready to swallow them up. But just as they came to the whitened edge of the first great wave, it seemed to melt away, as if it had been merely a show or a reflection. No sooner did they pass through one wreath of foam, however, than another still more threatening rose up. They were in constant fear. Moreover, through the clear water they could see the bones of many people who had perished, strewn on the bottom of the lake.

The Master of Life had decreed that the two of them should pass safely through, for they had both led good lives on earth. But they saw many others struggling and sinking in the waves. There were old men and young men, and women too. Some passed safely through, and some sank. But it was only the little children whose canoes seemed to meet no waves at all. Finally every difficulty was passed, as if in an instant, and they both leaped out onto the happy island.

They felt that the air was food. It strengthened and nourished them. They wandered over the blissful fields, where everything was made to please the eye and the ear. There were no storms. There was no ice, no chilly wind. No one shivered for want of warm clothes. No one suffered from hunger, no one mourned the dead. They saw no graves. They heard of no wars. There was no hunting for animals, for the air itself was food.

Gladly would the young warrior have remained there forever, but he was obliged to go back for his body. He did not see the Master of Life, but he heard his voice in a soft breeze. "Go back," said the voice, "to the land where you came from. Your time has not yet come. The duties for which I made you, and which you are to perform, are not yet finished. Return to your people and accomplish the duties of a good man. You will be the ruler of your people for many days. The rules you must observe will be told you by my messenger who keeps the gate. When he gives you back your body, he will tell you what to do. Listen to him, and you shall one day rejoin the spirit whom you must now leave behind. She has been accepted, and will be here always, as young and as happy as she was when I first called her from the land of snows."

When the voice had ceased, the young man awoke. It had been only a dream, and he was still in the bitter land of snows, and hunger, and tears. ◆

1. RESPONDING TO THE TALE

a. A *quest* is a long, difficult journey in search of something noble, ideal, or holy. Would you call this young man's journey a quest? Why or why not?

b. What was he looking for? What did he find?

c. Why do you think the author does not give the young man a name? What is the effect of leaving him nameless?

2. ORAL LANGUAGE RETELL THE TALE

Think about the events in the tale and how it is told. Jot down notes on the storyline that detail what happens from beginning to end. Use these notes to help you retell the tale to a partner. Remember to use an expressive voice, pauses, and volume to create the best effect.

SELF-ASSESSMENT: Make a tape recording of your retelling. Listen to the tape. How could your retelling be improved? How have you changed the tale by telling it orally?

3. READING COMPARE STORIES

Read the next selection. With a small group, compare "The White Stone Canoe" and "Savitri and Satyavan." Copy the following chart into your notebook and record your ideas. What conclusions can you draw about these two tales?

	THE WHITE STONE CANOE	SAVITRI AND SATYAVAN
characters		
setting		
main idea		
point of view		
use of language		
storyline		
ending		
personal opinion		

Great love stories often involve great sacrifice. What stories or movies can you think of with this theme?

✻ SAVITRI AND SATYAVAN

HINDU MYTH RETOLD BY MADHUR JAFFREY

Once upon a time there lived a King and Queen, who after many years of being childless, gave birth to a daughter.

She was the most beautiful baby the parents could have hoped for, and they named her Savitri.

When Savitri grew up and it was time for her to marry, her father said to her, "Dearest child, we hate to part with you. You have given us the greatest joy that humans can ever know. But it is time for you to start a family of your own. Is there any man you wish to marry?"

"No, father," replied Savitri, "I have not yet met a man I would care to spend my life with."

"Perhaps we should send for pictures of all the nobles in the country. You might come upon a face you like," said the King and he sent his court painter to bring back portraits of all the nobles and rulers in the country.

Savitri examined the portraits, one after the other, and shook her head. The men in the portraits all looked so very ordinary, even though they were all emperors, kings, and princes.

The King then said to his daughter, "It might be best if you went to all the big cities of the world to find a husband for yourself. I will provide you with the proper escort of men, elephants, camels, and horses. Good luck. I hope you can find a man to love."

Savitri set out with a large procession of men, elephants, camels, and horses. In her effort to visit all the cities of the world, she had to cross many oceans and deserts. She did this fearlessly. But she never found a man she could love.

Pronunciation guide:

Savitri:
Sa-vit-ri

Satyavan:
Sat-ya-van

GOALS AT A GLANCE

■ Develop a modern retelling of an ancient myth.
■ Prepare and present a debate.

181

When she returned home, her father said to her, "You have looked in all the big cities of the world and have found no man that you wish to marry. Perhaps you should now search through all the forests of the world."

Savitri set out again with a large procession of men, elephants, camels, and horses, and began searching through all the forests of the world. She did this fearlessly.

She had looked through the last forest and was just about to return home when she came upon a young man who was cutting wood.

"What is your name?" she asked.

"Satyavan, your highness," he replied.

"Please do not address me as *your highness*," she said, "my name is Savitri. What do you do for a living?"

"I do nothing much," the young man replied. "I have very old, blind parents. I live with them in a small, thatched cottage at the edge of the forest. Every morning I go out to cut wood and gather food. In the evening I make a fire for my parents, cook their dinner, and feed them. That is all I do."

Savitri returned to her father's palace and said, "Dearest mother and father. I have finally found a man to love and marry. His name is Satyavan and he lives in a cottage by a forest not too far from here."

"But will you be able to live a simple life in a simple cottage?" asked her father. "This young man obviously has no money."

"That makes no difference at all to me," Savitri said. "He is capable, honest, good, and caring. That is what I respect and love him for."

The King sent a message to the couple's cottage saying that Princess Savitri wished to marry their son, Satyavan. When Satyavan arrived home that evening with his heavy load of wood his parents said, "There are messengers here from the King. Princess Savitri wishes to marry you."

"I love the young lady in question," replied Satyavan, "but it will be impossible to marry her. She has money, jewels, elephants, camels, and servants. What can I offer her?"

Tears rolled down the faces of his parents. "Son," cried the mother, "we never told you this, but long ago, before you were born, your father too was a ruler with a kingdom of his own. His wicked brother blinded us and stole our birthright. You should have been born a prince and heir to the kingdom, quite worthy of the beautiful Savitri. We have fallen on hard times, but if you two love each other, why should you not marry? Who knows what the future has in store for anybody?"

So a message was sent back to the King saying that Satyavan had agreed to the match.

On the day of the wedding, the King and Queen held a huge reception. Everyone of any importance was invited.

That is how it happened that the wisest Sage in the kingdom appeared at the scene.

Just before the wedding ceremony, the Sage took the King aside and whispered, "It is my duty to warn you. The young man your daughter is to marry is decent and of good character, but his stars are crossed. He will die very shortly. This marriage would be a tragic mistake."

The King felt ill when he heard this. He called his daughter and told her what the Sage had said, adding, "Perhaps it is best to call the marriage off."

"No, father," Savitri said solemnly, "I will marry Satyavan, whatever our future may hold."

Savitri was no fool, however. She had heard that the Sage knew of heavenly remedies for earthly problems.

"Oh dearest Sage," Savitri said to him, "surely there is a way I can prevent my husband from dying. You, in your great wisdom, must offer me some hope. There must be something I can do?"

The Sage thought deeply, "You can extend your husband's life by fasting. Eat nothing but fruit, roots, and leaves for a year, and Satyavan will live for those twelve months. After that he *must* die."

With a sense of doom hanging over the bride's family, the wedding did take place. The groom and his parents were told nothing of what the future held for them.

Savitri began to lead a simple life with her husband and parents-in-law. Early each morning, Satyavan set out for the forest to cut wood and to forage for food. When he was gone, Savitri made the beds, swept the house, and shepherded her in-laws around wherever they wished to go. She also prayed and fasted.

One day Savitri's mother-in-law said to her, "Child, we know how rich a family you come from. Since we have lost our kingdom, we can offer you no fineries but Satyavan does collect enough food for all of us. We have noticed that you eat just fruit, roots, and leaves and never touch any grain. That is not a healthy diet. We are beginning to worry about you."

"Oh, please do not worry about me," begged Savitri. "I love to eat fruit."

The twelve months were almost over. On the very last day, Savitri got up with her husband and announced that she would accompany him into the forest.

"Child, what will you do in the forest? The work is hard and there are all kinds of dangerous animals," said her mother-in-law.

"Do stay at home," said Satyavan, "the forest is not a comfortable place."

"I have travelled through all the forests of the world. I was not uncomfortable and I was not frightened. Let me go with you today."

Satyavan had no answer for his wife. He loved her a lot and trusted her instincts. "Come along then, we'd better start quickly. The sun is almost up."

So they set out toward the heart of the forest.

Once there, Satyavan climbed a tree and began to saw off its dried-up branches.

It was a scorchingly hot day in May. The trees had shed the last withered, yellowing leaves. Savitri looked for a cool spot to sit down and just could not find any. Her heart was beating like a two-sided drum. Any moment now the year would end.

"Ahhh…" came a cry from Satyavan.

Savitri ran towards him, "Are you all right?"

"I have a piercing headache."

"Come down from the tree. It's the heat. I will run and find some shade." Savitri found a banyan tree and helped Satyavan towards it. Many of the banyan tree's branches had gone deep into the earth and come up again to form a deliciously cool grove. The leaves rustled gently to fan the couple. "Put your head in my lap," Savitri said to Satyavan, "and rest."

Satyavan put his head down, gave a low moan, and died.

Savitri looked up. There, in the distance coming towards her, was Yamraj, the King of the Underworld. He was riding a male water buffalo, and Savitri knew that he was coming to claim Satyavan's soul. She turned to the banyan tree and implored, "Banyan tree, banyan tree, look after my husband. Shield him and keep him cool. I will return one day to claim him."

Yamraj took Satyavan's soul and started to ride away. Savitri followed on foot. She followed for miles and miles. Yamraj finally turned around and said, "Why are you following me, woman?"

"You are taking my husband's soul away. Why don't you take me as well? I cannot live without him."

"Go back, go back to your home and do not bother me," Yamraj said.

But Savitri kept following.

Yamraj turned around again, "Stop following me, woman," he cried.

Savitri paid no heed to him.

"Well, woman," said Yamraj, "I can see that you are quite determined. I will grant you just one wish. As long as you do not ask for your husband's soul."

"May my in-laws have their sight back?" asked Savitri.

"All right, all right," said Yamraj, "now go home."

After several more miles Yamraj glanced back. There was Savitri, still following.

"You really are quite persistent," Yamraj said. "I'll grant you one other wish. Just remember, do not ask for your husband's soul."

"Could my father-in-law get back the kingdom he lost?" Savitri asked.

"Yes, yes," said Yamraj, "now go, go."

Several miles later, Yamraj looked back again.

Savitri was still following.

"I do not understand you. I've granted you two wishes and yet you keep following me. This is the last wish I am offering you. Remember, you can ask for anything but your husband's soul."

"May I be the mother of many children?" Savitri asked.

"Yes, yes," Yamraj, said. "Now go. Go back home."

Several miles later Yamraj looked back only to see Savitri still there. "Why are you still following me?" Yamraj asked. "I have already granted you your wish of many children."

"How will I have many children?" Savitri asked. "You are carrying away the soul of the only husband I have. I will never marry again. You have granted me a false wish. It can never come true."

"I have had enough," Yamraj said. "I am quite exhausted. Here, take back your husband's soul."

Savitri rushed back to the banyan tree so her husband's body and soul could be joined again.

"Oh banyan tree," she said, "thank you for looking after my husband. In the years to come, may all married women come to you and offer thanks and prayers."

Satyavan opened his eyes and said, "My headache has gone."

"Yes," said Savitri, "thanks to the kind banyan tree that offered us its shade. Let us go home now where a surprise awaits you. I will not tell you what it is."

Satyavan put his arm around his wife's shoulders and they began to walk slowly back home.

----

1. RESPONDING TO THE MYTH

a. In your notebook, retell this myth in six or seven sentences. Compare your retelling to a partner's.

b. Were you surprised by any of the characters or their actions? Explain.

c. What does this myth teach the reader about resolving conflict?

d. Does this myth emphasize, or downplay, the gap between the rich and the poor? Explain fully.

2. WRITING MODERN RETELLING

If this myth were set in a contemporary Canadian city, how would it change? Rewrite this myth with a modern spin. You can change the way characters behave or feel, what they want, and what happens to them. For example, would Satyavan feel reluctant to marry Savitri because he thinks, at first, that she is of a higher class? But try to give your story a similar message and theme. Share your first draft with your classmates, asking them to help you revise it. As you edit your work, check to make sure that your use of verb tense is consistent. If you start a story in the past tense, it should usually remain in the past tense.

STRATEGIES

3. ORAL LANGUAGE PREPARE A DEBATE

Is Savitri's life controlled by others or by herself? Form two groups and prepare arguments for each side. As you prepare your argument and then debate, remember to

- review the facts in the story
- think about your opinion or the position you'll be taking
- summarize your information and position
- prepare a persuasive argument about two minutes in length
- work co-operatively with others on your team to develop three arguments that support, but don't repeat, each other
- revise your argument
- memorize and practise delivering your argument
- speak persuasively, slowly, and clearly
- listen carefully to everyone's arguments, especially the opposing team's
- prepare your *rebuttal* (your response to the argument of an opposing team member)

SELF-ASSESSMENT: Do you think you presented a convincing argument? In your rebuttal, did you respond to the arguments of the others, or just repeat your previous argument? What part of your debate could have been improved?

Why do you think seawater is salty? Tales such as this pourquoi *tale attempt to explain the world around us.*

The Magic Millstones:
Why the Sea Is Salt

Icelandic Pourquoi Tale by Margaret Mayo   Illustrations by Louise Brierley

When the world was first made, the water in the sea was fresh and not the least bit salty. And it would be like that today if King Frodi had not been so greedy and unkind.

In the long-ago times, Frodi, King of the Northlands, owned some magic millstones. They looked the same as other millstones that ground up oats or barley. Just two round, heavy stones. It was said, however, that the stones could grind out whatever their owner wished, *if he knew how to make them turn.* But, though the king and his servants tried and tried to move them, the millstones could not be turned.

King Frodi was forever saying, "If only I could turn those millstones, I would grind out so many good things for my people! They would all be happy and peaceful and rich!"

Then one day, two tall, golden-haired women dressed in long, white flowing robes came to see King Frodi. They were powerfully built, like giants, and yet they were splendidly beautiful.

188

"And what can I do for you?" asked the king.

"Nothing!" answered the two women. "We have come to do something for you! We know how to make the magic millstones turn!"

Then the king was a happy man. "Bring the millstones!" he called to his servants. "Set them up here! Quickly!"

"What shall we grind for you?" asked the two women when the millstones were finally brought in. "Think carefully!"

"Grind peace and happiness for my people," cried the king. "And some gold too."

"These are good wishes," said the two women.

They touched the magic millstones. "Grind, grind! Peace and happiness for the people!" they chanted. "And gold too! Grind on! Grind on!"

From that moment, there was happiness and peace among all the king's people, throughout the land. But King Frodi didn't know about that, because he didn't move out of the room. He just sat there, watching the grains of bright yellow gold pour out from between the stones and pile up on the floor. He had never seen so much gold in one place before—and he wanted more of it, lots more!

After a while, the two women said, "Now it is time for us to rest."

"No!" cried King Frodi. "Keep grinding! Keep grinding!"

So the two women kept on chanting, and the heap of gold grew bigger.

The king could not keep his eyes off it. "I want enough gold to fill the room," he thought. "No, enough to fill the castle. No, the city. Lots and lots of gold."

But as the two women grew tired, they chanted more slowly, and the gold only trickled out. Then the king was angry. "Why did you come to my castle if you did not wish to grind for me?" he said. "Grind faster! Faster!"

Then the two women chanted faster, and the grains of bright yellow gold began to pour out again. All day they kept on chanting and grinding, and all day the king watched.

When evening came, the two women said, "We are very tired. We *must* rest for a while."

But the sight of so much gold had changed the king.

"You may rest for as long as it takes to say 'King Frodi!'" he said. "Listen: 'King Frodi!' There, you have rested. Now grind away. Faster! Faster!"

"King Frodi is no longer a good man," said one of the women. "He is greedy and unkind."

"He must be destroyed!" said the other.

Then they chanted, "Grind, grind! Strong, fierce warriors to fight King Frodi, Grind on! Grind on!"

And warriors, all fully armed, leapt out from between the millstones. ten...twenty...thirty of them! They surrounded the king, and with their sharp swords they killed him.

But what then? Here was a band of fierce warriors in a country that had been given peace and happiness.

"We can't stay here!" declared the fiercest of the warriors. "Come! Let's take the women and the magic millstones and sail away to another land. Then we shall have everything we want."

So the warriors took the millstones and the two tall, golden-haired women. They boarded a ship and ordered the sailors to set sail, and when the sailors saw the warriors' fierce and awful strength, they had to obey.

When the ship was some distance out at sea, the fiercest warrior said to the two women, "Now turn the millstones and show us what you can do!"

"We are tired," they said. "Let us rest for a while."

"Rest? You shall have no rest! Grind on!" ordered the warrior. "Grind what you like! Salt! Anything! But grind on! Grind on!"

Then the two women touched the millstones. "Grind, grind!" they chanted. "Salt! More salt! Grind on! Grind on!"

And pure white grains of salt poured out from between the stones, until there was a huge pile of salt on the deck.

"That's enough!" cried the fierce warrior. "Quite enough! Stop!"

But the two women only chanted faster and faster, and the salt flowed out over everything and everyone, and the ship began to sink. Even then they went on chanting, faster and faster: "Grind, grind! Salt! More salt! Grind on! Grind on! *And never cease from grinding!*"

And the weight of the salt was so great that the ship sank below the water and down, right down to the bottom of the sea, taking with it the millstones and everyone on board.

Those magic millstones are still lying there at the bottom of the sea, and they are still grinding. So that is why the sea is salt.

----

1. RESPONDING TO THE TALE

a. Why is the sea salty? Retell this story in a few sentences to a partner.

b. What is the message of this tale? Do you think the message is relevant today? Explain. List five morals the tale teaches (they don't all have to be serious).

c. In your notebook, write a paragraph to define the characteristics of a pourquoi tale.

2. ORAL LANGUAGE STORYTELLING

Have you ever read or heard any other tales that explain why seawater is salty? What reasons did they give? What other reasons could be given? Jot down a few ideas for alternate explanations. Choose one idea and develop it into a tale for telling out loud. Write the tale as simply as possible, with an easy-to-remember storyline. If one line leads naturally into the next it will be easier to memorize your story. Practise telling your story out loud. You may want to make a few changes to the tale to make it easier to tell.

Tell your story to your class, using gestures and an expressive voice, varying volume and tone. Refer to your written version as little as possible.

HOW TO CREATE A COMIC BOOK

Goals at a Glance
● Adapt a story to comic book form. ● Use drawings and dialogue to tell a story.

Have you ever wanted to create a comic book? Well, take one of the tales in this unit, such as "The Magic Millstones," and follow this process to adapt the tale into a new and fun format.

Grab Some Comic Books
If you want to create a comic book, first you have to know how they work. Select two or three comics, and flip through the pages, noting

● how the pages are laid out
● how the story is broken into a series of pictures
● how the reader knows what the characters are saying and thinking
● how background information is provided
● what special effects the artist uses to create interest.

Form Your Creative Team
Perhaps you're thinking that creating a comic book is an impossible task. How can one person do all the necessary writing and drawing? Don't worry! Comic books are usually created by a team of writers, artists, and editors. That's why your first step should be to form your own creative team. Here's one way in which you might divide up responsibilities:

Writing: One person can work on the story, dividing it into pieces, figuring out the dialogue, and creating a script.

Drawing: Working from the script, someone else (with artistic ability hopefully) can create the drawings. The first step is to make a rough draft that shows sketches of what each page will look like. At the final draft stage, the artist needs to remember to make dialogue balloons large enough to hold the text.

Lettering: Someone with neat handwriting can write the words into the drawings. (Or someone with computer skills could scan the drawings, input the text, and create an on-screen version of the comic book.)

PROCESS

Colouring: Someone can colour each panel of the comic.

Editing: Someone should make sure the illustrations and text support one another, and should proofread the text before it's added to the final art.

Choose a Story

A comic book is a blend of story and art. Though each element is important, the starting point is always the story. In creating a comic book, there are two options—writing an original story, or choosing a story that already exists. The advantage of choosing an existing story is that some of the work has already been done for you!

Consider the tales in this unit and which one would make the most exciting comic book. Discuss all the tales with your group, and decide together which one should be adapted. The following suggestions describe how you might adapt the tale "The Magic Millstones" into a comic book.

Prepare Your Adaptation

Read "The Magic Millstones" carefully, thinking about how you can transform the tale into a sequence of drawings that will tell it in an interesting way.

- Photocopy the tale so you have a working copy on which you can write notes.
- Use a highlighter to show which sentences need to be illustrated, which lines of dialogue you want to include, and key words that the artist and writer should keep in mind.

- Divide the story into sections, one for each panel or frame. Each panel should add something to the story. Most panels will include words—either narrative (written at the bottom of the panel) or dialogue (written in speech balloons). The number of panels you'll need will depend on the length of your story. The writer and artist should discuss this, deciding on how many panels are needed to tell the whole story.

Draft a Script

Although the artist may be itching to start, your comic book will be a lot better if you take some time to draft a script. This is a task for the writer, though other group members should be involved in offering ideas, reviewing, revising, and editing the script.

The script gives a written description of each panel of the comic, including narration, dialogue, and instructions to the artist. Here's an example:

> *Panel #4 is a larger panel and should show the two golden-haired women and King Frodi. The King has a surprised expression.*
>
> **Narration:** *One day, two visitors arrived.*
> **King:** *What can I do for you?*

At the beginning of the script, you might include a list of all the characters, with a brief description of each one.

Develop a Storyboard

Now the artist gets to work! Using the script, the artist creates a *rough draft*—a series of rough sketches showing what the comic will look like.

Avoid detail in the drawings—you can even use stick figures. The rough draft needs to show how many panels will be used on each page,  and the approximate size and position of the drawings. Include some of the text to ensure that you are leaving enough space.

As a group, review the rough draft for potential problems, such as panels that contain too much text. You might ask someone outside of your group to give you feedback. Is the story easy to follow? Are more images, dialogue, or narration needed? Can the panels be made more interesting?

At this stage the artist could also create detailed, coloured drawings of each character. This will allow the group to make final decisions on details such as clothing styles, facial features, and colours.

Finish Your Comic Book

Once your team has revised the storyboard as necessary, you can begin work on the final version. Use several large blank sheets, folded in half and stapled in the middle, to create a booklet that resembles a commercial comic book.

- Using a ruler, the artist can carefully draw an outline for each panel.
- The artist completes each panel according to the rough draft, leaving the right amount of space for text.
- When finished, the artist can pass it to the letterer, who adds the text.
- The comic book then goes to the person adding colour.
- Use correction fluid or tape to cover up mistakes. If necessary, you can do a replacement panel on another piece of paper, cut it out, and paste the whole panel over the one with the mistake.
- Use the outside of the booklet for a front and back cover.

Self-Assessment

How does your comic book compare with the tale you adapted? What was gained or lost in the transformation of story to comic book?

The checklist below can help you assess the process you followed to create your comic book.

❏ We analysed comic books to learn their characteristics.
❏ We drafted a script to describe each panel of our comic.
❏ We created a rough draft that included text and drawings.
❏ Our comic book retold the most important aspects of the tale we adapted.

What happens when Water comes to visit, bringing all his friends?

WATER, MOON, AND SUN

A Nigerian Pourquoi Tale

RETOLD BY ANN PILLING

ILLUSTRATIONS BY KADY MACDONALD DENTON

Long, long ago Sun and Moon got married, and for a while they were very happy together, and very busy setting up house. But the time came when they wanted to see their friends again, and their very best friend was Water.

"Hey!" Sun called to him, across the Earth. "What about paying us a visit? It's a long time since we saw you."

"I'd love to come," Water called back, in his deep gurgling voice, "but can I bring my friends? There are a lot of them, I'm afraid. I think your new house will be too small for us."

"Not at all," said Sun. "We'll build a whole new village, with dozens of huts and a big fence all around, to keep out the wild animals. That's it, we'll build a special *kraal*, just for you. Do say you'll come. We miss you."

195

So Water agreed, and set off to visit Sun and Moon. With him went all the creatures in the sea, the tiny sardines, and the massive whales, the razor-toothed sharks, and the glowing rainbow fish, the crabs, and the lobsters.

Sun and Moon were excited. They could hear Water's great roaring miles away, long before they could see him. Then they spotted him, flowing like a broad blue ribbon around the hills and through the forests, then charging, broader and mightier still, across the thirsty plains. At last he swirled in, covering their feet.

"It's wonderful to see you again, dear friends," he boomed, "and what a marvelous new village you've built."

"Er, yes," Moon said rather nervously, as Water and his friends swished about, exploring every corner of the kraal, and a crab took a sly nip at her toes.

"Is everybody here?" called Sun, above the roaring of Water. "I'm afraid we're getting rather short of space." He and Moon had already retreated outside their hut, to one corner of the kraal. The inside was useless, for all the furniture was floating around.

"Not quite," shouted Water, above the din, and in swept two whales blowing their water spouts madly, and a great big hippopotamus, which immediately squashed poor Moon against the fence.

"Help!" she shouted. "You've filled up the kraal. There's no room for anything else. Stop, Water, stop!" But Water didn't hear her. He was much too busy welcoming all his friends. Sun and Moon looked down at the scene in alarm, at the bobbing jellyfish and the wriggling eels, at the proud sea horses as they went riding by. Then a couple of flying fish came zipping along, and they ducked their heads.

"It's no good," wept Moon, "the kraal's full to overflowing. I'd simply no idea that Water had so many friends. We can't stay here. I'm leaving." And she took a great leap into the sky. Sun, who loved her, followed, landing even higher, and Water was left down on Earth, filling the great kraal with all his fishy friends.

And that is why there are lakes and rivers and seas all over the world, and why Sun and Moon shine down on them from up above, Sun fierce and hot by day, Moon, more gently, by night.

----

1. RESPONDING TO THE TALE

a. Did you guess what the ending of this tale would be? If yes, at what point did you guess?

b. Is this tale serious or humorous? Which details from the story support your opinion? How does the language used influence the tale's tone?

c. What do you like about this tale and its illustration? What do you dislike? Which description or phrase is your favourite? Explain fully.

d. Why do you think this tale developed? What other tales from other cultures are you reminded of?

2. LITERATURE STUDIES   USE PERSONIFICATION

How is **personification** essential to this myth? Try telling the tale without using personification. What other tales can you think of that use personification? Which characters are personified? What human traits do they have?

> **Personification** is a literary device that gives human traits to non-humans, for example, Water can speak, think, and have friends.

With a partner, brainstorm some ideas for a modern tale involving personification. Choose one idea to develop further.

SELF-ASSESSMENT: In your notebook, write down a definition of personification, and provide an example other than this tale.

3. LANGUAGE CONVENTIONS COMPOUND SENTENCES

A good tip to follow as you're writing is to avoid long strings of short, simple sentences. One of the easiest ways to avoid these is to join the sentences using *and* or *but*. For example, "Then a couple of flying fish came zipping along. They ducked their heads." could be changed to a compound sentence, "Then a couple of flying fish came zipping along, *and* they ducked their heads."

In a compound sentence, both clauses are given equal weight. Review this tale to see how Ann Pillings has used compound sentences. Check your writing for opportunities to use compound sentences.

STRATEGIES

4. ORAL LANGUAGE READERS' THEATRE

With a small group, develop a readers' theatre script for the tale. Begin by listing your characters, including a narrator who will say all words not spoken by characters. You may wish to use several narrators so that one person does not need to read all the lines.

Develop a script based on the tale, suitable for an audience of your classmates. Try to develop a script that flows well, and leaves no questions unanswered. Choose the roles you wish to play, and read the parts aloud. Rehearse your reading at least once, before presenting it to your class. Remember to think about how the voices should sound. For example, at one point in the story, Water's voice is described as a "deep gurgling."

You may want to use a video recorder to tape your presentation. How does developing and presenting the tale as a readers' theatre help you and others understand the tale?

In the tales of many cultures the trickster character plays an important role. What do you know about characters like Discord, Raven, Anansi, Coyote, Pan, and...

That Wascawwy Wabbit:

Bugs Bunny as Trickster

Essay by DAVID CREIGHTON

The Warner Brothers studio in 1938 saw the birth of Happy Rabbit, a cute little fellow with buck teeth. But his godfather, Mel Blanc, didn't care for his name and gave him a new one, Bugs Bunny.

On with the show, this is it!

The world first heard Bugs's Brooklyn accent (lent by Blanc) in the 1940 short, *A Wild Hare.* He grew into a sophisticated young performer, simply superb (or "supoib"). Yet according to Elmer Fudd, he was a "wascawwy wabbit" who used dastardly means to defeat his foes. Didn't he drop a piano once on Yosemite Sam, when both were trying to win the hand of a wealthy widow?

Bugs did his bit during World War II, appearing in several cartoons promoting the sale of war bonds. He also had a brief operatic career, memorably recorded in the classic cartoon, *What's Opera, Doc?*

GOALS AT A GLANCE

■ Analyse the content and features of cartoons.
■ Write an essay about cartoons.

199

Bugs is in direct line of descent from Hare, an animal that is the trickster in many cultures. Rabbits, after all, are ridiculously weak little fellows who survive by being constantly vigilant and smart. Also, their buck teeth, long ears, and powers of reproduction are sources of amusement. And to some Aboriginal peoples, few creatures were more vital as sources of food and clothing.

One of Bugs's ancestors came from southern Africa, a Hare trickster who became known in America as Br'er Rabbit. In Joel Chandler Harris's Uncle Remus stories, we read about an ongoing battle of wits between him and Br'er Fox, who set a tar doll in his path one day. As the figure seemed insolent, Br'er Rabbit butted it and became hopelessly stuck in the goo. "All right, you've got me," said Br'er Rabbit, "and now you can chop off my head if you like but don't, please don't toss me in the briar patch!" With a mean grin Br'er Fox did just that—and in the thorny briars, of course, Br'er Rabbit was perfectly safe once more.

Bugs reminds us that tricksters are still very much with us. Cool and in command, always ready with a one-liner, he forever wins out, whether it means impersonating a sheep or plugging Elmer's shotgun with his fingers.

Although Bugs retired from active cartoon-making in 1963, he appears in reruns every Saturday morning. The mythology of this buffoonish bunny is most reassuring, showing us how easy it is to outwit oppressors and bask in the sun, munching carrots.

Well, th-th-th-th-that's all f-f-f-folks.

---

1. RESPONDING TO THE ESSAY

a. Do you agree with David Creighton that Bugs Bunny is a trickster? Explain your answer. What evidence does the author give to prove his point?

b. What is the main idea or thesis of this essay? How does the author develop an essay that supports this thesis?

c. Do you think this essay could change the way you look at *Bugs Bunny* cartoons?

2. MEDIA MESSAGES ANALYSE CARTOONS

Next time you have a chance, watch some *Bugs Bunny* cartoons.
Answer these questions in your notebook for one particular cartoon:

- What's the cartoon called? What do you think of the title?
- What happens in this cartoon? (Write five or six sentences to describe it.)
- If Bugs outwits another character, how does he do it? Why does he do it? Has he outwitted this character before? Why doesn't this character learn not to mess with Bugs?
- What is the funniest line in this cartoon? Who delivers it?
- What is your opinion of the dialogue in this cartoon?
- How would you describe the artwork in this cartoon?
- How would you describe the voices and the sound effects?
- What is the message of this cartoon?
- What is the purpose of this cartoon?
- Who is the audience? What makes you think so?
- How is this cartoon like or unlike other cartoons in content and design?

3. LANGUAGE CONVENTIONS CONJUNCTIONS

Reread the essay and examine how the author has used **conjunctions** to connect related ideas. Authors may use conjunctions within one sentence:

> In many tales the trickster plagues other characters, *although* in some tales the trickster is helpful.

Sometimes an author links one sentence with another sentence by beginning the second sentence with a conjunction:

> Coyote is a trickster given credit for many good deeds. *But* he can be just as mischievous as other tricksters.

Many people consider beginning sentences with *and* or *but* grammatically incorrect. However, many writers may do so for effect. What effect might Creighton have been hoping to achieve with his use of conjunctions?

> **Conjunctions** are words—such as *and, but, or, because, although, when, if*—that link related words, phrases, clauses, or sentences to one another.

4. ESSAY CRAFT ESSAY ABOUT CARTOONS

Think of another aspect of cartoons that you feel strongly about, and that would make a good topic for an essay. For example, you could write about violence in cartoons, the portrayal of women, cartoon humour, the value of cartoons as educational tools, or any other topic of your choice. Remember there are two (or more) sides to every argument or topic. You can take either position, but you must be prepared to defend it.

Generating Ideas

Begin with a statement that establishes your position on the topic. Jot down notes for three or four arguments that support your position. You may also want to take the offensive—state the opposing argument and then offer evidence that disproves it.

Outline

Use these notes to develop an outline for your essay. Consider the most effective arrangement of ideas.

First Draft

For every point on your outline, write one paragraph providing supporting examples. End your essay with a concluding statement that reflects your opening paragraph.

Revising

Read your essay out loud to yourself, slowly. Listen for awkwardness. Is your thesis easy to identify? Do you state your thesis in the first paragraph? Do the following paragraphs offer supporting evidence? Is your argument reasonable and persuasive? Do you use connecting words to link related ideas? Revise your essay so that each paragraph flows into the next.

Final Draft

Create a final draft on computer or by printing neatly. Use your spell checker to check spelling. Share your essay with another classmate, asking if your argument is persuasive.

SELF-ASSESSMENT: Grade your essay according to some of the points mentioned under the Revising head. What grade do you think your essay deserves? Explain.

What do you know about pandas?
Do you know how they got their black markings?
This legend offers an explanation.

THE LEGEND OF THE
PANDA

Chinese legend by Linda Granfield

ILLUSTRATIONS BY SONG NAN ZHANG

L ong years ago, Dolma, a young shepherdess, lived with her sisters in the Wolong Valley, deep in the mountains of Sichuan province.

Each day, Dolma led her small flock of sheep up the steep slopes of the nearby mountain. The rat-a-tat of woodpeckers echoed as Dolma and her companions travelled past frosty waterfalls and over moss-covered rocky paths to the fragrant meadows.

While the sheep grazed, Dolma collected herbs to make medicines for the villagers. She also gathered mountain blossoms—red and gold poppies, gentians as blue as the mists that veiled the mountaintops, and purple violets that lifted their tiny faces to the sunlight.

On a morning when the air was sweet with spring, a young animal crept from the nearby evergreen forest. "Will you join our flock, little Beishung?" laughed Dolma.

By the trickling stream, the white panda cub nibbled tender shoots. His hunger satisfied, he frolicked among the sheep and lambs like a furry acrobat celebrating the end of the bitter winter. And each day thereafter, the white cub joined Dolma's flock to feed and play.

As she had so often, one day Dolma left her flock to gather herbs. Among the dewy grasses, she filled her basket and returned to the meadow. Dolma smiled to see her peaceful flock.

Suddenly, a snow leopard pounced from a tree. With teeth bared, he attacked the white cub. "Beishung!" cried Dolma, as the sheep fearfully bleated.

The leopard's sharp claws tore at the helpless little Beishung. Yet Dolma, without a thought for her own safety, grabbed a stout branch and rushed forward to beat the leopard mightily.

The wounded cub withdrew weakly into the flock. The angry leopard, eager to claim a life, turned upon Dolma. Moments later, the shepherdess lay lifeless upon the trampled grass, the basket's blossoms and herbs strewn about her.

Great were the lamentations in the Wolong Valley when the people learned of Dolma's death. Heavy was the grief of all the Beishung. They knew of Dolma's kindness to the cub, and of the brave act that had saved him from the leopard's claws.

On the appointed day, the sorrowful villagers gathered with Dolma's heart-broken sisters to bury the shepherdess. Grey clouds hung heavily over the mountains as the white cub led the Beishung to join the funeral procession.

As the bamboo grasses rustled in damp winds, the mourners smeared themselves with ashes. The Beishung wiped their tear-filled eyes with sooty paws and hugged themselves as they wept. They covered their ears against the loud lamentations and, wherever the animals touched their snowy bodies with ash, the black soot stained forever the thick white fur.

Dolma's sisters were convinced they could not live without her. As the sisters' cries reached the snow-capped mountaintops, the earth beneath their feet spoke to them with fierce rumblings, as if it, too, were mourning. The villagers fell back in awe as the earth suddenly split wide and received the four loving sisters. Where the meadow once lay rose a mountain of four peaks that reached beyond the clouds.

And this is exactly why to this day, the giant panda, the "bamboo-eater," wears the black marks of mourning in memory of the brave shepherdess, Dolma. His home and refuge is in the protective forests of Siguniang, the "Mountain of the Four Sisters."

Author's Note

Giant panda fossils found in Asia reveal that the mammal appeared nearly two million years ago. Pandas belong to their own subfamily within the bear family. In China, the panda is called daxiong mao, meaning "large bear cat."

The panda has the digestive system of a carnivore, or meat-eater; however, through the centuries, it has adapted to a vegetarian diet and feeds mainly on the leaves and stems of bamboo. In fact, the panda spends most of its waking hours eating up to twenty kilograms of bamboo each day. Its flexible forepaws allow the panda to hold onto its food. Strong flattened molars and powerful jaw muscles enable the panda to crush tough bamboo stalks, and a thick lining protects the panda's esophagus from bamboo splinters.

The giant panda has thick, coarse fur that protects it from the cool, damp climate of the Chinese forests. Some scientists believe that the panda's black markings provide camouflage in the shadows of the forests; others think the colouring warns other animals to keep away from the panda's territory.

The panda leads a solitary life of eating and sleeping, except in the spring when mating may occur. One or two tiny cubs, covered in fine white fur, are born in August or September. After one month, they develop their black panda markings. The young live with their mother until they're about eighteen months old. Then the pandas are on their own as the mother leaves to breed once again.

Scientists estimate that fewer than one thousand pandas remain living in the wild in China today. As people develop more land, the bamboo groves are destroyed and the panda has less to eat, and a smaller area to inhabit. Climate changes and the natural life cycle of the bamboo in some areas have left the panda with little to eat. Despite strict laws, hunters continue to trap and kill the panda as its pelt becomes increasingly valuable.

Efforts to save the endangered panda—the international symbol for the World Wildlife Fund—have been well-documented. The WWF is an agency that has been working on panda conservation in China since 1980. A captive breeding program at Wolong, China's largest panda reserve, has been successful in recent years: thirty-six cubs have been born since 1987, and twenty-one have survived past six months.

There are plans to create new reserves in China, and to establish links between isolated panda populations. Special programs continue to alert the world of the decreasing number of pandas, and recent technology provides more options in the fight to save the endangered panda.

----

1. RESPONDING TO THE LEGEND

a. How does Linda Granfield establish Dolma's goodness from the beginning of the legend? Find evidence within the whole story. What words would you use to describe Dolma? Why did you choose those words?

b. Discuss the illustration. Does it reflect the story's mood? Does it help you understand the story? Do you find it appealing?

2. LITERATURE STUDIES UNDERSTANDING LEGENDS

What do you know about **legends** and their features? What other legends have you read? How are they like or unlike "The Legend of the Panda"? As a class, discuss the features of legends, and this example of a legend. Does knowing the features of legends change your understanding of "The Legend of the Panda"? Explain fully.

> A **legend** is a story from the past, such as *Robin Hood,* that has been widely accepted as true. Sometimes legends explain a natural fact, such as how mountains were formed. Legends often include magical elements.

3. WRITING LEGENDS

Use your understanding of legends to develop a short, two-page legend. You could retell a legend you're familiar with, or create a modern legend— such as The Legend of the VW Bug, or The Legend of the Computer Chip. Begin with a description of the main character(s), as Granfield has. End with an explanation of how something came to be. Add illustrations you've created or found. Share your first draft with a classmate, asking for help revising it. Remember to use your dictionary or computer spell checker as you revise.

4. RESEARCHING SUMMARIZE INFORMATION

Reread Linda Granfield's note on page 206, and think about the statistics she gives the reader about panda bears. Think about the tone of her writing, and the information she has included. Who do you think her audience is? What do you think her purpose is? Does she write objectively, or emotionally?

Use the following tips to help you write a report on another endangered species:

- Before you begin your research, develop questions that provide a focus for that research. This can save you time.
- Use the Internet or library resources to locate information on an animal of your choice. Use the animal's name as a search word. Look for general information about the animal and its habitat; why the species is endangered; what is being done to protect it; and what else could be done.
- For the purpose of this report, do not use any publication that is over two years old, since the information needs to be up-to-date.
- Contact environmental organizations through e-mail or by phone.
- Use index cards to make notes on facts, quotations, and theories. Write a paragraph that summarizes the information in your own words. A *summary* is a brief statement that gives the main details.
- On each card, record information about each source—author, title, publication date, Web site. This data will help you later when you have to provide a source list or bibliography.
- Organize your index cards into the order you wish for your final report.
- Write a two-page report modelled on Granfield's. Begin by describing the animal and its habitat. Then write up your information in a manner that others will easily understand.
- Prepare a final draft that includes answers to all the questions above, as well as one or two images—photos or drawings.

SELF-ASSESSMENT: Review your report, and compare it to Granfield's. Have you summarized information clearly? Is there any information that you've neglected to include? Is your presentation straightforward and comprehensible?

One decision may change your life, as the young hero, Paris, finds out in this myth.

PARIS
and the
GOLDEN APPLE

GREEK MYTH BY ETH CLIFFORD

"The child must die," the old woman cackled.

Queen Hecuba stared at the old woman, then held the baby close.

"You have heard her prediction," King Priam said in a low voice. "Our son will bring death and ruin to his family, to all of Troy. He must die that others may live out their lives in peace."

"No," Hecuba said stubbornly. "It was only a dream. I have had dreams before."

"Not one such as this, my lady," the old woman insisted.

Hecuba had dreamed that the tiny Paris, who lay so quietly in her arms at this moment, had turned into a burning torch that set all Troy aflame. The old woman, a dream prophet, had then said that a terrible end would come to Troy if the baby were allowed to live.

Priam went to Hecuba and took the baby from her. "I shall do what is necessary," he said.

Hecuba wept as Priam left the room. She saw, even as the tears rolled down her cheeks, that the King's eyes filled, too. Much later, when Priam returned, Hecuba gave him a searching glance.

"I had not the heart," Priam answered the look. "I gave the boy to a shepherd. He will leave the child on the slopes of Mount Ida. He will not live," Priam added sadly.

But instead, the shepherd raised Priam's son as his own. The young boy lived the life of a shepherd and did not know that his father was a king.

When he was a young man, Paris fell in love with Oenone, the river god's daughter. She loved him in return, for even the gods knew Paris was

GOALS AT A GLANCE

- Develop understanding of characters.
- Plan and present a dialogue.

209

the most handsome of all mortals. Life for Paris and Oenone was sweet and pleasant on Mount Ida.

Then one day, life for the young lovers changed suddenly. The morning began as usual. Paris, dozing in the morning sun while his flock of sheep grazed on the slopes of the mountainside, heard a soft voice calling him. He turned over and stretched at the sound of his name.

"Paris! Paris!" the voice repeated again and again.

Paris opened his eyes and smiled. When he saw Hera, the goddess of heaven, standing over him, he murmured, "If I am dreaming, let me dream on."

With Hera were two other goddesses. "We have come to ask you to make a judgment for us," Hera told the young man. In her hands a golden apple glittered and glowed in the sunlight. On it Paris could read the words *To the Fairest.*

"Know that there is a contest among the gods to pick the most beautiful goddess," Hera went on. "The gods have narrowed it down to Athena, Aphrodite, and me. But they cannot decide among us. Help us, Paris. Choose a winner."

Paris turned from Hera to Athena, the goddess of wisdom. Then he looked at Aphrodite, the goddess of love. "How can I decide?" he asked finally in despair. "How can a mortal man succeed when the gods have failed?"

"I can help you decide," Hera announced. "Give me the golden apple, and in return you shall have power and riches beyond measure. I shall make you master of the world. You shall be a mighty conqueror of nations and the most honoured warrior in history."

Before Paris could answer, Athena spoke up. "What are power and riches without understanding and knowledge? Give the apple to me. Then your wisdom shall bring you the respect and admiration of all humans through the ages."

Aphrodite saw that this offer pleased Paris and spoke quickly, "But Paris, what are any of these things—power, fame, riches, knowledge— without love? No man can live without love. Give me the apple, Paris, and I shall help you find the most beautiful woman in the world, a woman so lovely men would gladly die for one glance, one soft word, one tender touch..."

"Does such a woman exist?" Paris asked.

"She exists," Aphrodite answered, holding out her hand, palm up, ready to receive the golden fruit from Paris. "She exists, and she is yours when the apple is mine."

The dazed Paris put the apple in Aphrodite's waiting hand. The goddess laughed joyfully and held the apple high above her head.

"So this is the judgment of Paris!" Hera cried in terrible anger. "You shall rue this day."

"You have made two powerful enemies," Athena added darkly.

Aphrodite smiled as Hera and Athena stormed away. "Never fear," she told Paris. "I shall protect you."

"And the most beautiful woman in the world?" Paris reminded the goddess.

"She shall be yours. You have my promise. Leave these mountains, Paris, and go to Sparta." Tossing the golden apple in the air with delight, the goddess disappeared.

Neither Aphrodite nor Paris had given any thought to Oenone, who had been hiding in a nearby grove of trees.

Now, with the goddesses gone, Oenone stepped forward. "Paris," Oenone said, "I beg you. Do not go. If you do, you will die, and many men and a city will die with you."

Paris smiled. "Can you read the future, then?" he teased.

"You will die," Oenone repeated.

Suddenly Paris grew angry. "I'm tired of living a shepherd's life," he shouted, although he had been content enough before the goddesses came. "It's time for me to see more of the world. I shall go to Sparta as Aphrodite directs."

"If you leave me now," Oenone announced, "you will beg for my help when it matters most. And I shall refuse to help you, Paris."

"My mind is made up," Paris said shortly.

◆ ◆ ◆

When Paris arrived in Sparta, he found that Aphrodite had spoken the truth. The most beautiful woman in the world did live in Sparta. Her name was Helen. What Aphrodite had failed to tell Paris was that Helen was already the beloved wife of Menelaus, King of Sparta.

"We bid you welcome," Menelaus greeted Paris.

Helen smiled, and Paris's heart leaped within him at the sight. Suddenly no one existed for Paris except Helen—not Oenone, whom he had once loved, nor Helen's husband Menelaus. Before her marriage, many men had tried to win her, but Helen had never responded. Now, as if she were bewitched, she allowed Paris to speak words of love.

"Leave Menelaus, and come away with me," Paris begged.

"I cannot," Helen replied, but still she listened.

"Menelaus leaves for Crete tomorrow," Paris whispered. "While he is gone, come away with me."

"I cannot," Helen repeated. But when Menelaus left for Crete, Helen fled to Troy with Paris.

When Menelaus found that his wife was gone, he swore he would not rest until Helen returned to Sparta.

Menelaus sent word to all the kings and princes of Greece. "Before Helen married, we took an oath that we would band together to protect her if the time should come when that might be necessary. That time has come. I ask your help in rescuing Helen."

Achilles, King of the Myrmidons and bravest of all Greeks, was first to answer. Then others joined the cause. Among them were the huge Ajax the Great; Diomedes, King of Aetolia; Odysseus, who left his wife and child unwillingly; Nestor, King of Pylos; and Agamemnon, King of Mycenae, brother to Menelaus.

Time passed slowly while Menelaus and the Greeks prepared to attack Troy. Two years went by before a fleet of over one thousand ships stood ready to sail from Greek shores. More than one hundred thousand men looked to Agamemnon for direction, for Agamemnon was commander-in-chief of the war party.

The Trojans, too, prepared for war. King Priam had discovered that Paris was his son. However he felt about Paris's actions, he made up his mind to stand by the son who had been saved.

For nine years, the Greeks laid siege to Troy. But the city, protected by strong, high walls, was not touched. It was well defended by Hector, oldest son of King Priam, and by Paris and the other brave Trojans.

At last Odysseus called a council of Greek warriors. "We cannot take Troy by force," he said. "So we must take it by trickery."

"And what does Odysseus mean?" Menelaus asked.

"The goddess Athena has helped me draw up a plan," Odysseus answered. "Let's have one of our artists design a huge wooden horse..."

"Have you gone mad?" Agamemnon yelled. "Are we children that play games with wooden horses?"

"Hear me out," Odysseus pleaded. "We will have the horse built in such a way that one hundred warriors will be able to hide inside. In the dark of the night we will leave the horse outside the walls of Troy. In the morning, our ships will pretend to leave. When they see Greek ships sailing away, the Trojans will think we have lost heart for battle. We will also leave a man behind to be captured. When the Trojans bring the wooden horse into the city, the man will let our soldiers out to destroy the Trojan army. Troy will be ours, and Helen will be returned to Menelaus."

"The goddess Athena helped you with this plan?" Agamemnon asked in surprise.

"The goddess of wisdom herself," Odysseus replied firmly.

"Why does Athena help us instead of the Trojans?" Menelaus asked.

"Long ago, Paris chose Aphrodite over Athena," Odysseus answered. "Athena swore that she would get even with him."

Menelaus was impressed. "Let's start to build our wooden horse at once," he said.

◆ ◆ ◆

And it came to pass just as Odysseus had promised. The horse was built. Odysseus, Menelaus, and other warriors hid inside. The Greek ships moved away from the shores.

A cry of victory rose from the throats of the Trojans when they saw the fleet vanish into the mists at sea. "We have won! We have won!" they shouted.

"Not so," said one of the priests. "It is a trick. I fear the Greeks, even when bringing gifts."

"What? Do our eyes betray us then? Are not the Greek ships passing from sight?" the Trojans called out.

They did not listen to the priest and opened the gates of Troy. People streamed out of the city to see the strange wooden sculpture the Greeks had left behind. Then a group of Trojan soldiers captured a Greek soldier, the man left behind by Odysseus as part of his plan.

"Save me," the Greek soldier babbled. "They left me here. I am lost."

"Tell us, Greek," one of the Trojans asked. "What is the meaning of this huge wooden horse?"

"It is an offering to Athena," the Greek answered.

"Then let us take this offering inside the gates," another Trojan shouted. "It is not right that an offering to Athena be left here on the shores of the sea."

Once again the Trojan priest raised his voice in warning. But, overcome with joy at their victory, the Trojans would not listen. Pushing and pulling, Trojan soldiers rolled the giant wooden horse inside the city.

That night they celebrated late and long. And while they sang and danced and gave thanks to the gods, the Greek soldier crept to the wooden horse. He opened the bolts that locked a door in its side and motioned quietly for the Greek soldiers to come out. Silently the Greeks ran through the city. They opened the gates of Troy, and the Greek soldiers, who had returned in their ships under cover of darkness, slipped into the city.

A terrible battle followed. But the Trojans, taken by surprise, were not prepared to fight an enemy inside their walls and were beaten.

Paris killed the great Achilles, who all men said could not be defeated. But he himself was badly wounded by another Greek soldier.

Knowing himself to be dying, Paris's thoughts turned to Oenone. "Send for Oenone," Paris begged.

At first Oenone would not come. Then, overcome with memories of her husband, she went at last to Troy.

"Sweet Oenone," Paris pleaded when he saw her. "I know you have the art of healing. Only you can help me now."

"Why doesn't Paris ask Helen for help?" Oenone answered coldly.

"Please," Paris said softly, tossing his head from side to side in pain. "I am dying, Oenone. I pray you. Help me."

Oenone moved back, away from Paris's reaching hands. "Once, a long time ago, I told you that you would beg for my help when it mattered most. And I said that I would refuse."

"Will you stand by and let me die?" Paris moaned.

"There are many ways of dying," Oenone answered with bitterness. "I died ten years ago. Can you ask a dead woman for help?"

Paris knew now that there was no one to save him. He turned his face away from Oenone, and his spirit fled from his body.

Oenone wept beside his body. "Oh, Paris," she sobbed. "When the goddesses came that fateful day, why did you give the golden apple to Aphrodite? How different our lives could have been."

Oenone looked up, Queen Hecuba had entered the room. Looking down at Paris, she said sombrely, "Do not long for what might have been, Oenone. Paris could not have changed his fate. It was ordained at his birth that he would be a burning torch that would set all Troy aflame. Now the prophecy has come true. The king is dead; Troy is destroyed. And Menelaus has reclaimed Helen."

So the story of Paris ended, and the city of Troy vanished into the mists of time.

----

1. RESPONDING TO THE MYTH

a. With a partner, discuss the myth, and develop a time line of the events. Make a chart to help you understand all the characters and their roles. Include names, where they go, and what they do.

b. Are there elements of this myth that you find hard to believe? Explain fully. How are these elements an essential part of myths?

c. Would you describe Paris as a hero? Explain your answer.

d. What was the worst mistake made by a character in this story? Have you ever had to make a difficult choice? What helped you? Do you think Paris made the right or wrong choices? Explain.

e. How are characters in this selection rewarded or punished? Do you think this myth is intended to teach a lesson?

2. MEDIA MAKER CHARACTER CONNECTIONS

Answer the following questions in your notebook:

- Who are the main characters in this myth?
- How would you describe their behaviour? Their personality?

A **logo** is an identifying symbol or image, sometimes including a name or word, used in advertising.

Design a **logo,** or symbol, for one of the main characters. Your logo should represent the role the character plays, as well as his/her personality. Begin with notes, and a rough sketch. Does your sketch reflect the character to your satisfaction? Work on a final draft. Share your finished logo with your classmates. Can they guess who your logo represents?

SELF-ASSESSMENT: Examine your logo and your original character description. Have you accurately reflected the character?

3. ORAL LANGUAGE PRESENTATION PLANNING

With a partner, or in small groups, plan an oral presentation of a conversation between any of the following characters:

- Queen Hecuba, King Priam, and the prophet
- Hera, Aphrodite, Athena, Paris
- Helen and Paris
- Paris and Oenone

Begin by choosing one of the above groups, and discussing the events in which they're involved. Jot down some ideas about what they may say before, during, or after the events. Use your notes to develop a script. Assign roles to each group member. Practise your lines, and rehearse together.

Remember to stay in character as you say your lines. Use volume, an expressive voice, gestures, and movements. Once you're satisfied with your performance, share your dialogue with the whole class.

4. LANGUAGE CONVENTIONS ANALYSE ADVERBS

Look through the myth and list all the words ending in *-ly* that you find.
How are these words used? What do these words have in common?
How does the *-ly* ending change a word? What does the *-ly* ending mean?

In your notebook, write a sentence using the following words with
an *-ly* ending:

daring	nervous
smart	speechless
honest	nice

Do you find that the meaning of the word can sometimes change slightly,
when *-ly* is added? For example, would you use *smart* and *smartly* to convey
a similar meaning?

REFLECTING ON THE UNIT

SELF-ASSESSMENT: ORAL LANGUAGE

As you worked on this unit what did you learn about
- debating?
- retelling tales?
- developing dialogue?
- storytelling?
- giving oral presentations?
- presenting readers' theatre?

List three goals for improving your oral presentations.

LITERATURE STUDIES

Compare the characters in two tales, for example Dolma and Savitri,
or Paris and Dolma. How do their actions and personality differ?
What happens to each character? How are they punished or rewarded?
Which one do you admire more? Explain fully.

VISUAL COMMUNICATION

List the country of origin of each tale you experienced in this unit, including
those you read outside of this anthology. Develop a map that shows where each
tale originated. What conclusions can you draw about the popularity of stories?

WRITING

Write five interesting questions you would like to ask one of the characters
in this unit. Ask a partner to write answers to your questions. Then discuss
how the questions might have been improved.

MEDIA MIX

FAST FORWARD

UNIT AT A GLANCE

When Movies Cost a Nickel

What early memories do you have of going to the movies? In this memoir, Braithwaite recalls his first experiences with movies, long, long ago.

Memoir by Max Braithwaite

The best thing about Prince Albert was the Strand Theatre on Central Avenue. It was a temple of delight, an arena of excitement, a steam bath of emotions, a great place to be on Saturday afternoon. Movies on Saturday afternoon cost a nickel for kids, and on Friday night they cost a dime. So, of course, we always wanted to go on Friday night. But there weren't enough dimes to go around.

We'd line up at Dad's chair after lunch on Saturday and he would dig deep into his pocket with his big hand and produce a handful of change. Then, with a long finger, he'd poke among the dimes and quarters and coppers, looking for nickels. (I remember that there was always a shiny lucky quarter in that big, lean hand. Dad had carried it in his pocket since he was a schoolteacher in Ontario.) Then he'd dole out the nickels, and we'd be off.

For a long time Denny, my younger brother, got in free, so my other brother Hub and I would take him with us. Dad, who paid little attention to these niceties, didn't know about the free ticket and so he gave us a nickel for Denny, too. Which meant a whole raft of cent candy, licorice plugs, licorice whips, jawbreakers, and candy kisses to be munched during the performance.

We worked this racket until long after Denny was six. He was a skinny kid and small and the ticket-seller got used to letting him in free. But they changed ticket-sellers, and when we appeared the new one asked,

"How old is the little red-headed boy?"

"Oh, he's just five," Hub assured her.

GOALS AT A GLANCE

- ◼ Write a movie memoir.
- ◼ Describe and analyse stereotypes in movies.

But he hadn't reckoned on Denny's pride of accomplishment in having achieved his sixth birthday three months earlier. He elbowed his way to the front with fire shooting from his eyes and stated defiantly, "I'm not five. I'm six!" That was the end of our nickel's worth of goodies during the show.

Inside that dark theatre it was bedlam. Every kid that came considered it a duty to make as much noise and create as much mayhem as possible. We always arrived at least a half-hour before the show started, and for some silly reason they let us in (the practice of making kids line up outside on the sidewalk evidently hadn't been considered). So, we whiled away the time wrestling, stealing each other's toques and mitts, shoving each other under the seats, chasing each other up and down the aisles, and yelling our heads off.

Then—at last—would come the long-awaited signal. The lights would go out, and the trademark of the Union Operator would flash on the screen.

Charlie Chaplin in *Modern Times*.

Charlie Chaplin in *The Gold Rush*.

And the roar was such as greets a tie-breaking home run in the ninth with two out. And when the movies began there was still no need to be quiet. There was no talk or sound—except what came from the eager piano player in the pit—and all the dialogue was printed on the screen. So you could cheer with the good guy, scream at the bad guy, and laugh your head off at the funny guy without ever interrupting the action.

And what action! It was all action then. We'd see at least four items. A feature, usually starring William S. Hart, or Doug Fairbanks, or Hoot Gibson, or Milton Sills, or Thomas Meighen. They were the greatest: plenty of fist fights, thousands of blank cartridges blazed away, break-neck chases, crashing aircraft, exploding ships. Talk about violence! They were loaded with violence.

And then came the serial. Continued from last week, when the heroine, always in riding breeches, had been bound hand and foot and locked inside a shack which was perched precariously on the edge of a cliff. The villain, bad luck to him, had planted a charge of dynamite—they used more dynamite in the movies than they did in construction in those days—and was lurking behind a boulder, ready to push the plunger down and blow shack and heroine to eternity.

But it never worked out that way. The hero, you see, was on the way. He always got there in the nick of time and saved her life. Then she would throw her arms around his neck, and kiss him, and flutter her eyelashes, and such a "boo!" went up from the disgusted boys in the audience as could be heard clear down River Street.

And then there was the comedy, which we all loved. One- and two-reelers, featuring Charlie Chaplin, or Fatty Arbuckle, or cross-eyed Chester Conklin, or wistful Harry Langdon, or deadpan Buster Keaton. There was always a chase with automobiles just missing each other on busy streets, with men piling out of them and flying through windows, and lots of pratfalls—the pie in the face came much later—and the Keystone Cops, and the Mack Sennett bathing beauties.

It was all pantomime and it killed us. I have never heard such laughter as arose from those Saturday afternoon audiences. Never since have I laughed so hard that I couldn't get my breath, that my stomach pained, that I literally fell out into the aisle. Yes, I admit it, more than once our bladders couldn't stand the strain, and many a wet-legged kid staggered embarrassed out of the Strand. No generation of kids ever laughed as hard as we did, I'm sure, and none had so much to laugh at. It was truly the golden age of laughter.

----

1. RESPONDING TO THE MEMOIR

a. Why was going to the movies so appealing to Max and his brothers? Are movies still as appealing today? Do you look forward to going to see a movie more than watching a video? Explain your answer.

b. How do you think movie theatres and going to the movies have changed since movies cost a nickel? How have they stayed the same? What makes you think so? Develop a Then and Now chart and list as much detail from the selection as you can.

c. Have you ever tried to get into a movie by lying about your age? Discuss this experience with a partner, explaining the situation and what happened. What did you learn from this experience?

d. This article gives you a glimpse of the early history of movies and movie theatres. What do you think movies will be like in the future?

2. MEDIA MESSAGES STEREOTYPES

In his description of the movies, what *stereotype* (an oversimplified picture of a group of people) does Braithwaite describe? Discuss this stereotype with a partner. Do you think the stereotypes in movies have changed much since? Explain fully.

Now, discuss one movie you've both seen that involved some kind of stereotype. What was the purpose of the stereotype? Who might be offended by this stereotype? What could the movie's creators have done instead? Do you both feel as strongly about this movie's use of stereotypes? Explain fully.

STRATEGIES

3. WRITING MOVIE MEMOIR

Write your own movie memoir, explaining what going to the movies means to you. Begin by jotting down answers to some of these questions:

- What do you enjoy about going to the movies?
- What do you dislike?
- Who do you like to go with? Why?
- What's the best thing that ever happened to you at a movie?
- What was your most exciting movie moment? the funniest? the saddest?
- How do you behave in the theatre?
- How do you wish others would behave?

Organize your notes into an outline and then write a first draft of your memoir. Remember that in a memoir you are relating personal experiences, thoughts, and feelings. Exchange memoirs with a partner, and discuss the similarities and differences in your movie experience.

SELF-ASSESSMENT: Reread your memoir and think about its organization. Do you think the flow of the memoir could be improved? Could you use linking words between sentences and paragraphs more effectively?

What do you expect a "satiric article" on car chases to be about?
Read on to find out if your guess is correct.

HOLLYWOOD'S
New Rules for
Car Chases

Satiric Article
by Pierre Berton

Since every major film now released by Hollywood contains an obligatory car chase, the Academy of Motion Picture Arts and Sciences has felt it necessary to lay down a set of regulations for independent film producers.

USE OF POLICE CARS

1. During a police car chase, the police are to be shown as dangerous incompetents. Each film must use a minimum of seven cars (the median number is twelve), all of which are to be destroyed as the result of police stupidity and bad driving.

2. At least one pursuing police car must skid off the highway and roll down the bank into a shallow pond. Wet police officers emerging from the car must wave their fists and make other futile gestures.

3. When chased by a patrol car on a hilly, winding highway, the fugitive car should avoid one of the hairpin turns by plunging straight down the slope to make a perfect four-tire landing. The patrol car will attempt to follow suit but will turn end-over-end and burst into flames.

GOALS AT A GLANCE

- Respond critically to the satire.
- Model the selection to write a satire.

225

A chase scene from *Lethal Weapon*.

POINTS OF INTEREST

1. Four-Lane highways. All chases on four-lane highways will take place in the wrong lane with both pursuer and pursued trying to avoid oncoming cars. A minimum of eight cars (median eleven) will be knocked sideways off the highway.

2. Car ferries. Every fleeing car will attempt to reach a car ferry. As the ferry leaves the dock, the fugitive car will leap the gap and land on the deck of the ferry. The pursuing patrol car will attempt the same feat and plunge instead into the water. A wet police officer will emerge, shout imprecations, and wave her fist at the ferry.

3. Storefronts. All storefronts along the line of the chase will be equipped with large plate-glass windows. Police cars that fail to make a tight turn will skid into other police cars, which will hit parked cars, hurling them through the plate glass windows of (a) soda fountains, (b) ladies' hair-dressing parlours, (c) supermarkets.

INNOCENT BYSTANDERS

1. While travelling the wrong way down a superhighway, the chase cars will carom off other cars driven by innocent bystanders who will be forced off the highway to crash into lamp standards, the concrete median, or other innocent bystanders.

2. A runaway perambulator with a baby inside will be involved in all major car chases. In spite of several near misses, both baby and carriage will emerge unhurt with the baby chortling and gooing in high good spirits.

NOTE: These rules can easily be adapted for chases involving: (a) motorcycles, (b) bicycles, (c) roller-skates. Chases involving tracked vehicles require different rules, which will appear in our next bulletin.

----

1. RESPONDING TO THE ARTICLE

a. Explain Berton's tone and message. What is he saying about car chases? What is he saying about Hollywood movies? Do you agree or disagree? Explain.

b. Do you think Berton is being fair? Why or why not?

c. Why might Berton want to exaggerate his point of view?

d. How does this article highlight many of the stereotypes commonly found in adventure movies? Who's being stereotyped? How? Why?

2. WRITING DEVELOP A SATIRE

Reread this article and think about other rules Berton could have included for car chases. Share your ideas with a partner. Read the definition of **satire** at right and discuss how Berton uses satire. How can you tell he's being satiric?

> **Satire** is a type of writing that uses humour to point out what is wrong with an organization, person, or society.

Together, think about another aspect of movies that you could write a list of rules for. For example, you could write rules about how teenagers should be portrayed in movies. Like Berton, the tone of your rules should be satiric, or tongue-in-cheek. You want to make your reader think critically about your topic by exaggerating how Hollywood handles it. Use a similar format to Berton's for organizing your rules. Share your rules with another group, asking for feedback.

SELF-ASSESSMENT: Have you achieved a satiric tone in your writing? How can you tell?

Trick Shots

The last time you watched an action movie were you impressed by the special effects? Do you know how any of these special effects are accomplished?

Article by Ian Graham

A scene from *L'Homme à la Tête de Caoutchouc*, showing one of the earliest trick shots in motion pictures.

S ome of the early filmmakers wanted to show their audiences something magical, something that seemed impossible. Over the years, they perfected the basic special effects (sfx) techniques and continually improved them. How did these pioneers of movie special effects make people gasp with amazement?

When the French filmmaker Georges Méliès was making a movie in a Paris street in 1896, his camera jammed for a few seconds. When he watched the film, he was astounded to see people vanishing at the moment when the camera jammed. It gave him the idea of using the same effect to make actors seem to disappear or move from one side of the picture to the other in an instant. In 1901 he made a movie called *L'Homme à la Tête de Caoutchouc* (meaning *The Man with the Rubber Head*). In it, a scientist played by Méliès makes a living copy of his own head, places it on a table, and blows it up with a pump.

GOALS AT A GLANCE

- Research how special effects are developed.
- Develop a glossary of media terms.

First, he filmed himself as the scientist in his laboratory. Then he rewound the film and filmed his own head on the same piece of film. To make his head appear to grow larger, he simply moved closer to the camera. When the film was shown, Méliès as the scientist and Méliès as the disembodied head appear together.

Death rays from a spaceship in *War of the Worlds*.

War of the Worlds, made in 1953 by George Pal, included scenes of spaceships from Mars firing death rays at the Earth. The rays were painted straight onto each frame of the film. Three years later, *Forbidden Planet* featured an invisible monster terrorizing astronauts who had landed on an alien planet. When the monster was required to appear, it was visualized by a technique called rotoscoping. The monster was drawn by an animator on cels that were laid over an enlarged copy of each frame. Finally, each frame of film-plus-cel was rephotographed so that the animated monster became part of the film.

Matte technique, as this is known, is still used in film-making today. A matte may be a metal mask cut out to cover part of the film or, as in Méliès's case, a blank space left in a film so that a new image can be added later.

Astronauts on the *Forbidden Planet* face the enemy—a monster created by early animation techniques.

TRAVELLING MATTE

The modern equivalent of early matte techniques is the **blue screen travelling matte process.** In one of the *Back to the Future* films, Doc Emmett Brown's time machine, a de Lorean car, takes off from the road and flies into the distance. A model of the car was filmed in front of a blue screen. This was used to make a matte, or mask, consisting of the opaque silhouette of the car against a clear background. Next, the matte and a film of the background shot from a helicopter are printed onto another strip of film to produce a film of the background with a clear "hole" the precise shape of the car. This is used to make a counter-matte, with an opaque background and a clear area the shape of the car. The counter-matte and the film of the car are printed together onto a new film to produce a film of the car without its blue background. Finally, this is printed into the hole left in the background shot. The result is a film of the car flying through the air.

STOP MOTION ANIMATION

One of the most famous sfx experts was Ray Harryhausen. He specialized in a technique called **stop motion animation** using models and puppets. In 1933, he worked on a film called *King Kong* about a giant ape that escaped from its cage in New York and made off with the film's star, Fay Wray. The ape was actually a 45-cm-high model that Harryhausen photographed frame by frame, moving the model a fraction after each frame.

A new era in cinema sfx dawned in 1977 with the release of *Star Wars*. Dogfights between spacecraft and chases across the galaxy looked more realistic than ever before thanks to **motion control.** Each sequence was carefully planned so that the position of every spacecraft in the shot is known at every instant. Their flight paths were modelled on World War II films of combat between fighter planes to make them look authentic. Each spacecraft model was filmed by a camera on a moving platform controlled by a computer. When all the models had been filmed, the separate images were combined on one piece of film.

ANIMATRONICS

Modern movie puppets are often filmed "in real time"—moving realistically in front of the camera at the same time as the actors. They are usually made from a flexible latex (rubber) skin fitted over a metal skeleton. Cables similar to bicycle brake cables attached to the moving parts are operated by technicians to make the puppets move. Larger creatures are played by actors wearing creature suits. A mask over the actor's face is controlled by cables to make

King Kong towers above the skyscrapers of New York, yet he is only 45 cm tall.

Special effects spaceships in *Close Encounters of the Third Kind.*

the eyes blink, eyebrows rise, and mouth open and close. They are not controlled by the actor, who needs to keep both hands free. Instead, they are operated by a puppeteer by radio control. This technique is known as **animatronics.** One of the model aliens built for the film *ET* was controlled by animatronics. Another was an alien suit worn by a small person for scenes in which the alien had to be shown walking.

When the Teenage Mutant Ninja Turtles took on the bad guys on the movie screen, the actors playing the four wrong-righters wore animatronic turtle heads, each controlled by more than twenty motors operated by a puppeteer out of shot. Some of the dinosaurs that terrorized the characters in *Jurassic Park* were animatronic machines. Others were images created entirely by computers. In some scenes, where a dinosaur's head appeared, only the head was built with its animatronic control system and hoisted on a crane to make it move realistically.

MODEL MAGIC

Models are often used in scenes that are too expensive or difficult to film for real. A well-made model filmed cleverly can look very realistic, but filmmakers have to be extra careful when models are used with water or fire. Waves and

flames have a certain scale of their own and if a model is too small, any waves or flames in the same shot will make it look false.

Films made in the 1940s and 1950s about World War II often included scenes showing warships at sea. It wasn't always possible to film real ships, so models floating in water tanks were used instead. To make them look more realistic, the film was run through the camera faster than normal, so that

One of the animatronic heads created for the film *Teenage Mutant Ninja Turtles.*

tiny ripples on the water's surface were slowed down when the film was shown to look more like large waves. Even so, some of the model sequences used in these old films look false because of the scale of the waves compared to the ships. Nowadays, models used in water are rarely smaller than a quarter the size of the real thing.

Fire in the movies isn't always what it seems. When a Mercury space capsule had to be filmed re-entering the Earth's atmosphere for *The Right Stuff*, the sfx crew used a model of the capsule and a cylinder of nitrogen gas. The gas, released through the blunt end of the model capsule, would normally produce a white cloud, but illuminated by an orange light and blown along the model by fans, it looked as if the capsule was plunging into the atmosphere enveloped in fire as its heat shield burned away. ◆

British TV ads for electricity have used a series of models of talking animals that appear to move freely. The models are moved a fraction of an inch at a time and photographed, and the photographs are run together to make a moving film.

1. RESPONDING TO THE ARTICLE

a. What do you think makes filmmakers want to discover ever better ways of creating special effects (sfx) or "trick shots"?

b. Which types of movies do you think use the most special effects? Why do you think so? Where else can sfx be used?

c. Do you think there's any limit to what sfx can do? What kinds of sfx might be possible in the future?

2. MEDIA MAKER RESEARCH SFX

With a small group, discuss the processes used to create special effects. Which of the movies described in the article have you seen? What did you think of the sfx? What else would you like to know about these movies or sfx in general?

Find out more about how your favourite movie used sfx. Most modern movies have Web sites that you can visit. Or you can use library sources to find out more about sfx. Choose one process that you think is the most interesting, and write a one-page report describing how it's done and what effect is achieved.

SELF-ASSESSMENT: How well do you understand the process of creating a particular sfx? What else would you like to know about the process? Would you be able to create this sfx? What would you need?

3. WORD CRAFT DEVELOP A GLOSSARY

List any words from the article that are connected with movies or sfx. Add a definition for each word. Develop a personal glossary of media words and add to it as you work on activities in this theme. Use this glossary as a reference as you write reports, or talk about media.

BASED ON THE NOVEL

ESSAY BY GORDON KORMAN

I remember a conversation with a producer who was working on turning one of my books into a feature film. The more I heard, the more I became convinced that I had better savour the moment when "Based on the Novel by..." flashed on the screen, because it was going to be the only thing in the movie even vaguely reminiscent of what I wrote.

I think it finally sank in when the producer said, "Well, you know the scene where Steve—?"

"Wait a second," I interrupted. "Who's Steve?"

How ignorant of me to think that, as the guy who wrote the book, I should actually be able to recognize the hero, especially after they plotted, replotted, unplotted, added, excised, and replaced personnel like Harold Ballard. Can't tell the players without a scorecard.

Then I thought of the junior high school student who might someday be called upon to do a book report on my book. He would plough over to the video store and rent *that* movie, save time, and come up with a report destined to flunk with flying colours. (The character sketch of Steve would lay a particularly large egg.) Every one of us has beaten a deadline by condensing a lot of reading time into a ninety-minute movie.

All this is hypothetical, of course, because the proposed movie never got made—which is why I am not dictating this piece over the cellular phone in my Maserati. But it did get me thinking about book versus movie, and what makes a book so special, since it obviously isn't time efficiency.

GOALS AT A GLANCE

■ Analyse how a novel can be adapted to a movie.
■ Identify what influences the production of movies.

235

Lately, teachers have thrown us a curve. Now we have to read the book and see the movie, and compare the two. Teachers are very big on comparisons. Here it works. Almost invariably, the book gets the nod.

That's not to say that all the movies are bad. After the books, though, they're just somehow incomplete. The novel always seems to have something more—a greater depth, a different perspective, a more incisive insight and humour. There is something unique to the written word—to that relationship between author and reader—which cannot be reproduced any other way. It's more than just reporting or storytelling. It's *different*.

Readers participate in a novel. In a sense, it is almost a collaboration between them and the writer as, reading, they supply their own interpretation—the readers' draft. No two are ever alike. You can read the same book as someone else without reading the same book. (For instance, everybody who read *Lord Jim* and liked it read a different book than I did. That may be because I'm a poor "collaborator" with Joseph Conrad.) There is a feeling of accomplishment when you come to the end of a very good book—you have completed a successful collaboration. Don't expect royalties.

**These movies are all based on novels.
The novel *The Princess Bride* was written by William Goldman, who also wrote the screenplay. *Forrest Gump* was originally a novel, written by Winston Groom. The movie *My Left Foot* is based on the autobiography of Christy Brown.**

1. RESPONDING TO THE ESSAY

a. Reread the question at the top of page 235. Would you now change your answer? Explain.

b. What are the advantages of books over movies? Movies over books? Develop a chart to compare the two formats.

c. How do you think Gordon Korman feels at first about having his book made into a movie? How does he feel later on?

2. MEDIA MAKER ADAPT A NOVEL

Why would a director decide to make a movie out of a novel? What things need to be considered in this sort of adaptation? Think about how your favourite novel could be adapted to the big screen. In your notebook, jot down answers to the following questions:

- What makes it suitable for adaptation?
- Why would an audience find it appealing? How could it be made more appealing?
- What type of movie would it be?
- Which actors would you cast in the roles of the main characters?
- Who would you want to write the screenplay? Would it be the author of the novel or a screenwriter of a movie you've really liked?
- What parts of the novel might you cut? What parts of the novel would you be sure to include?
- What would you want to change? (You could change, for example, the title, point of view, setting, characters, storyline, theme, message.)
- What else do you need to consider as you adapt the novel?
- What else might influence the production of this movie?

Use your answers to these questions to write a proposal for adapting this novel into a movie.

PEER-ASSESSMENT: Present your proposal to your classmates. Do they agree that this novel would make a good movie? Explain your answer.

The Day the TV Broke

Poem by

Gerald Jonas

It was awful. First,
the silence. I thought I'd die.
This is the worst,
I said to myself, but I
was wrong. Soon, the house began to speak.
(There are boards in the halls
that creak
when no foot falls.
The wind strains
at the door, as if in pursuit
of someone inside, and when it rains,
the drainpipe croaks. Nothing is mute.)
That night, there came a noise from the shelves
like mice creeping.
It was the books, reading themselves
out loud to keep me from sleeping.
I can tell you I was glad to see
the repairman arrive.
Say what you will about a TV—
at least it isn't alive.

1. RESPONDING TO THE POEM

Discuss the poem and the experience it describes. What is the tone of the poem? What is the mood of the poem? Has the poet used description effectively? Have you ever had a similar experience? How did you feel? Explain.

2. LANGUAGE CONVENTIONS USING PRONOUNS

Pronouns are words that stand for nouns. Some common pronouns are *I, it, me, them, herself, that, those, any, some, everyone, who,* and *what.* Pronouns are useful when you're writing (or speaking), because they can help you avoid repeating a word over and over; however, be sure that your audience can tell what word the pronoun is replacing (its *antecedent*).

> **Vague:** Renata went with Mallory to her house. (Did they go to Renata's house or Mallory's?)
> **Vague:** I'm interested in movies, but I also like cartoons. I watch them all the time. (Does the speaker watch movies, cartoons, or both, all the time?)

How would you make both of these sentences clearer or more specific?

Check your use of pronouns in one or two recent assignments, and make sure the antecedents are clear. Be particularly careful with the pronouns *it, this, these, that,* and *those.*

*What would you like to see
on TV news shows?*

Good News

Editorial by Joseph Schrank

T he public television station is experimenting with new approaches
in presenting the news. I have a proposal for an entirely new kind of
television news program.

On this program there would be no catastrophes, no train wrecks, no
skyjackings, no burst water or gas mains, no fires, no wrecked school buses,
no auto smash-ups with pools of blood and corpses on the roadway, no
jailbreaks, no strikes, picket lines, riots, shootings, killings, war, murder,
robbery, fraud, extortions, kidnappings, and the like which comprise the
content of our daily news broadcasts. This program would be called
"Good News."

What *would* it show? It would show, for example, an unknown woman
going to work with a contented smile after a good night's sleep, a good
breakfast, and a goodbye kiss from a husband who loves her. It would show
someone finding a terrific bargain in the meat department, a child finding a
nickel in the street, a boy helping someone across the street, someone
giving up his seat in the subway or on a bus to an elderly person, someone
holding a door open for someone else, picking up a parcel for someone who
dropped it. Small acts of courtesy, politeness, and kindness.

"Good News" would show christenings, birthday parties, bar mitzvahs,
graduations, weddings, outings in the country or at the seashore or in the
parks, family visits, street flirtations—all with entirely unknown people.

GOALS AT A GLANCE

■ Analyse the factors that affect news production.
■ Create a good news report for TV.

It would show someone leaving a hospital cured, someone getting a raise in pay, someone being told by a doctor the results are negative, someone raising flowers successfully in a tenement window box or vegetables in a tiny backyard, someone successfully repairing a vacuum cleaner or opening a stuck window or repairing a plumbing leak. The happy events occurring all over the world every hour of the day that are utterly disregarded by all the newscasts on the grounds, I suppose, that good news is no news.

But my program would also show unusual events: someone picking up an empty cigarette package or a newspaper from the sidewalk and depositing it in the trash basket, a taxi driver saying "thank you," a *smiling* theatre box office clerk, someone on a supermarket checkout line with twenty items waving ahead someone with three items, two people hailing the same cab and then each insisting the other take the cab, a motorist slowing down and stopping at a corner without a traffic light to allow a pedestrian to cross, a politician withdrawing from a race on the grounds that the other candidates are better qualified for the job. On my program, only shows the critics liked would be reviewed. The weather prediction would be given only if fine weather is expected. (Oh, and the weather forecasters would not attempt feeble witticisms—they would just give the weather report.)

Good news! When the yearning arises for the customary television news diet of murder, mayhem, crime, and catastrophe, there would always be the "regular" newscasts to turn to. But "Good News" would show what else is happening all the time and at the very least would serve to restore some balance to the picture of the daily activities of the human species. And what a program for the millions of insomniacs to watch before bedtime!

No commercials, naturally.

----

1. RESPONDING TO THE EDITORIAL

a. What is the message and tone of Schrank's editorial? What does he think of regular news programs?

b. How does his second last line affect the message in the rest of his editorial?

c. Do you think Schrank thinks this proposal will be taken seriously by those who produce news shows? Explain your answer.

2. MEDIA MESSAGES ANALYSE THE NEWS

With a small group, discuss the news programs that exist now and Schrank's proposal. Would you like to watch a news program like the one Schrank describes? Do you think a news program like this would be successful? How does a TV station measure the success of a program? Why don't more TV stations run "Good News" programs? What would you propose to a TV station starting a new news program?

STRATEGIES

3. MEDIA MAKER PRODUCE A NEWS REPORT

Develop a TV script for a good news report about something that has happened in your school or community. Use the ideas in Schrank's editorial as a starting point, and then look for good news. Interview your classmates or neighbours to find out about recent events. Jot down notes as you collect information. Back at your desk, choose one event and write a short news item about it. Remember to answer the **5 W's** of journalism and to create a script that is objective and free of bias. Also remember that most TV news items are only about thirty seconds long.

> The **5 W's** of journalism are *who, what, where, when, why,* (and can also include *how*).

Read your news item to your class, using a visual to help your audience focus. As you deliver the news, remember to speak slowly and clearly, and look at your audience. If a video recorder is available, produce your script as a TV news report. You could co-operate with several classmates to create a "Good News" show.

SELF-ASSESSMENT: List three things news anchors should remember as they gather and deliver the news.

How We Make The TV Show

Behind the Scenes at *Street Cents*

Article from the
Street Cents Web site

Street Cents is based all across Canada. We have our main production centre in Halifax, Nova Scotia. That's where the studio segments are shot and where the show is put together. We also have producers working in several different Canadian cities. They put together the "field" segments, which are the stories that come from outside the studio.

Before the production season starts, we come up with ideas for topics. We have eighteen shows to do in a season and that means we need eighteen topics. Our researchers interview a group of teenagers from the Halifax area about the kinds of topics that interest them. We call them our teenage advisors. Then the researchers and senior producers have a meeting to pick the topics for the season.

Once a week during our production season, we have a brainstorming session with the entire editorial staff to come up with ideas for the stories that will go into a show. Then in a smaller meeting, we choose the stories from among all the ideas we get from our staff, viewer letters, and phone calls, and from this Web site. Before we go ahead and do them, we check with our teenage advisors to see if they like the stories. If not, we go back and pick new ones.

GOALS AT A GLANCE

- Write a letter in response to the article.
- Identify and correct run-on sentences.

Now our writers begin writing the studio script, and our field producers write and find kids to be in the segments from outside the studio. Usually there are three drafts of a show script before we go into production, so everyone from the hosts to the network boss in Toronto can have a say. Then the set designer, carpenters, wardrobe, props, and hair and make-up people meet to figure out how to make things in the script look real on TV.

The hosts rehearse the show with the director on a Sunday. They shoot the studio segments on a Monday and Tuesday. It takes a full two days to make it look good. The field producers take one day to shoot their segment and one day to edit it. Then all the elements are put together by the presentation producer in an edit suite. He adds visual effects and lots of sound effects to turn *Street Cents* into the show you see on TV.

Then we do it all over again the next week!

----

1. RESPONDING TO THE ARTICLE

a. What did this article tell you about producing a TV show that you didn't already know? What else would you like to know?

b. What do you think is the most important part of putting a show together? Who do you think has the most important job? Justify your answer.

c. With a partner, discuss the show *Street Cents*. Have you ever watched it? What is its purpose? Who is the audience? What is your favourite feature of the show?

2. LANGUAGE CONVENTIONS RUN-ON SENTENCES

A run-on sentence is formed when two sentences are improperly joined. To fix a run-on sentence, add the proper punctuation, or change the wording to make it a single sentence.

> **Run-on:** I'd recommend the movie to anyone, the special effects are great!
> **Better:** I'd recommend the movie to anyone; the special effects are great! **Or:** I'd recommend the movie to anyone because the special effects are great!

Read through the selection and make a list of words used to join *independent clauses* (complete thoughts). Then look through an example of your own work to make sure you haven't created run-on sentences. Correct any run-ons with the correct punctuation or a conjunction.

3. WRITING A FORMAL LETTER

On *Street Cents* the hosts often read letters from kids across Canada, who write to ask questions, or complain about a product. Think of something you would like to ask or complain about. Jot down ideas for a letter.

Now, write a formal letter to the people at *Street Cents*. Begin with a rough draft, and then revise, edit, and proofread. Check your paragraphs—each should begin with a main idea, and have supporting sentences. Make sure you have a paragraph for each idea in your letter. Remember not to use slang in a formal letter. You should also use complete, grammatically correct sentences, and correct spelling.

Use a computer to help you produce a neat copy with no errors. As you work on your final draft, remember the format of a formal letter:

(Your name and address here)

April 21, 2005

STREET CENTS
POST OFFICE BOX 3000
1840 BELL ROAD
HALIFAX NS B3J 3E9

Dear *Street Cents* Producers:

I really enjoy watching your program. I find it very informative and...

Sincerely,
(your name)

Last Chance
Comic Strip by
Charles Schulz

Peanuts   **by Charles Schulz**

© 1985 United Feature Syndicate, Inc.

Drink Milk, Love Life

Commercial Script
from the Dairy Farmers of Ontario

Opening shot of the top half of a nearly-filled glass of milk. Milk logo on upper left of screen. Milk is poured into the glass.

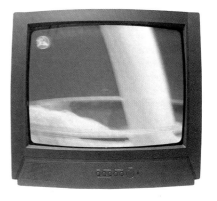

Cut to shot from inside the glass. Computer animated shapes in the form of human figures rise from the milk and play soccer. Lyrics from "Drink Milk" song begin, as does running text feature listing nutrient information for the product.

Lyrics
Drink milk
Love life
Grab that freshness
Good as cold has ever tasted
Drink milk
Love life
Drink milk

GOALS AT A GLANCE

■ Respond critically to commercials.
■ Analyse commercials and their messages.

247

Running text

250 ml of 2% milk contains:

Energy 129 calories (546kJ)

Protein 8.6%

Carbohydrates 12.4 g

plus these % of Recommended

Daily Intakes:

Vitamin A 11%

Vitamin D 44%

Thiamin 8%

Riboflavin 25%

Niacin 10%

Vitamin B 66%

Folacin 5%

Vitamin B-12 45%

Pantothenate 11%

Calcium 29%

Phosphorus 22%

Magnesium 14%

Zinc 11%

Cut to **close-up** of teenaged girl, profile.
She is drinking heartily from a glass
of milk labelled "Milk Energy."

Cut to close-up of teenaged boy, profile.
He is kissing the side of a full glass of
milk, also labelled "Milk Energy."

Cut to three teenagers standing together,
facing forward, each raising a full glass
of milk in a "Milk Energy" cup.
Boy in middle holds a soccer ball.
All are smiling. Above their heads
are the words, "Drink Milk. Love life."

1. RESPONDING TO THE COMMERCIAL

a. What is this commercial selling (besides milk)?

b. What image does the ad create?

c. What does the image have to do with the product?

d. Do you think this commercial is effective? Explain why or why not.

e. What effect do you think the running text, listing the vitamins and minerals, has on the audience?

2. MEDIA MESSAGES   COMMERCIAL MESSAGES

With a small group, discuss your favourite commercials and why you think they're effective. What language does the advertiser use? Are there catch phrases, such as "This may be your last chance" or "Batteries not included." Develop a list of phrases that you've heard in commercials. What else do you often hear in commercials? How do the advertisers try to sell their products? What images do the advertisers often use? How do advertisements make people feel?

Opening shot is the first scene or image the viewer sees.

Cut to indicates an abrupt change from one shot to another.

A **close-up** is a shot that focusses on one thing—such as a person's mouth.

Read the title and by-line of this selection. What arguments do you think could be used for either side?

The Two Sides of Advertising

Debate by Edith Rudinger and Vic Kelly

Advertising is a bad thing because it

…misleads the shopper by making claims which are exaggerated, if not untrue

…deliberately sets out to deceive

…gives precious little information but tries to persuade

…puts up prices, especially newspapers and magazines

…spoils TV programs by getting between the things we really want to see

…persuades people to buy things they do not need or really want, and sometimes things they cannot afford

…makes people dissatisfied

…undermines our values and our attitudes towards some of the most important features of life (e.g. courtship, love, marriage, motherhood, personal relationships)

…is wasteful of money that could be spent on better causes

…spoils our language by cheapening words like "love" and taking away the meaning from words like "fire"

…endangers health by making exaggerated claims about, for instance, aids to slimming, health foods, toothpastes, drugs, patent medicines

…is anti-democratic, because advertisements make it harder for people to choose freely

GOALS AT A GLANCE

■ Participate in role-playing.
■ Justify own opinions.

Advertising is a good thing because it

...gives shoppers useful information to help them choose wisely
...ensures that shoppers know what they are buying
...forces the manufacturers to take care that their products are of a good standard
...encourages competition between manufacturers, and so keeps prices down
...reduces prices by increasing sales
...pays for TV programs and keeps down the cost of newspapers and magazines
...makes TV, newspapers, and magazines brighter and more interesting
...raises our standard of living and increases our enjoyment of life by encouraging us to buy things attractively presented to us
...contributes to the economic growth of the country as a whole
...is an essential feature of a free, democratic society

You may be able to think of more arguments on both sides.

- -

RESPONDING TO THE DEBATE

Discuss this selection with a partner. Are there any points on either side that you strongly agree or disagree with? Explain. Together, role-play an argument two people might have about whether advertising is good or bad. Use points from the selection, as well as your own.

Check out how some advertisers try to grab the attention of their audience.

What's the Message?

Print Ads from Canadian Magazines

When the party's this big, you invite the neighbours. CANADA

A fiddler keeps the dancers swinging. Join us at one of the many Soiree'99 festivals and events.

A rich and storied history. A unique culture. And awesome natural beauty. These things we brought to Canada 50 years ago. This year we celebrate them with Soiree'99, a rollicking year of festivals and events across our province. And we want all of Canada to join us. There'll be jigs and reels and friendly folk. Our party. Our country. Our way. Join us for Soiree'99. Dancing shoes required.

For your free Travel Guide and Festival and Events Guide or to make reservations for your stay, call Kelly at

1 800 563 NFLD

E-mail: info@tourism.gov.nf.ca   Internet: http://public.gov.nf.ca/tourism

Proud Sponsors of Soiree'99

NEWFOUNDLAND & LABRADOR

GOALS AT A GLANCE

- ■ Analyse the effectiveness of ads.
- ■ Write a letter to an advertiser.

Behold.

Her
    splendour
        weaves a
            delicate spell
                which enchants
                    my soul,
                        holding that
                            part of me
                                here forever.

Yukon
Magic & Mystery

Yukon
Tourism

1-800-78-YUKON www.touryukon.com/rc.html

Could this be the **original spice girl?**

With its gleaming skyscrapers and sophisticated shopping malls, modern Singapore is truly the face of New Asia. Yet the old Asia is never far away: sensitively preserved Colonial, Chinese, Malay and Indian quarters offer exciting glimpses of the past. And when you need a break from exploring, remember that Singapore's rich culinary heritage makes it one of the world's most exciting places to eat. Whether you're sampling satay in one of our renowned food stalls or devouring a spicy curry in Little India, a vacation in Singapore is one that you'll savor forever.

NEW ASIA

Singapore

So easy to enjoy, so hard to forget.

For a free video and information, call the Singapore Tourism Board at 800.944.8778 or visit our website at www.singapore-ca.com

Eight species of whales are on Canada's List of Wildlife at Risk. World Wildlife Fund is working to establish marine protected areas for these and other species not yet endangered, including the killer whale. This will help safeguard the planet's wildlife and wild places. And that's critical to protecting the web of life that sustains all life, including yours. So do something for yourself and support WWF Canada. To find out how, visit www.wwfcanada.org or call 1-800-26-PANDA.

Their future is our future.

Photo: T.H. Brakefield/First Light

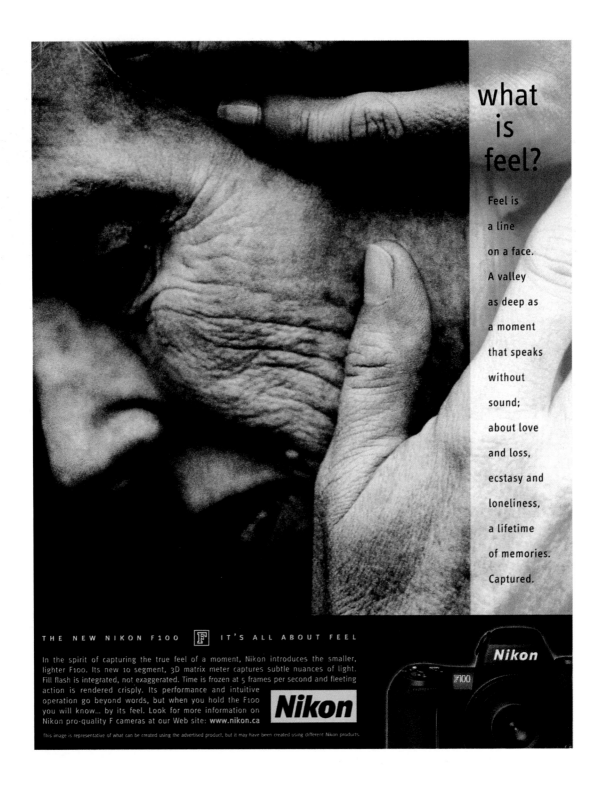

It was a good idea:
Cross the seas with lines of ships.
Cross the land with lines of steel.
Tie the lines, draw them tight,
and make a smaller world.

Forty years ago a simple idea
changed the world: the box.
The standardized container,
which could be moved at
unheard-of speed, from
trucks to trains to ships.
From land to sea.

Almost overnight,
the world became smaller.
But world trade grew bigger.
Fourteen times bigger, so far.
And as trade grows,
so do railways.

In North America, more freight
volume moves by train than
by any other mode, and rail
container traffic has been
growing at double-digit rates.
Rail is twice as fuel-efficient
as road transport. One train
moves as much as 280 trucks.

Every year Canadian Pacific
moves 150 million tons
of goods across Canada
and the US Midwest and
Northeast, over 15,900 miles
of railway lines.

Which are closely tied
to our shipping lines.

It's a small world.
And a perfect place for trains.

CANADIAN PACIFIC
Energy Transportation Hotels

www.cp.ca

----

1. RESPONDING TO THE PRINT ADS

a. Which of these ads do you find the most appealing? Why?

b. How effective are these ads? What makes them effective?

c. What is the purpose of these ads?

d. What type of magazine do you think these ads come from?

e. How do some advertisers take advantage of trends, or current events?

2. WRITING A FORMAL LETTER

Look through magazines and newspapers for other print ads. Choose one
that makes you react strongly, whether in a positive or negative way.
Perhaps it's an ad that makes you laugh or cry or rage. Think about why you
like or dislike the ad. Jot down notes describing your reaction. Now, use
these notes to write a formal letter to the advertiser. (For help writing
formal letters see page 245.)

HOW TO CREATE

PRINT ADS

Goals at a Glance

- Use appropriate persuasive techniques. • Select vivid and effective language.

The information below can help you create a magazine advertisement, but it applies equally well to other forms of advertising, such as posters and billboards.

Before you start, keep in mind that ads developed by professionals are the result of teamwork among writers, art directors, and their clients. You might try a team approach for your own ad.

Define Your Purpose

When you create your own magazine ad, your first task is to define your purpose. Do you want to convince readers to buy or use something, to vote for someone, or to change the way they think about something? Follow these steps:

1. Choose the product, service, or idea that will be the focus of your ad.
2. Decide what kind of message you want to send. Do you want to use the direct approach, telling your readers exactly what to do? Or will you be subtle, creating a positive or negative atmosphere meant to influence their behaviour?
3. Target an audience. Like professional advertisers, you should direct your ad at a specific group of people. Consider such factors as age, income level, and gender.

Check Out the Competition

Before you design your own ad, pick up a few magazines and see what other advertisers are doing. (You'll also find a sample of ads on pages 252-257 of this book.) Note the ads that seem to catch your attention best. What part of the ad (image, slogan, *copy*—or text) caught your interest?

As you flip through magazines, remember to examine ads that you don't like. Try to figure out why they are making a negative impression. This will help you to learn what to avoid when

PROCESS

you create your own advertisement.

Pay special attention to the ads that seem to have the same purpose and/or audience as yours.

Select an Approach

As you know, magazine advertisements are carefully designed to grab the reader's attention and communicate a persuasive message briefly and effectively. But there are many different ways of achieving those goals. Try one of the approaches described in the following list:

- Use humour to entertain the reader and make the persuasion seem less obvious.
- Include facts and figures if you want to convince your reader through logic.
- Try a testimonial, in which a famous person endorses something, to create a strong positive impression.
- Use positive, appealing words and images in your ad which will become associated with the product or idea you are promoting.
- Use the bandwagon approach to encourage the reader to fit in with the crowd.
- Take advantage of your reader's hidden fears, showing how your product or idea can protect against disaster or embarrassment.

Design Your Ad

Once you have a general approach in mind, you can start thinking about the specifics. Most ads can be broken down into three elements: the visual, the slogan, and the copy. Though all three elements are related, it's usually easiest to consider each one on its own. In each case, remember to keep your purpose and audience in mind.

The Visual: Most ads use at least one carefully selected photo or illustration to make a strong statement. Through the visual element of your ad, you can nudge the reader's feelings. For example, a heartbreaking photo of people in a crisis can prompt someone to become a volunteer or contribute money. Here are some questions to ask when you develop your visual:

- Will I use a photo or illustration?
- What colours will help me communicate my message?
- Will my visual include people?
- How large will my visual be?

The Slogan: A slogan is a phrase that sums up the message in a memorable way. It can be as short as one word and is almost never longer than a single line. The slogan is just as important as the visual, and is usually placed in a prominent position. Ask yourself these questions as you develop your slogan:

- What is the key idea I want the reader to know?
- What words would best communicate the idea?
- How large will my slogan be, and what typeface will I use?
- Where will I position my slogan?

The Copy: In addition to the slogan, most ads also include descriptive text (known as *copy*) that supports the message. Writing ad copy is similar to writing poetry or song lyrics—the idea is to use language carefully so it has a strong effect. You should also consider using figurative language (e.g., simile, metaphor, personification). Think about the following:

- What background information do I want the reader to know?
- What concrete nouns, lively verbs, vivid adjectives and adverbs can I use to make my copy effective?
- Is it appropriate to use special techniques such as alliteration, assonance, simile, and metaphor?
- How much copy should I use and how big should it be?

Put the Elements Together

Now it's time to combine your visual, slogan, and copy into one ad. Before you move to this final stage, it's helpful to create full-size rough sketches to preview your ad. This will allow you to experiment with the size and positioning of the different elements. Remember—all three elements should work together to persuade the reader.

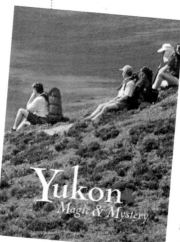

Make your finished version as professional-looking as possible. You might generate your slogan and copy using a computer. In fact, with the right software you can design your whole ad on-screen and print a colour copy.

Self-Assessment

How effective is your magazine ad? What improvements could you make?

- ❏ I had a clear purpose and audience for my ad.
- ❏ I selected an approach that was appropriate to my message.
- ❏ I carefully considered each element of my ad: visual, slogan, and copy.
- ❏ My ad persuasively communicates my message.

PROCESS

Sometimes thinking of that million-dollar idea is just a matter of…

TWISTING the
Familiar

ARTICLE BY FAITH POPCORN

One warm summer's day, when we were watching the world go by, it seemed as if every man, woman, and child had an ice cream cone clutched in their hands. "How clever a cone is," we thought. "How utterly convenient." Yet these carriers haven't really changed since they were invented at the World's Fair in St. Louis in 1904.

Why not expand on this handy, hand-held concept? Make taco cones and fill them with chili? Or crisp rice cones piled with Chinese chow mein? Or English muffin cones cradling peanut butter and jelly, cheese and onions, or even an herb omelette?

This is Twisting the Familiar.

Something comfortable turned into something new. Novelty without threat. It's a way of building on what the consumer already knows and likes, without taking away any of the benefits normally found in a favourite product.

Think of McDonald's Chicken McNuggets (much-loved fried chicken, only bite-sized, easier to eat). Or, Nabisco's Teddy Grahams (a double-twist: teddy bear charm enhanced by graham cracker taste and vice versa). Great ways to ease a wary consumer into new products.

Another way of Twisting the Familiar is with an exaggeration of the norm. The Alice-in-Wonderland syndrome.

• Giant sizes, such as huge mushroom-shaped muffins or plate-sized cookies.
• Miniatures, such as bite-sized pizzas, mini-Mars ice cream bars, baby veggies, espresso-for-one machines, itty-bitty Cuisinarts.
• New and different colours, such as tomato pasta, ink-black pasta, white bell peppers, hunter green KitchenAid mixers.
• New packaging, such as the highly successful juice paks, or European mayo in a toothpaste-like tube (why not tubes of salad dressing base or salsa?).

The central premise of Twisting the Familiar is that the consumer world doesn't have to be the way it is. There are no absolutes. The trick is to challenge the assumptions, change the ground rules.

If you know that as many people like "salty" as "sweet," then look at some of the traditional sweets and ask why. Why are all frozen ice pops sweet? Instead of fudge or banana coconut, why not frozen V8 on a stick? Why are most yogurts sweetly fruit-based with globs of jam? Why not cool cucumber/mint or crunchy vegetable yogurts for lunch or a snack? And those diet shakes that are substitutes for meals. Why should you have to drink a sweet chocolate, vanilla, or strawberry dinner? Why not tomato-basil, herbal chicken, or wild mushroom, all closer to soup?

This works conversely, too.

Why are most chewing-gums spicy (cinnamon) or refreshing (spearmint) or child-oriented (bubble gum)? Isn't there an opening for a premium chocolate chewing gum (Godiva sugarless?), orange expresso, or cappuccino gum?

Examine popular eating habits and you might find familiar twists. Plenty of people eat muffins for breakfast and slather them with butter and jam. Why not make life easier—and make microwavable muffins with a center nugget of butter and/or fruit preserves or chocolate spread. Or make cereal bars with a milky/creamy centre.

If more people like *hors d'oeuvres* better than main courses, try creating a frozen dinner of mixed appetizers. And think of adding chunks of sundried tomatoes for texture or *jalapeños* for pizzazz to that familiar bottle of ketchup. (By the way, putting ketchup, mustard, and relish in plastic squeeze bottles a few years back was perfect Twisting the Familiar.)

In other words, question everything.
• Why does shampoo come in bottles? Why not in bars, like soap?
• Why does cereal always come with two wrappings, inner bag, outer box? Why not just the bag, like Pepperidge Farm cookies? Or canisters, like bread crumbs? Or in big burlap bags, to be scooped out like oats or rice in days of yore? And how come no one has realized

that cereal grains are sprayed with pesticides? Great opportunity for organically-grown cereal.
• Do products really need to have packaging at all?
• Why can't those brown padded mailing envelopes come with reusable closures?
• Why haven't cameras shrunk like calculators, so you can carry one around in your wallet? Or, why can't a camera double as a Walkman? Why aren't there cameras with mini-tape recorders in them so you can identify each shot (great for real estate agents, insurance adjusters, etc.)?

Twisting the Familiar is letting your imagination wander across the marketplace. It's being free of fixed images, those static ideas of "It's always been this way." It's taking a hard look at everything to see what should be reshaped for this coming decade.

And it's reshaping things for a better world.

---

1. RESPONDING TO THE ARTICLE

a. Which idea in the article is your favourite? Explain why.

b. What is the tone of this article? What is its message? Justify your answer.

c. With a partner, discuss some of the questions the author raises. What answers would you give to these questions?

2. MEDIA MAKER GENERATE IDEAS

With a small group, generate other marketing or packaging ideas. Then choose one idea and develop a marketing plan for it. Or take one of Faith Popcorn's ideas, and develop a plan for it. Discuss this one idea thoroughly. Together, list the advantages and disadvantages of the idea. Brainstorm solutions to any possible problems. List steps that would need to be taken to get your idea to a target market for testing. If possible, take those steps. Then evaluate the results of your market research.

SELF-ASSESSMENT: When working with others, do you offer ideas? Do you listen to others? Do you take helpful notes? Do you respect the rights of others to voice their opinion?

The Internet: The Newest Medium

Article by Catherine Rondina

One day, the Internet may be your home's complete media centre. It's beginning already. You can listen to the radio, check out your favourite TV shows, watch videos, research all kinds of topics, or communicate with your friends. In fact people you've never met can become your friends, through the Internet. Will the Internet of the future be all the media you'll ever need? What do you think? Follow Cathy as she takes you on a tour of the hottest new medium.

Hello cyberpals, my name's Cathy, and I'm a Net Wizard. Well, maybe not a wizard, but I do know a lot about how the Internet works. I'm here to tell you a little bit about the Net and how to have fun with it. I'm sure you've heard of the Internet, you're probably already surfing every minute you can get. Did you know it's also called the "Information Superhighway"? Well, you can probably figure out why. It's jam-packed with information, travelling at super fast speeds.

Everybody seems to be using the Net these days, surfing in cyberspace, riding the waves to visit computers all over the world. I've been surfing for almost four years now and I even have my own Home Page. I created it myself, with a little help from my friends. You can create a Home Page, too.

GOALS AT A GLANCE

■ Develop a glossary of terms.
■ Analyse main and subordinate clauses.

264

Check out these pages from a popular Canadian Web site run by the Aboriginal Youth Network.

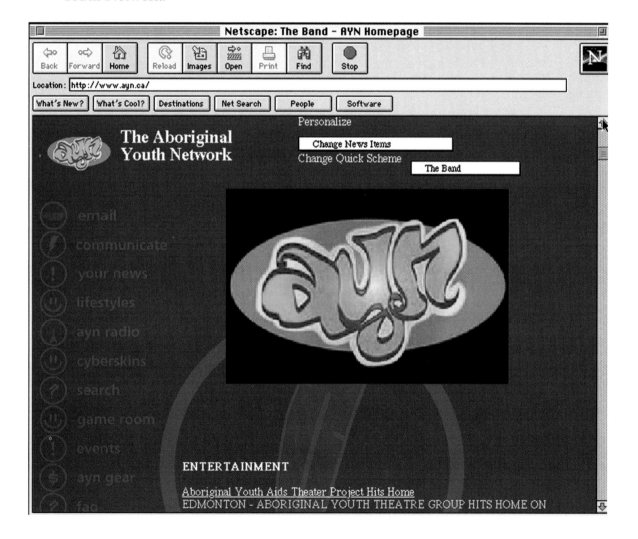

The best way for you to decide about how you want your Web page to look is to visit some other sites. You could just *surf the Net* (browse through a bunch of Web sites connected to a personal interest) or you could visit particular Web sites. You'll need to know their Web addresses, called **URL**s (Uniform Resource Locators). Basically, it's like a phone number on the Web. Once you understand the letters and symbols, the rest is easy. For example, say the Web site is located at:

http://www.infoaccess.on.ca/cathyr/html

http tells you that my site is on the World Wide Web, which most surfers use.

www.infoaccess.on.ca tells the computer where on the Web my site is located, or what service provider I use. A service provider is the company I'm online with.

cathyr tells you the name of my specific file, or it can be a directory for the site.

html means that the file is formatted for the Web, so don't try to download anything from the site and use it on any old dinosaur of a computer.

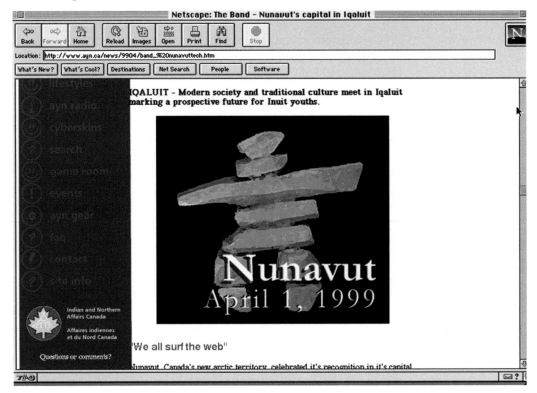

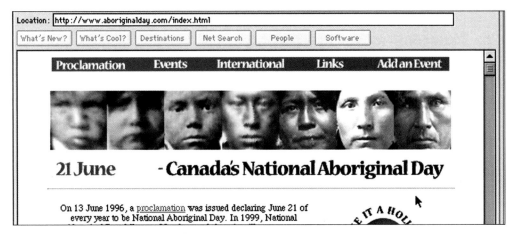

Location: http://www.aboriginalday.com/index.html

What's New? What's Cool? Destinations Net Search People Software

Proclamation   Events   International   Links   Add an Event

21 June   - Canada's National Aboriginal Day

On 13 June 1996, a proclamation was issued declaring June 21 of
every year to be National Aboriginal Day. In 1999, National

Now that we've got the hard part over with, here comes the fun—creating your own Home Page. Whenever you visit a site on the Web, the first thing you see is a Home Page. It's sort of like a welcome mat at your front door. This is where you start to explore the site. You want to make it look interesting, so fellow surfers enjoy their visit. For example these are the options on my home page:

- Best music e-mail sites—here I recommend my favourites
- Musical Games—games I made up, like matching groups to their songs
- All About Me—Cathy, you can talk with me in real time on this site
- Mix and Match Games—just fun stuff
- Sports Desk—some of the latest stats for my favourite teams.
- e-mail—please write!

On my third page I have a lot of crazy, fun things to do. You can play a game where you have to finish the words to a famous song, or you can help me name my twenty goldfish. I created a site on which you can see pictures of my favourite singers by pressing SuperSingers, or you can help me with some math problems I've been having by visiting Weird Math. See what I mean? You can put in anything you want to. I also have a counter on this page so you can see how many visitors I've had on my Home Page. I check it almost every day!

I like to have kids write back to me so I invite them to e-mail their comments to me. I think having my own Home Page is great. I really like to work on it and I add new things to it all the time, but my favourite thing is making new friends in Cyberspace.

Happy surfing!

1. RESPONDING TO THE ARTICLE

a. Do you strongly agree or disagree with any of the author's statements? Explain.

b. What do you like about the Internet? What do you dislike?

c. What do you think the future of the Internet will be like?

d. What questions would you like to ask the author about the Internet?

2. WORD CRAFT   GLOSSARY OF TERMS

Many of the words in this article are specific to the Internet, or have specialized meanings for Internet users, such as *cyber,* or *surfing.* Reread the article and list these words, with a definition. Use the word's context, or a dictionary to help you define the word. Where do you think these words come from? What other meanings do some of these words have? Write about your own experiences on the Internet, using some of these words correctly.

3. LANGUAGE CONVENTIONS   CLAUSES

A *main clause* is a group of words that has a subject and a verb, and can stand on its own as a sentence. A *subordinate clause* is a group of words that has a subject and a verb, but that cannot stand as a sentence without another clause. Subordinate clauses often begin with a *subordinate conjunction,* such as *although, because, since, when, that,* or *who.* For example:

I went fishing with my uncle when I was young.

When you use a sentence with a main and a subordinate clause, be sure to put the main idea you want to express in the main clause, and the less important information in the subordinate clause. Notice how the meaning of the sentence above changes when the clauses are reversed:

I was young when I went fishing with my uncle.

Look for sentences with subordinate clauses in the selection, and rewrite them with the clauses reversed, as above. What difference does this make to the meaning of the piece? Now, check through your own writing to make sure you have used main and subordinate clauses correctly.

REFLECTING ON THE UNIT

SELF-ASSESSMENT: MEDIA
As you worked on activities in this unit what did you learn about
• movie production?
• television news?
• commercials?
• advertisements?
• the Internet?
• stereotypes?
• special effects?
• marketing?

VISUAL COMMUNICATIONS
Compare two of the images within this unit. Do you know who produced them? What is the purpose of these images? Who is their audience? What special techniques were used? What is their message?

ORAL LANGUAGE
With a partner, discuss the importance of any one of the media covered in this unit. What would we do without it? What makes it more or less important than another type of media?

WRITING
Choose one of the media (movies, TV, commercials, ads, Internet) discussed in this unit, and write a paragraph describing what you think it might be like one hundred years from now. Who will be using it? What will its purpose be? How will it be better? Worse?

ISSUES

"To talk goodness
is not good—only
to do it is."

Chinese proverb

DO THE RIGHT THING

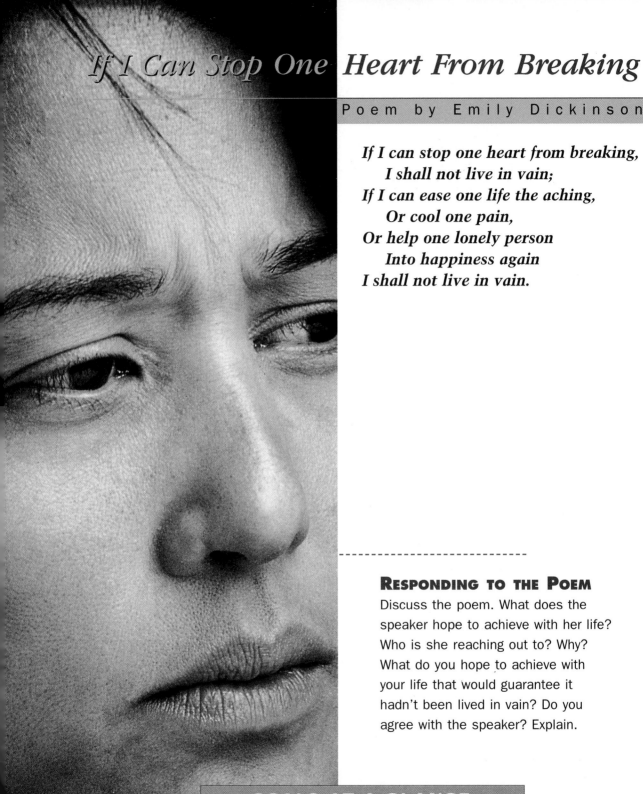

If I Can Stop One Heart From Breaking

Poem by Emily Dickinson

If I can stop one heart from breaking,
   I shall not live in vain;
If I can ease one life the aching,
   Or cool one pain,
Or help one lonely person
   Into happiness again
I shall not live in vain.

RESPONDING TO THE POEM

Discuss the poem. What does the speaker hope to achieve with her life? Who is she reaching out to? Why? What do you hope to achieve with your life that would guarantee it hadn't been lived in vain? Do you agree with the speaker? Explain.

GOALS AT A GLANCE

- Locate ideas in texts to develop interpretations.
- Use oral skills to participate in discussions.

Can you think of a situation when cheating might be justified? In this futuristic story, a young man must decide.

And the Lucky Winner Is...

Science Fiction Story

BY MONICA HUGHES

The heliolites soared above the river valley, clustering, separating.

To Jon, squinting up into the sunshine, they were like a cloud of brilliant butterflies. For just a moment he wished he were up there with them, but only for a moment. The one time he'd soared he'd felt so nauseated that he'd barely made it back to solid earth in one piece. The nausea, along with a hatred of crowds, seemed to be the flip side of his "gift." He'd gladly trade the shameful hidden skill of telekinesis for the chance to soar with his sister and his best friend. To be skilled in telepathy and telekinesis, gifts useful only to spies and other servants of the state, was a burden he would happily cast off. To be like Peri. To be free...

Peri, strapped in her harness, watched the city swing beneath her, a slowly rotating jigsaw of ceramic roofs, solar panels, and streets, with the river cutting a random furrow through its geometric order. Directly below her she could see Jon, a dark dot on the field by the bridge. Kid brother, isolated as usual from the crowd.

She felt the chill of cloud-shadow on her cheek an instant before her heliolite lost power. Automatically she compensated, manoeuvring neatly into the thermal that rose from the hot ground of the bluffs above the river. Around her the others moved smoothly into place on the funnel of warm air.

This was the best moment, soaring like a bird in the silence of the thermal. Without worry, at one with the air, she swung in her harness, leaning into the thermal, following it around. She forgot about her math test, so awful, but totally essential if she could ever hope to work in the space

---

GOALS AT A GLANCE

- Analyse the setting of a futuristic story.
- Use evidence to develop opinions about characters.

273

program, about her brother Jon, more silent and separate from their friends every day, about Nev. Did Nev really love her as much as she loved him? As much as he said... Or was it really only a Senior Year relationship that meant no more to him than trying to beat her at squash or soaring? Everything was left behind in the wrinkled land below, as Peri soared in the silence.

Then the sun slid from behind an obscuring cloud to reactivate the tiny engines on the wing tips. She engaged the jets and soared out of the thermal, away from the crowd, up, up, to that breathtaking instant before stalling. Then she plunged and regained speed in a shiver of nylon wings. It was a tricky manoeuvre, one she had just perfected. Up here she was the best, and it felt good.

Over her shoulder Peri glanced at the others, just breaking free of the thermal like a cluster of firework stars. Something was badly wrong! One heliolite seemed to hesitate at the thermal interface, shuddered, and plunged suddenly toward the ground. She saw its colour, a royal blue zagged with a lightning line of gold. Nev's!

In a single frozen instant she saw the tiny figure of Jon scurry across the field. Do something, Jon! her mind screamed. Reach out with your telekinesis. Grab him. Defy gravity. You can do it!

But Jon wasn't God, and Nev's heliolite continued to spin downward like a twisting maple key. Instinctively Peri cut the power to her props and followed it down in a steep frantic dive.

The nylon shivered and the wind screamed through the titanium frame as she approached the ground. She could see Nev's 'lite, broken below her, Jon running towards it. Now the ground was rushing towards her. She soared briefly to absorb speed and, in a series of roller coaster moves, came to a stop fifty metres away. Her fingers fumbled stiffly at the harness buckles. Come on. Come on. At last she was able to wriggle free, to run stiff-legged across the rough turf towards the broken heliolite. The fifty metres seemed forever.

"Nev! Nev!" She stumbled in the grass and Jon caught her arm.

"He's alive, Peri. I can still sense his life force. But..."

Nev lay still. His eyes were not quite closed and she could see a glint of white between the lids. He looked horribly not there, as if the Nev she knew were in some other place and this was only a shell.

The medics arrived, to slip a rigid collar around his neck, to ease a stretcher sheet under his body, wrapping him carefully and light-zapping the sheet to stiffness. She watched the cocoon that was Nev loaded aboard, watched the copter take off. Then she stood numbly, with the wind drying her lips, until Jon put his arm around her and helped her climb to the top of the bluffs, where the others waited outside the heliolite rental agency.

They crowded around. "What happened?" "What went wrong?" "How's Nev?" But there were no answers.

Hours later, in the hospital, Peri tried to explain to Nev's mother what had gone wrong. "We'd been trying out a new manoeuvre. I guess he didn't..." She stammered and was silent under the contempt in Mrs. Wright's eyes.

"If it hadn't been for you...you're always leading him on with your reckless ideas. Those crazy heliolites—they should be banned. What if he dies? What if he never walks again? Oh...oh..."

Peri flinched from her anger and her pain. "I'm sorry, Mrs. Wright. I'd give anything in the world for this not to have happened."

"Why do you want to do these crazy things? How come you can't be more like your brother? For all he's a year younger than you, he's got more sense, he's not so foolish as to..."

"That's not fair, Mrs. Wright." Jon stood protectively in front of Peri. "Nev's every bit as crazy about helioliting as Peri, honestly."

Then the doctor came and there were involved explanations about the realities of spinal cord injuries. Nev's mother began to cry, her mouth open in an ugly square.

Peri swallowed her own tears. "Oh, please don't cry, Mrs. Wright. It'll be all right. They've got new techniques. Microsurgery and electric stimulation. It'll be okay." She turned to the authority in sparkling white, the silver caduceus winking in his left lapel. "Isn't that true, doctor? Tell her."

"Indeed, we have made amazing advances in the field of nerve regeneration in the last twenty years. Biochemistry. Electrical stimulation. It's a very lengthy process, of course. Labour intensive. Expensive."

Mrs. Wright twisted her fingers together. "I've got medical coverage. That'll take care of it, doctor."

"Your insurance will certainly cover the tests we've done so far and your son's stay in hospital for the next few days. You need have no concern on that account. Beyond that...well, talk to your insurance agent. You're looking at something in the neighbourhood of a quarter of a million dollars." The doctor's buzzer beeped.

"A quarter of a..."

"Excuse me. We'll have an opportunity to talk later. In the meantime, a visit to the accounting office will make procedures clearer to you."

He hurried away, leaving them standing in the middle of the waiting room.

Mrs. Wright turned on Peri, her mouth tight. "See what you've done. You've ruined both our lives with your stupid reckless games. A quarter of a million! How will I ever...?" She scrubbed her eyes angrily. "Oh, go away. Get out!"

Peri tried to protest, but Jon took her arm and pulled her along the corridor and through the doors into the sunlit grounds of the hospital. "Don't cry. Don't pay attention to her. It's not your fault."

"Perhaps it is. I'm much better aloft than Nev. But he always wanted to catch up."

"It was his choice. You didn't twist his arm."

"Maybe I could leave school and get a job. Just to help pay for Nev's treatment."

"Mum and Dad'll never let you. Not in a million years. Besides, what about the space program?"

"That doesn't matter. Nothing matters except Nev getting better. Oh, Jon, what are we going to do?"

Peri put on a bright face to visit the hospital the next day, but it slipped off at the sight of Nev cradled in a paraplegic bed.

"Nev, I'm so sorry. It's all my fault."

He managed a grin. "You sound just like my Mom! I told her and I'm telling you and then let's forget about it, okay. I wasn't trying to copy your crazy stunt, I'm not that dumb. One of the struts snapped, that's all."

"Are you sure?" Relief flooded through her, followed by shame that it should make a difference. After all, it didn't help Nev a bit whether it was her fault or not.

"Quite sure. And the doctor had a bit of good news. Something called the Hi-med Lottery Fund. To help poor slobs like me who can't come up with a quarter of a million to get my legs back."

"Then it's okay?"

"Not exactly okay. But my National Security Number goes into the lottery locally for a bed in the neurological unit here. Every time there's a draw I get a chance."

"There can't be that many people with spinal cord injuries right here in town. The odds must be pretty good, don't you think?"

"I'm betting on it." Nev managed a grin and she grabbed his hand and held it against her cheek, turning her face away so he shouldn't see her tears.

When visiting time was up, Peri went in search of the doctor whose name was on the chart at the foot of Nev's bed. She found him in the cafeteria, coffee cup in hand.

"Please, can I talk to you about one of your patients, Nev Wright?"

"Are you a member of the family?"

"N...no. Not exactly."

"Then I can't discuss the patient with you."

"It's not that. I mean, I don't want to ask you about Nev. But the program...the lottery?"

"Yes? Do sit down, Miss...er..."

"Peri Stanley. I don't understand how the lottery works."

"It's an experimental program. A real step forward in the democratization of medicine, we believe. Any major procedure or experimental protocol consuming over a hundred thousand dollars in excess of medical insurance coverage is supported by the province, the clients being chosen by lottery."

"Yes, I know that bit. But how does it actually work?"

"Nev's National Security Number will be submitted to the city lottery foundation. Every month, during the regular drawings for prizes in the provincial lottery, several numbers are drawn randomly from those submitted by the City hospital system. If Nev's number is drawn, then his worries are over. Free medical treatment, physiotherapy, whatever's needed to get the boy back on his feet."

"And the odds, doctor? What are Nev's chances?" Peri burst out.

"There are enough funds to admit three persons a month to the centre."

"Three people? Out of how many? There can't be that many people with spinal cord injuries."

"You'd be surprised. Several hundred. Of course he can try again, up to two years. The chances of rehabilitation after that time become minimal."

"Three out of several hundred?" Peri choked on the words.

"Better than nothing." The doctor smiled wryly and got to his feet. "And you can always try to raise the money yourselves. People do, you know. Bake sales, marathons, that sort of thing. Excuse me, I must go. Good luck."

Luck, thought Peri miserably as she left the hospital. That's what it's going to take. Monumental, stupendous luck. Then she stopped so suddenly that the door swung against her shoulders as the person behind her pushed through.

"Pardon me."

"Sorry." Peri walked back home, her mind furiously going over the possibility. Jon. And his gift for telekinesis. Moving things with his mind. Small things, like dice. Or maybe the numbers in a lottery?

"You're crazy!" was Jon's reaction.

"You can change the odds, Jon, you know you can."

"But that's cheating, Peri. I won't cheat. And suppose someone found out. Can you imagine what my life'd be like if I ever let people know what

I can do? The Government'd probably draft me or use me in experiments. I wouldn't have a life of my own. It'd be horrible."

"I know telekinesis is rare, but don't you think you're a bit paranoid about the Government. After all..."

"I've heard stories of people simply vanishing. Sucked into the system to be used. After all, Peri, they use dolphins to carry bombs and mines. Why should they be more fussy about people?"

Peri wrapped her arms around her chest and shivered. "I know, Jon," she said in a small voice. "But what about Nev?"

That was it, wasn't it? Jon thought gloomily, after he'd got away from his sister's pleading. What about Nev? He found himself reliving the nightmare moment when he realized that the heliolite was out of control, that his telekinetic power was useless, that he could no more stop the falling heliolite than he could stop the spin of Earth.

But now there was something he could do. Change the odds in the provincial lottery and undo the damage that his failure to help Nev had caused.

It's wrong, an inner voice told him clearly. Once you start using your powers to cheat, there's no end to it, is there?

Yes, but this is different.

No, it isn't. It's no different from always winning at backgammon, even if you don't try to throw double sixes.

His mind seesawed miserably to and fro between the opposite and irreconcilable facts, and he found himself hating Peri for having had the stupid brilliant idea in the first place.

Three days later the ambulance brought Nev home to his mother's apartment in the same block where Jon and Peri's family lived. He arrived in a flesh-coloured, permeable plastic body cast and a variable slant chair-bed.

Jon tried a light touch. "You're looking great. Apart from that bruise on your forehead." Stupid, he thought savagely. That the best you can do?

"And apart from being numb from the hips down I guess I'll survive." Nev sounded just as unreal.

"You'll be into rehab in no time," Peri burst out. "I've had this fabulous idea to beat the odds so that your number will come up right away."

"How are you going to do that?"

"Telekinesis."

"You, Peri? You've got as much psi ability as a plasti-brick wall."

"She's thinking of me, Nev. It's crazy. The numbers are probably generated in a computer concealed in a sealed vault somewhere."

"But they aren't, Jon." Colour flooded Nev's face. "I asked about it in hospital. The lottery's run in public, with a live audience, and one of those old-fashioned bingo machines that throw up the numbers randomly. Anyone can go and watch. Mostly they give out prizes, but they run the Hi-med Lottery at the same time."

"Nev, are you saying you think it'll work? You really want me to try it?"

"Of course he does," Peri shouted at him. "You can't not. Jon, you're my one and only brother, but I swear I'll never talk to you again if you don't at least try to help Nev."

"Take it easy, Peri. Back off. It's Jon's decision." Nev interrupted.

"I don't even know if I can do it to order, or if it's like dreams, something that just happens."

"It'll be okay, Jon. I'll help you practise. All we need to start working is Nev's National Security Number." She pushed up his sleeve and ran her thumb over the digits tattooed there. "24-2-30…your birthday. I remember that part. Four days before mine. Then 005193…right?"

"Eleven numbers. Think you can handle that many, Jon?"

"I dunno, Nev. But I can try."

Now that the choice was out of his hands, Jon pushed the guilt and worry to the back of his head and concentrated on honing his telekinetic powers. Peri wrote the numbers zero through nine over and over again on table tennis balls and put them in an antique pickling jar that their mother used as a vase, and Jon began to practise plucking out the digits of Nev's security number in order. After three weeks Jon had a permanent headache and Peri was nervous enough to jump out of her skin.

"It's no good. My brain's turning to mush, and my psi abilities aren't getting any better. Like I said in the beginning—I don't think it's a thing you can force." John sighed. "I'm afraid it's hopeless."

"It's my fault. I've been pushing you too hard. Why don't you take a rest. After all it's three days…" Her voice wobbled. "Three whole days till the lottery."

Peri and Jon waited in line outside the convention centre until the doors were opened and the crowd pushed in.

"We've got to get close to the front." Jon warned her.

"I know." Peri gasped, the wind knocked out of her as an elbow-jabbing woman pushed past them.

They managed to get seats in the front row close to the enormous number-generating machine. It was edged with garish fluorescent lights, red, orange, blue, and purple, which flashed on and off in rhythm with the latest hyperpunk.

Jon groaned. "It'll be hard to concentrate with all that going on."

Peri squeezed his arm. "You'll manage. I know you will." She turned, so he wouldn't see her face and guess how nervous she really was, and stared around the hall.

The seats were filling up fast. Streamers hung from the ceiling, twisting in the air-conditioning. LOTTOLOTTOLOTTO they spelled endlessly. The crowd noises rose to beat the hyperpunk. The lights flashed. She could feel the tension zapping at her nerves, tightening her skin. Her stomach flipped uneasily.

"Surely not all these people have friends needing help?" She turned back to Jon.

"I'll bet not one of them is here for the Hi-med Lottery. Take a look at the program."

"Win a Mazda hovercraft...a home fusion unit...but this isn't what we're here for."

"Down near the end." Jon pointed. "Three rehabilitation places at Healing Hands Medical Unit. Just before drawing the numbers for the Provincial Lottery. That's what everyone's here for, I guess, the big prize— a tax-free year for the whole family."

As he spoke the lights and sound mercifully dimmed and the Master of Ceremonies glided out into the spotlight, a smooth-faced android familiar to Peri from news and weather reports on the local channel. There'd been an occasion, Peri heard a woman in the row behind her whisper, when an irate loser had gunned down the lottery MC, so it was no longer a favoured post for a human, despite the publicity. If there should be another incident, well, androids were replaceable.

"Welcome to the twenty-ninth running of the new provincial lottery. I hope you all have your National Security Numbers on you—har-har. Today it may be your turn to win a home composter, a water purification unit, a super hovercraft. And, as I'm sure you all know, the big prize today is..."

"Jon, what about...?"

"Sh. He'll get to it. Just listen."

"And folks, between the draws for the home composter and the big prize, we will, as usual, draw three places for hospital beds in the rehab unit of the City Hospital. The lucky winners will receive the very latest in scientific treatment absolutely free! So come on, all you folks here and at home watching this program—brought to you by the makers of NoZone, the cream that guarantees freedom from skin cancer—let's begin our evening of fun and excitement."

An hour and a half dragged by for Peri and Jon. The numbered balls flipped up and down on the current of air in the machine. Randomly one would pop out, and Smoothface would announce the number. As the eleventh and final number popped out, the central computer searched out the name and telephone of the lucky winner. Within a minute the audience was treated to a display of hysterical joy, brought by home videophone to the big screen above the stage. Instant win. Instant emotion. Between the draws the audience ate sushi and fried squid.

"Look, Jon. Something's happening."

Two workwomen in coveralls, who probably earned less in a year than Smoothface's owner earned in a night, wheeled on a smaller machine, decorated with fluorescent H's, which blinked frenetically on and off.

"...and now, folks, for those unfortunate few who have suffered traumatic accidents in the past year, the City Hospital's Hi-med Lottery brings you the Healing Hands Hope Chest! In this transparent container," Smoothface went on, "are the National Security Numbers of all those poor folks in need of a boost—a boost which we intend to give them tonight."

Peri could see that each of the balls in this container was much larger, large enough to have an entire NS number printed on its sides. This was going to be totally different from extracting the right digit from zero to nine, and getting it right eleven times. Finding the ball with Nev's number on it within a container of several hundred was like pinpointing one star in a galaxy with one's eyes shut.

"Jon, what'll we do?" She grabbed his arm.

"It's the dregs, I know. But I'll try just visualizing Nev's number and willing it up. Maybe it'll work. Maybe we'll have to call this a practice run for the next lottery, or the one after."

"But..."

Jon was no longer listening. He closed his eyes. Peri could see the muscle at the corner of his jaw quiver and tense. She doubled her fists in her lap so that the nails dug into the palms.

The balls began to bounce on the current of air within the machine, rattling as they moved randomly around. She stared and caught her breath in a gasp. Up the near rim of the container a single ball wriggled upward, against gravity, to bob on the air stream. She looked quickly around. Had anyone else noticed the unusual movement?

Most of the audience had left the stands for a drink of low-alcohol beer and a sushi snack. To them, this was the boring interlude before the main event. Those who remained were talking, joking, rustling their programs.

Some twisted theirs into paper airplanes and glided them towards the stage. Peri looked anxiously at Jon. Would this nonsense distract him? But it was all right. His eyes were still shut, concentrating.

Then she saw her. A woman dead centre in the front row was staring intently at the machine. Peri remembered her. The woman who'd jabbed her out of the way as they had jostled in the doorway. She could still feel the bruise on her ribs.

In a sea of munching mouths, her face stood out. Her eyes were narrowed, her forehead furrowed. She looked as if she wasn't even breathing.

Peri's eyes darted back to the number generator. Another ball was creeping up the side. It spun against the one she guessed that Jon was guiding and hovered beneath the narrow exit passage. Jon's ball jostled it, they spun apart and, as they ricocheted off the walls of the container, a third ball was hiccuped into the exit and rolled into the MC's outstretched hand.

"...and the lucky winner is...91-07-13-02547. In one moment we will see for ourselves..." A picture flashed onto the screen. A lean man propped in a wheelchair, neckbrace forcing his chin up, someone's hand holding the phone to his ear. Smoothface spoke into his mike. "Mr. James Rierdon. I guess they'll be calling you Lucky Jim tonight, eh, Mr. Rierdon? Free rehabilitation at the city hospital! Congratulations and big hand for Mr. Rierdon!"

As the screen blanked out there was a spatter of applause and then the crowd noise filled the hall like the wind against a diving heliolite. The balls began to bubble on their air jet. Up and over. Down and up. Again one ball edged up to the surface, stayed there, fighting gravity. A second ball rose beside it.

Like two gladiators in the ring, thought Peri. Each feinting, watching the other's move, ready to block it, to be the first beneath the narrow exit. She saw the MC's hand move. Both balls rolled towards the opening. And jammed. Neither gave a millimetre. Sweat ran down Jon's face. Six seats to her right Peri saw the woman's face glisten pallidly under the bright lights.

"Sorry folks." Smoothface smacked the side of the old machine. The woman's body jolted as if she had been hit. Peri heard Jon grunt in pain. "Little jam-up here," the android went on. "A bit more air to stir them up again and...here we are. The lucky winner is 15-11-03-47892!"

Once more a picture flashed on the screen, this time of a woman in her mid-twenties lying in a quadriplegic's harness.

"Congratulations on your win, Daisy Jones. Daisy's been waiting for electrotherapy and nerve surgery for a long eight months following a car accident. Remember, folks, your driving safety depends on a good computer program. Keep your module checked!"

Their opponent's face was dead white. She looked as if she might faint any second now. If she does, a small ugly voice said clearly in Peri's head, then we've got it made. Now she knew that Jon had the mental strength and the skill to pull Nev's number up. Third time lucky...

But Jon was on his feet, grabbing Peri's arm. "We're getting out of here."

"What's the matter? You're so near..."

At the door he turned and waited. The MC's smooth voice reached them faintly. "...And the lucky winner is...baby Alison Temple. Baby Alison was born with severe cerebral palsy. Now, with the latest techniques of muscle and nerve rehabilitation..." His voice was lost in a torrent of laughter and sobs. "Ladies and gentlemen, right here in the audience, here is Mrs. Temple, little Alison's mother! What a moment! Mrs. Temple, would you like to tell us exactly what you're feeling right now..."

Jon put his arm through Peri's and pulled her through the crowd, past the stalls selling lucky T-shirts, stuffed bean cakes, four-leafed clovers, and vials of moon dust. Tears ran down Peri's face and she brushed them away angrily.

They walked on until they came to the footbridge across the river. It was hung with paper lanterns, and the pleasure boats beneath looked like illuminated water beetles. Here Jon stopped.

"I could read that woman's thoughts, Peri. So strong. I could see her baby, and what treatment could do for her. I'm sorry. I'm really sorry. And it'd be the same the next time round, the next lottery, wouldn't it? Always the knowledge that if we cheated so Nev's number would come up it'd be at someone else's expense."

"How are you going to tell him?" Her angry tears splashed on the carpet. "What's the use of your esper skills if you can't even help Nev? I just hate you, Jon!"

He looked away from her anger, staring absently down at the strings of lights reflected in the water. They blinked on and off. White. Red. Green. Idly he switched the order. Red. White. Green. And back again. Suddenly he straightened up and whistled. His eyes sparkled. "Maybe I can do something for Nev after all, Peri." He walked quickly away from her through the brightly dressed crowd.

Three months later, when Peri and Jon were making their daily visit to Nev's apartment after school, Nev grinned at Jon. "I think you can tell her now."

"Really?"

"Tell me what? Hey, you two, what's been going on?"

"I got the idea on the bridge that night, the lottery night, looking down at the coloured lights. And it made me think about the damaged nerves in Nev's spine. And whether telekinesis would be useful. So I went to the medical library and did some reading, and...well, anyway, Nev and I've been working on it for the last while."

"Working on what?"

"This."

Slowly, thoughtfully, Nev wiggled his toes.

----

1. RESPONDING TO THE STORY

a. With a partner, replay Jon and Peri's argument for and against cheating on the lottery. Think about what else might have been said, and how they are both feeling at that point in the story.

b. Why does Jon decide not to use his special powers to win the lottery? What would you have done? Explain your answer.

c. Do you think it's fair for Peri to blame Jon when he refuses to continue cheating? How would you have felt if you were Jon? if you were Peri?

d. Do you think holding a lottery for health benefits is right? Explain your answer.

2. WRITING ANALYSE THE SETTING

Find evidence of when in the future this story takes place, and what the future is like. List some of the phrases in the story that show this.

Write a descriptive paragraph that describes the futuristic setting Monica Hughes has created. How is the future different from the present? What changes seem exciting or good? What changes seem bad? How are people different or the same? How is society different or the same? Why do you think Hughes created this sort of society of the future?

SELF-ASSESSMENT: With a partner, discuss your notes on the setting. Were there interesting or important points about the setting that you missed? List three techniques Hughes uses to develop the setting. How could you use these techniques in your own writing?

3. READING CHARACTER DEVELOPMENT

Reread the story and discuss with a partner how both Jon and Peri change through the story. What concerns do they have at the beginning of the story? At the end of the story, how have their concerns changed? Develop a time line that lists each event in the story, and shows how Jon and Peri have developed.

4. ORAL LANGUAGE ROLE-PLAYING

In a group, discuss the moral decisions each character makes. Discuss moments when you've been faced with similar decisions. What helps you to make your decision?

All our lives, everyday, humans are faced with moral decisions—do we cheat on the history test or accept a D? Do we shoplift that candy bar? Do we repay that debt, or forget it? What we decide may affect the rest of our lives. How can we decide? Here are some questions to ask yourself, next time you're faced with making choices:

- Will doing this act hurt me?
- Will doing this act hurt anyone else?
- Will I feel guilty or ashamed?
- Will I lose the respect or trust of those I love and respect?
- How much do I want to do this?
- What will be the consequences of this act?
- Are there any good reasons for doing this act?
- Would I do this act if my parents (or a teacher) were standing beside me?

Discuss these questions and add any others that you can think of. Test these questions by role-playing the following scenario:

A friend has told you in confidence that he's been having problems with his father and is thinking of running away. Should you tell a teacher? his parents? Should you offer him a place to stay while he works everything out?

Can you think of a time when doing the right thing made others sit up and take notice? A young man does what he feels is right, and his actions serve as...

SIGNPOSTS

ON THE
Journey

Anecdote by Steve Buist

When raising teenagers, there are not a lot of signposts on the highway of life that tell a parent how the journey is progressing.

Those that do pop up on the horizon are often negative—poor grades, failing grades, no grades. A bad attitude or trouble with friends, perhaps even trouble with the law.

Maybe that's why parents of teenagers spend seven years holding their breath, crossing their fingers, and repeating over and over, "No news is good news. No news is good news."

I have a sixteen-year-old son. To a sixteen-year-old man/child, life can be condensed to four basic necessities: a reliable TV converter, a comfortable couch, the need to remain horizontal (and motionless) on said couch for hours at a time, and the need to practise driving the car as much as possible. (There are only two subgroups of children that enjoy a trip to the grocery store—those under the age of five who think the visit might end with candy in the checkout line and sixteen-year-olds with a learner's permit.)

The other night, my son attended a banquet where he works. He looked quite handsome and strapping in his suit and snappy coat. I had forgotten how tall he's become but, of course, we rarely see him upright (see above, basic needs one to three).

When I arrived to pick him up from the dinner, he started to get in the car, then stopped, looking distracted. "Just a minute," he said.

GOALS AT A GLANCE

■ Examine media stereotypes.
■ Analyse the use of simple sentences.

I pushed open the door and asked him what was wrong as he walked towards the parking lot.

"I think those guys are going to try and beat up another kid," he said.

I watched him walk over and step into the middle of the fray. I couldn't hear what was being said but the crowd started to disperse.

Later, he would tell me it was the second time that night he had stepped in.

I then saw him take a smaller boy under his wing and walk him back to the front door. He made sure the boy was getting a ride home and then told him to stay by the front, where the adults were standing.

When my son finally got back in the car, he told me that the boy is often the target of bullies, and just as often, my son comes to his defence. I knew none of this until the other night. It was one of the most satisfying signposts that has passed by us on our journey.

In the overall scheme of things, it may not have been much. It won't feed hungry kids or bring world peace.

But he did a good and decent thing. He did the right thing.

I learned that he's making the right choices. And I couldn't be prouder. He needs to know that.

----

1. Responding to the Anecdote

a. The author begins the anecdote with a description of a teenager. To what extent do you think this characterization is true? Explain.

b. The father relating the anecdote suggests that his son's actions served as a "signpost on the highway of life that tells a parent how the journey is progressing." What other "signposts" are there? Explain fully.

2. Language Conventions Simple Sentences

A simple sentence uses a noun and a verb, and not much else. Simple sentences contain no clauses. For example, each of the following are simple sentences:

> The black dog sneezed. The plane crashed. I love you.

Reread the selection. Which sentences do you think are the author's most powerful and effective sentences? Are any of these "simple sentences"? Why are these sentences effective?

Reread some of the stories you've written. How could you use simple sentences to improve a piece of your writing?

3. MEDIA MESSAGES STEREOTYPES

In the media, teenagers are often stereotyped in a particular way. With a partner, compile a list of adjectives which you think could be used to describe the stereotypical teenager. Discuss television shows, or movies that feature people of your own age. Do you think any of these characters are stereotypes of teenagers? Explain fully. Think about commercials and how teenagers are often portrayed. Look through magazines or newspapers for articles and ads about teenagers. What is their message? Is there a hidden message? If so, what is it?

With your partner, develop an oral report that shows how you feel about media stereotypes of teenagers. Include specific examples of characters and situations.

In your report you might consider the following. To what extent do you think this portrait of teenagers is justified? How is this stereotype positive or negative? Why does this stereotype exist? Does one media form show teenagers in a more positive light than others? Explain.

SELF-ASSESSMENT: Did you draw any conclusions about media stereotypes of teenagers? Why do you think knowing about stereotypes is important?

THE LONG

Journey

Short Story by Sue Mann

"Hey, Walter, are you planning on staying all day?"

"Huh? Oh yeah, sure."

The auditorium is rapidly emptying, and with it comes a thick blanket of silence. Enveloped in my own thoughts, I have missed most of the assembly, but that isn't important. Now we have the next six minutes to go to our lockers and our first class, but I already have the books I need.

Thinking back over the past month, I remember numerous times when I wasted hours upon hours of valuable time, lying in front of the television or just daydreaming. Our English teacher gave the assignment five weeks ago.

"This short story is, in your own way, to symbolize something. Just make sure that someone with a little intelligence, namely me, will be able to recognize what you are trying to show. Have your story, with at least two thousand words, completed by April 21."

Today is April 21.

Three days ago I began to get worried about the story. I know I shouldn't procrastinate the way I do, but you know how it goes. When the assignment doesn't have to be handed in for two or three weeks, or even a week, it seems like a long way off. I always excuse myself by saying that I work better under pressure, but for some reason it didn't work that way last night.

Last night I still hadn't begun to write the stupid story. I mean, I had tried, but success had evaded me. Well, I was sitting there with the radio on, because of course I work better with noise in the background, trying to make my pen write a story. On my seven or so previous attempts, I could

> Does the saying "Don't put off 'til tomorrow what you should do today" have personal significance for you? Read how the character in this story learns its meaning the hard way.

GOALS AT A GLANCE

- Write an e-mail letter to a character.
- Respond critically to the story.

get about one hundred or two hundred words and then my mind would go blank. Then I started thinking that I could use a story from a magazine as a model. I mean, I could use the plot for an idea and maybe even use some of the phrases and incidents. For three hours I browsed through my old magazines and read all the short stories in them, along with jokes, cartoons, and the eye-catching articles. From the beginning I could tell that it was going to be more or less a waste of time because the only magazines I had were *Time* and *Sports Illustrated*, which aren't exactly literary magazines. But I just kept reading and losing time. Finally it dawned on me that my mother's *Good Housekeeping* magazines are rather well-known for their interesting short stories, at least around my house. Maybe I could find one making use of symbolism.

The twelfth *Good Housekeeping* that I picked up had *the* perfect story in it, and it was even written by a man. By this time I had read eleven magazines, and it was 11:30. I sat for an hour or so trying to figure out how I could change it, but still maintain the plot and the use of symbolism. When it got to be one o'clock my leaden eyelids were becoming too heavy for the weary muscles that hold eyelids up. Of course I had stayed up rather, well, very late the previous night because of a history report I handed in yesterday, a day late.

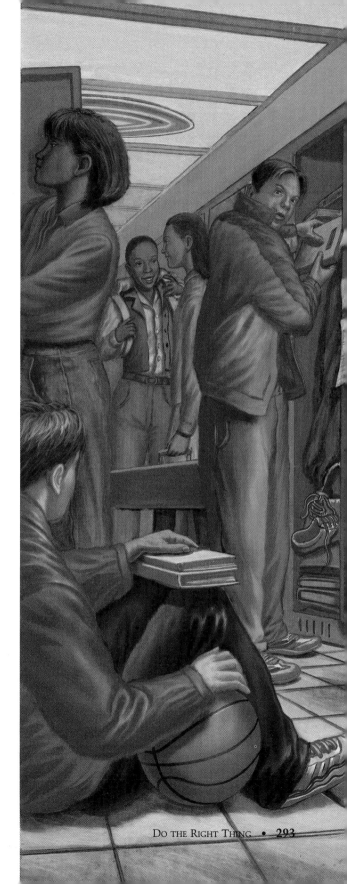

Then I got to thinking: "This is not only an old issue, but this magazine is written for and usually read by women." Since my English teacher is a man, I could see no earthly reason why he would ever read the story. The fact that he was a bachelor prodded me on even more. After about two more minutes of deliberation, I recopied the story in my own handwriting, changing only the names of the characters.

Sled
by Walter Milburn
All the adventure of the night and snow lay before him:
if only he could get out of the house....

Now I'm sitting in this auditorium seat. How can I possibly turn this in as my own work? The decision is weighing heavily upon my mind. I begin my journey through the endless corridors of the school.

"Beat Bears." We played them last week. That sign ought to be taken down. It's only taking up space now... Could I be put in jail?... *The Miracle Worker.* I hope this year the senior-class play is a more effective performance than it was last year... How could anyone ever know?... Jim got a new pair of shoes. It's about time. His old ones were falling apart... Who would know? I'll know. I haven't stolen since I was eight...until now... This door needs a good job of lubrication and the glass isn't exactly immaculate. My parents pay enough taxes. Why can't things be kept in good condition?... If by some stroke of misfortune...but, no, what possible way?... Here's Room 23. The "2" is almost one-quarter of a centimetre taller than the "3"... My seat, middle row, second from the back.

"Please pass in your stories."

I don't think I can.

"Well, Walter, isn't yours completed? Your grade can't take that."

"What? Oh, I, I must have been daydreaming. Here it is."

Well, I did it. I had to do it. If I failed English this semester, my parents would be more than mad. What's done is done. He'll never know the difference, and my parents will be happy.

"Now, class, I'd like to read this story to you. I told my aunt, who used to be an English teacher herself, about the assignment I gave, and she said that she had kept a story, written by one of her former pupils, on file because it is an excellent example of symbolism. The pupil is now a well-known author, and the story has been published.

"'Sled,' by Thomas E. Adams. 'All the adventure of the night and snow lay before him: if only he could get out of the house...'"◆

1. RESPONDING TO THE STORY

a. What reasons does Walter give to explain his procrastination? Have you ever used the same reasons? What other reasons have you used to explain why you have put off a task?

b. What do you think will happen to Walter next? What do you think should happen to Walter next?

c. Why do you think the author called the story "The Long Journey"?

2. WRITING E-MAIL

Imagine that you are a friend or relative of Walter's. What would you say to Walter to help him deal with his tendency to procrastinate? In your journal, write an informal e-mail message giving Walter some good advice about how to get work done on time. Remember that in e-mail messages you can use more informal language, and incomplete sentences.

3. LANGUAGE CONVENTIONS INCOMPLETE SENTENCES

To understand what an *incomplete sentence* is you need to understand what a *complete sentence* is! Complete sentences come in many shapes and sizes, and usually include at least a subject and a verb:

- Let's go!
- Where have you been all day?
- If you want to go to the movie, we need to leave right now.

However, some complete sentences consist of only one word, or a verb but no subject:

- Stop!
- Fire!
- Danger!
- Watch out.
- Come on.
- Don't.

Notice how many of these are commands or warnings.

Still, it's easy to detect incomplete sentences, because they leave the reader hanging. An incomplete sentence could consist of an incomplete thought, or simply a sentence fragment (part of a sentence being used as a complete sentence):

- If you want to go.
- Running through the park.
- Sunshine on the tiled floor.
- You.

Can you think of any occasions when these incomplete sentences might be used?

Halting Hatred

Young People Are on the Front Lines of the Battle to Banish Racist Attitudes

Newspaper Article
by Shaun Chen
YOUNG PEOPLE'S PRESS

Racism. Stop it!

This short, simple slogan was part of a campaign to promote the U.N. International Day for the Elimination of Racial Discrimination, on Sunday, March 21.

It sums up the message that thirteen-year-old filmmaker Andrea Ibsen wants to get out. The situation "is improving, but we still have a lot more to do," she says.

Ibsen and two of her classmates, Kate Dougall, thirteen, and Jamie Arfin, fourteen, were the youngest of ten winning teams from across Canada in the Stop Racism National Video Competition in 1998.

Their submission depicted children playing at a nursery accompanied by messages such as: "Everyone is the same; all these babies are beautiful."

It's a Wrap: Andrea Ibsen, centre, and her friends Kate Dougall, left, and Jamie Arfin made a winning video for the Stop Racism National Video Competition in 1998. Their submission showed youngsters of diverse backgrounds playing at a nursery.

Dougall says the point of their video was to show that human beings are not genetically coded with racist attitudes. "Children pick up racist ideas from their surroundings," she explains. "They don't say, 'I'm not playing with you since you're black,' because they don't really know about racism."

According to Dougall, education begins with "the younger generation, the roots. And if you grow up with all sorts of cultures that you can experience, you have less bias."

In Sioux Lookout, teenagers at Queen Elizabeth District High School are also fighting racism. Donovan Kakepetum, eighteen, is one of many First Nations students who have moved to Sioux Lookout for secondary education at Queen Elizabeth. Kakepetum says racial divisions are further fuelled by stereotypes. To combat stereotyping, a number of activities with a cross-cultural appeal were organized at the school in commemoration of International Day for the Elimination of Racial Discrimination, including classroom activities and a concert featuring both local entertainers and a First Nations rap artist from Winnipeg.

Back in Toronto, the Urban Alliance on Race Relations hosted a conference titled Race, Ethnicity and Youth Gangs, at Central Neighbourhood House.

Hana An, twenty-six, a project co-ordinator at the alliance, says the purpose of the conference was to brainstorm solutions to the ever-increasing problem of youth gangs and racism. "We want to tackle all types of issues that racism stems from," says An, who launched the Youth for Diversity project at the conference. This undertaking will allow young people to come up with alternative solutions to these problems, she says.

"Because Toronto is growing so fast, there are rising problems among the diverse groups we represent and an increase in violence and negativity."

Tasneem Alibhai, eighteen, a member of the Scarborough (Greater Toronto Area) Youth Council, says the solution is to encourage youth to mobilize in the empowerment of racial minorities.

"Women didn't have the right to vote at one point here in this country," she says. "But just look at us today and it is evident how much society has progressed in just one century."

Alibhai says more people of Asian and African descent need to fight their way into the mainstream media in order to break down social barriers.

"How many black reporters have you seen on television recently?" she asks. "And how many

Give Peace a Chance: Hana An of the Urban Alliance on Race Relations helped organize a conference on youth groups.

times have you seen a brown model in a magazine ad?"

The Scarborough Civic Centre celebrated the International Day for the Elimination of Racial Discrimination on Friday, March 19 at an event sponsored by the Scarborough Youth Council and the City of Toronto East Community and Race Relations Committee.

Though the day was celebrated early, its *raison d'être* was not lost on the participants.

"March 21 is an important day in our history," says planning committee member Nafisha Budhwani, eighteen.

On March 21, 1960, the Sharpeville massacre occurred in South Africa. Sixty-nine black protestors were killed by police during a peaceful rally against apartheid.

The United Nations declared March 21 as the special day in memory of those who died.

"We should be proud that Canada was the first country to organize an official national campaign," says Reza Kajbaf, eighteen, another committee member.

Hedy Fry, secretary of state for multiculturalism and the status of women, launched the 1999 campaign during South African President Nelson Mandela's visit to Canada in September, 1998.

"The mission was to get young people involved and also to empower them to help us, as a society, eliminate racism," Fry says.

Racism is a barrier to social progress, as it "traps us as individuals, [preventing us from realizing] our potential in the long run." ◆

1. RESPONDING TO THE ARTICLE

a. Do you think "halting hatred" is possible? Explain your answer.

b. Which statements in this article would you agree with? Which would you disagree with? Explain your point of view.

2. VISUAL COMMUNICATION DEVELOP AN IMAGE

Think about the title of this article, and its meaning. Imagine a single visual image that would reflect the title, for example, a painting or collage of symbols connected with peace, or perhaps a sculpture that depicts one of the people in the article. How would this image also reflect the people, and their goals, described in this article? In your journal, jot down notes describing and explaining your image. Once you've created your image, give it a title, and display it.

STRATEGIES

3. ORAL LANGUAGE PLAN A PROJECT

In a small group, discuss the article, and what the students and organizations tried to achieve. Together, choose one problem in your school, and develop a plan for helping to solve it. For example, you might decide to develop a video about smoking, form a committee to welcome new students, stage a play about violence, or create a school code of behaviour.

Use this checklist to help you develop your plan:
- What's the problem?
- How can your group help solve it?
- What is your goal? Do you think you can achieve it?
- What steps will you take to achieve your goal?
- Who will you need to ask for help?

Use the school's Web site or newspaper, or create posters—to announce your project, ask for help, and keep people informed about what your group is doing.

SELF-ASSESSMENT: Are you able to work co-operatively with others to complete a project? Do you share the duties of group work? Do you respect the opinions of others? Do you consider your own ideas objectively when presented with alternatives?

What did you do the last time someone asked you to do something you'd rather have avoided? Read on to find out what Trish does.

Babysitting Helen

Short Story by Kathy Stinson

It wasn't till Trish was talking on the phone to Gavin about their plan for Saturday that her mother told her she would be babysitting that night. Trish covered the mouthpiece. "I can't, Mom. I'm going out with Gavin."

"I already said you'd do it."

"Without even asking me?"

"Barb Stanley needs someone to stay with Helen for a few hours."

"Gavin, can I call you back? Yeah, love you too, bye." Trish picked her books up from the counter and hugged them to her chest. "You said I would babysit Barb's *mother*? That weird old lady who came for lunch and kept going 'Isn't that marvellous?' every time she made the wooden gull flap its wings?"

"It's just for a few hours. Barb said Helen will probably sleep the whole time. And Trish," her mother argued, "you do see Gavin every day."

Trish stomped upstairs to her room. Didn't mothers know anything about *love?*

Trish shoved her homework and a couple of tapes into her knapsack, just in case Gavin wasn't home when she called him from Helen's. She threw on her coat and flung her knapsack over her shoulder.

Helen was awake when Trish arrived. She was watching TV. Four brightly coloured barrettes—pink and red rabbits—were stuck haphazardly into her wispy white hair. Her brown sweater was on inside out.

Barb ushered Trish into the kitchen. "Mom had a longer nap than usual this afternoon," she said. "She wanted to make a cake this morning. I guess it tired her out. I'm sorry," Barb explained, "but with the long nap..."

"Does she know who I am?" Trish interrupted. "Won't she think it's kind of weird having a babysitter?"

"I'm afraid Mom doesn't know who many people are any more," Barb said. "And you can just tell her you came over to watch TV."

Trish shook her head. "What's with the barrettes?"

"My granddaughter left them here last weekend." Barb scribbled a phone number on a pad by the phone. "And for some reason, Mom has decided there's going to be a party tonight. So, just play along, okay? She'll get tired soon without anything actually happening." As she slipped out the back door Barb added, "Don't let her out of your sight for more than a few minutes, eh? She gets into things."

Right.

"Thank you for coming, Trish."

In the living room Helen was fixed on the TV. Trish sat down where she'd be able to watch them both. Crayons and old-fashioned stickers were scattered over the coffee table. Barb must have dug them out of some old box for the granddaughter's visit last weekend, Trish figured. And that must be her, the granddaughter—the little girl in the photo on the piano.

"Are you here for the party?" Helen said.

"Um, yeah."

"Your outfit is lovely."

Trish glanced down at her jeans and the old sweatshirt she only wore when she knew she wouldn't run into anybody that mattered. "Thanks. Um. You look lovely too."

Helen laughed. She was a tiny woman but her laugh came from deep inside and went on and on. Trish wondered what she'd said that was so funny.

"Would you just look at that!" Trish followed Helen's gaze to the TV, where a mechanical pink rabbit was marching across the screen beating a drum. "Isn't that the darndest thing?"

For the next fifteen minutes Trish and Helen watched *Golden Girls.*

Helen sat quietly through the funniest bits and laughed when nothing funny was happening at all. She seemed to like the commercials better than the show, and when the battery bunny started across the screen with his drum again, Helen laughed and exclaimed, "Would you just look at that! Isn't that the darndest thing?"

Trish pretended to laugh along at the boring rabbit with its ability to keep on going and going and going.

When the rabbit stopped, Helen got up and looked out the window. "Where is everyone?"

"Barb just went out for a little while," Trish said. "She'll be back soon. Why don't you come watch the rest of your show?" Or better yet, she thought, why don't you go to bed so I can call Gavin?

"Where do you live?" Helen demanded to know. Before Trish could answer, Helen asked, "You live at the bottom of our garden, don't you?"

"Well actually," Trish said, "I live up the street. You know the Carters? They're my parents."

"At the bottom of our garden," Helen said. "That's just what I thought." Then she wandered away in the direction of the kitchen.

Trish could hear canisters being moved around on the counter and the scraping of a chair across the tiled floor. Don't leave her alone, Barb had said. But she couldn't check up on a grown woman like she was some two-year-old. As a peach-skinned model on the TV smoothed moisturizer onto her cheeks, Trish concentrated on the sounds in the kitchen. When something heavy banged against the counter and onto the floor, Trish leapt from her chair, thinking 911.

She found Helen standing on the counter. "Dear, would you just pass me that tin of beans that fell?" Helen said.

Trish held up a hand, as if it might keep Helen from falling, and retrieved the tin from under the edge of the cupboards.

"Helen, it's time to come down now." Trish's heart had stopped beating, but from her mouth came her calm trying-to-reason-with-a-three-year-old voice. "Take my hands, I'll help you."

Helen turned back to the open cupboard. "But I haven't found what I'm looking for."

If Helen fell, she'd break something for sure. And if she broke a hip— well, didn't old people get pneumonia and die if they had to stay in bed for too long?

"What are you looking for?" Trish asked, fighting not to cry. "Maybe I can find it for you."

Helen stared into the cupboard for a long moment. "I've forgotten."

Her knees shaking, she reached her hands down to Trish. "My mind—"
She leaned against Trish as she lowered herself to the chair pushed up
against the counter. "It's not what it used to be, you know."

Surprised at how little Helen weighed, Trish lifted her the rest of the
way down. She felt Helen's feet touch the ground, a rush of relief. She
wanted to hug Helen. She wished, unexpectedly and momentarily, that her
own mother was there to hug her.

Trish picked the canisters up off the floor, where Helen had set them
out of her way, and returned them to the counter. "Would you like a piece
of chocolate cake?"

"Would that help my mind, do you think?"

"It can't hurt," Trish said. "You get some plates and I'll cut the cake."

Trish was pushing the knife through the layers of chocolate when Helen
said, "I don't think we can do that yet." She touched her hands to the pink
and red rabbits in her hair. "Everyone isn't here."

"Right." Trish followed Helen back to the living room.

Helen picked up the photo of Barb's little granddaughter on the piano.
"We used to have such lovely parties. She adored getting all fancied up."
Helen held the photo closer to her face. "I don't remember that dress
though."

"Who do you think—?" Trish swallowed. "Who is that in the picture,
Helen?"

"Why, it's Barbara. Do you know Barbara?" She set the photo back on
the piano. "Of course, you live in the bottom of the garden don't you. You
can go home now if you'd like."

"No, I think...I think I'd like to stay—" Trish took a deep breath, "for
the party."

Helen smoothed her skirt and sat down in front of the TV. "I love
parties, don't you?" There was effort in her words. When the battery bunny
came on she said, "Would you just look at that. Isn't that the darndest
thing?" But her eyes were without laughter. Trish knew how upset and out
of control little kids got when they were up much past bedtime. Would
Helen get like that if she got overtired trying to stay up, waiting for something that wasn't going to happen?

"Maybe you'd like to go to bed now," Trish suggested.

"You know I can't miss the party." The look in Helen's eyes reminded
Trish of a TV movie she'd seen in which a girl, all dolled up, was starting
to realize no one was going to show up for her party. "Not," Helen said,
composing herself, "after you've gone to so much trouble."

Trish looked at her watch. Barb wouldn't be home for another two hours. Should she—could she—try to give Helen her party?

Trish slid onto the piano bench and slowly, softly, started to pick out the notes of the first party song that came to her. *Hap-py birth-day to you, Hap-py birth-day to you...* Standing beside Trish, Helen began to move her head back and forth to the rhythm. *Hap-py birth-day, Hap-py birth-day...* Helen swayed, her eyes closed, and a trembling smile on her lips, as Trish played.

It's working, Trish thought. If this will keep Helen happy, I'll play all night. But in the middle of the next time through, Helen stopped moving and opened her eyes. Her expression was cross.

"What is it? Do you want me to stop playing?"

"Your playing is lovely." Helen placed her hands on her hips. "But it's not much of a party without hats, now is it."

Party hats? She'd never find any in this house. Trish picked up the TV guide. "I wonder if there are any good movies on tonight."

"Every good party," Helen insisted, "has hats."

What was it with this party thing? Helen couldn't concentrate on anything for more than two minutes, but she was determined there was going to be a party—with hats. Trish sighed. Party hats. Party hats.

In the kitchen cupboard she had seen paper plates. She'd brought pencil crayons for her map homework—Helen was supposed to be asleep—and of course, there were the stickers and crayons too.

"Look," said Trish. "We'll make hats." She knelt beside the coffee table. "With these stickers, we'll make beautiful hats."

"I can make a hat!" Helen grabbed a plate and a sticker. "You live in the bottom of the garden, don't you."

"Yes," Trish said. "Will you come and visit me there some day?"

"That would be lovely, dear." Helen rubbed the sticker over her tongue.

"Not too much," Trish said. "You'll lick off all the glue."

"I know that!" Helen laughed from deep inside.

Trish watched as Helen stuck stickers on her paper plate, licking and sticking, licking and sticking, one after another till two paper plates were covered. Please, energetic bunny, you've got to wear down soon.

Trish tied Helen's hat around her head.

"You too," Helen insisted.

"There," Trish said, her hat in place. "Now, ready for bed?"

"Don't be so silly." Helen planted herself firmly beside the piano. "The party is just beginning!"

Helen swayed through the first round of "Happy Birthday." The second time Trish played it, Helen's feet were lifting off the ground. The third time, she was swaying in circles, a spring in every step.

Trish played on as Helen danced. And then Helen began to sing.

Happy birthday to you, Happy birthday to you. Her voice was strong, her face radiant. *Happy birthday, dear Ed-ward*, she belted out, *Happy Birthday to yoo-oouu!*

When Barb came home, Trish was watching *Saturday Night Live* and colouring in the continents on her geography map. Beside her on the sofa, Helen was asleep, chocolate cake crumbs on her chest, homemade party hat perched on her head.

Barb eyed the three plates on the coffee table. Each held a fork, a few crumbs, and a birthday candle. "Did you have company?"

"I'm—not exactly."

Barb rummaged in her purse. "I'm sorry if Mom gave you a hard time."

Trish crumpled the money Barb handed her into the pocket of her jeans. "She's a neat lady." Careful not to disturb any of the stickers, Trish slid the hat Helen had made for her into her knapsack. "I'll come back and party with her any time." Trish opened the door to leave. "Barb?" she asked, "Who is Edward?"

"Edward? My father's name was Edward." Barb looked at Trish, puzzled. "Why?"

"That's who the party was for tonight," Trish said.

"Dad died two years ago."

"But when was his birthday?"

"November 24th. That's—"

Trish nodded. "Tonight."

From the sofa came a contented sigh. Barb and Trish turned. Helen was smiling in her sleep. ◆

1. RESPONDING TO THE STORY

a. Does Trish's mother have the right to offer her daughter's time and services? Prepare an argument for either side and role-play both sides of the argument with a partner.

b. Do you think Trish finds it easy or hard to help Helen? Explain what thing was the most difficult for Trish to do? Why do you think so?

STRATEGIES

2. STORY CRAFT DYNAMIC CHARACTERS

Many short stories and novels feature *dynamic characters*. A dynamic character is one who changes in some significant way between the beginning of the story and the end. The character may change or grow emotionally, spiritually, or intellectually. For example, an author could begin with an innocent or immature character, and have her grow as she faces problems or obstacles. Can you think of examples from your reading of dynamic characters? How does the character change significantly? What or who makes him change?

To what extent does Trish undergo a change in this story? Trace the development of her character by clearly outlining what she is like at the beginning of the story and then contrasting this with what she becomes by the end of the story. Discuss your ideas with a classmate.

SELF-ASSESSMENT: Check the stories in your writing portfolio. Do you think you've developed dynamic characters? How could you change your stories to make your characters more dynamic?

3. WORD CRAFT DESCRIPTIVE WORDS

Trish exhibits a number of admirable traits in the way that she cares for Helen. Compile a list of words that describe Trish's admirable qualities. Using a thesaurus, or the thesaurus function on a computer, find synonyms or related words for each of the words in your list. Be sure to include only those words that can justifiably be used to describe Trish. On your list, include evidence from the story to justify your choice of synonyms. Compare your list with a partner's.

4. WRITING DIARY ENTRY

At the end of the story, Trish never explains why she is willing to go back and "party with [Helen] any time." Why do you think she's willing to go back? Write a diary entry from Trish's perspective explaining why you are prepared to return and spend more time with Helen. Remember to stay in character, and use events from the story to support your opinions and ideas.

5 RESEARCHING DISEASES AND THEIR TREATMENT

With a partner, research a disease, such as alzheimer's, dementia, osteoporosis, or another condition, that is more likely to affect a senior citizen than a younger person. You could use the Internet or library resources. Find out the symptoms of the disease, and how it can be prevented or treated. In your report, consider the following questions as well:

- How do you think people with this disease would prefer to be treated?
- What could you do to help someone with this disease?

When I finally
got her attention
"Size seven and a half, please"
as I reached for the shoe.

Contempt, veiled
as laughter:
"You can't afford those!"

At that moment
I resolved to try on
every size seven and a half
in the store.

Not that I would ever buy —
only that I would try.

She needed to know
I had the right,
if I chose to
try and buy whatever
she had to show.

Very politely, "The grey pumps, please."
"The Almalfi in green."
(I hate green)
Canvas deck, why not.

When she was finally
surrounded by boxes,
her face truly red,
I left shoeless.

■ Analyse the events and ideas of the poem.
■ Exchange ideas.

RESPONDING TO THE POEM

With a partner, discuss the poem and what happens. Who do you think the speaker is? Why do you think the clerk has decided she/he can't afford the shoes? Who do you think is right in this poem? Explain your answer with supporting details. What would you have done in the speaker's place?

Birdfoot's Grampa

Poem by Joseph Bruchac

The old man
must have stopped our car
two dozen times to climb out
and gather into his hands
the small toads blinded
by our lights and leaping,
live drops of rain.

The rain was falling,
a mist about his white hair
and I kept saying
you can't save them all,
accept it, get back in
we've got places to go.

But, leathery hands full
of wet brown life,
knee deep in the summer
roadside grass,
he just smiled and said
they have places to go to
too.

GOALS AT A GLANCE

■ Demonstrate an understanding of the poem.
■ Examine how an author uses imagery.

1. RESPONDING TO THE POEM

Discuss this poem and its meaning with three or four classmates. What emotions do the two characters in the poem display? What does the speaker learn? How does he change? What is the poem's message? Do you think the poet delivers this message effectively? Explain.

Retell the events of this poem, in your own words. How does your retelling affect the effectiveness of the poem's message? How does the form and language of the poem help the poet send a message about nature?

STRATEGIES

2. POET'S CRAFT USING IMAGERY

Read the poem out loud. List those phrases that use strong images. With a partner, discuss their meaning, and why they appeal to you. Do you and your partner find the same phrases appealing? Which senses do the images appeal to?

Think of other selections and their use of imagery. Why is it important to use imagery? What does the author achieve with this use? In your journal, list ten everyday objects and use imagery to create strong and realistic descriptions.

Review your writing portfolio. Is there a poem that could be made stronger with the addition of strong images? Is there an essay that could be more interesting? Experiment with imagery in your writing. In your journal, record phrases other authors use that appeal to you strongly. These may spark your own creativity.

3. EDITOR'S DESK CONSTRUCT SENTENCES

Rewrite the first stanza of the poem on one line of your notebook or journal. What do you notice about this stanza? Now rewrite the other two stanzas in the same manner. How are the other stanzas similar? Different? Do you think these stanzas are grammatically incorrect? Would you change any of the punctuation within the stanzas?

Do you think the poet's punctuation and sentence structure are effective? How would you describe his sentences? Are they simple? Run-on? Complex? Compound?

Use this poem as a model to write your own three-stanza, three-sentence poem. Make each stanza a complete sentence, with independent and subordinate clauses, and modifying adjectives. Try to make each sentence at least thirty words long. Read your stanzas aloud to get a sense of their rhythm. (Read Bruchac's poem aloud and consider its rhythms.) Your poem could be about nature, or about doing the right thing. And perhaps, like the speaker in this poem, your speaker will have a change of heart at the end of the poem.

*How far would you go
to protect a friend?*

The Last Leaf

Script
by **Henry Gilford,**
based on
a Short Story
by **O. Henry**

CHARACTERS

ANNOUNCER

JOHNSY,

(Her real name is Joanna, and she is a very sick, young girl.)

SUE,

Johnsy's roommate, an artist, like Johnsy

THE DOCTOR

BEHRMAN,

an old artist, a friend of the girls

THE SET:
Sue and Johnsy's one-room apartment. There are two small beds, a table, chairs, an easel, and paints. Through the window can be seen the wall with the vine.

GOALS AT A GLANCE

■ Write a script based on a short story.
■ Examine and interpret paintings.

313

A C T   O N E

ANNOUNCER: Sue and Joanna are young artists. They live in a one-room apartment in an old house. Joanna, who is called Johnsy by her friends, has always wanted to go to Italy to paint the beautiful Bay of Naples, but she is very sick. As the play opens, she is lying in bed and the doctor is examining her.

DOCTOR: *(Holding Johnsy's hand)* You can't let this illness keep you down Johnsy. You've got to fight to get well and out of bed.

SUE: She won't eat anything, Doctor. I've made her soup, and even cooked a chicken. Won't you tell her to eat, Doctor?

DOCTOR: You need to eat, Johnsy. You need strength to battle this sickness of yours. Soup is good for you. So is chicken. You'll have to eat, if you want to get out of bed.

SUE: That's what I keep telling her, Doctor. She won't listen to me. Maybe she'll listen to you.

DOCTOR: You had better listen to Sue, Johnsy. She is your nurse, and she is a good nurse. A good friend, too, I think. *(Putting his instruments back into his bag)* I'll see you in the morning. *(Pause)* I'm trying to help you, Johnsy. Sue is trying to help you. You have to try, too.

SUE: Thank you, Doctor.

DOCTOR: *(As they walk to the door)* She's a very sick girl.

SUE: Is she going to die?

DOCTOR: I can't say. That's up to her.

SUE: What does that mean, Doctor?

DOCTOR: Well, the truth is that I don't give her much chance.

SUE: Oh! *(Pause)* Is there anything, anything I can do? Isn't there something you can do, Doctor?

DOCTOR: I'm afraid not. It seems to me that she wants to die. She doesn't want to live anymore. I would say that she has one chance in ten of coming through this illness.

SUE: But Johnsy has so much to live for! She's young. She wants to paint the Bay of Naples.

DOCTOR: The Bay of Naples? That's a long way from here. If there were something else, something right here, next door, across the street, she would have a real chance.

SUE: The only thing she wanted badly was to paint the Bay of Naples.

DOCTOR: It isn't enough. Too far away. Sorry. I'm doing my best, Sue. Maybe you can get her to think about something new. That would help. She has to have something, anything, to keep her alive.

SUE: I wish I knew. I'll try, Doctor. Thank you.

DOCTOR: Don't thank me. I haven't done anything. Try to get her to eat something. I'll see you in the morning. Good night.

SUE: Good night.

(The doctor leaves. Sue looks at Johnsy for a minute. She picks up her drawing board, tries to look cheerful, sits down beside Johnsy, and begins to draw.)

SUE: I said I'd have this drawing finished for the office by morning.

JOHNSY: *(Opens her eyes, looks towards the window.)* Twelve.

SUE: Are you feeling better, Johnsy?

JOHNSY: *(After a moment)* Eleven.

SUE: The doctor said you'd be up and painting in no time.

JOHNSY: Ten. Nine. Eight.

SUE: *(worried)* What are you saying, Johnsy?

JOHNSY: Seven.

SUE: What are you counting, Johnsy? What is it?

JOHNSY: They are falling faster now. There were almost a hundred three days ago.

SUE: Please, Johnsy! I don't understand you at all. Are you all right?

JOHNSY: It made my head ache to count them. There were so many.

Now it is easier. There goes another. There are only six now.

SUE: Six what, Johnsy? Won't you please tell me?

JOHNSY: Six leaves on the ivy vine, the ivy vine growing on the wall. Can't you see them? Through this window?

SUE: *(Looks)* Of course I can see them. But why are you counting them?

JOHNSY: When the last leaf falls off the vine, I must go, too.

SUE: Nonsense, Johnsy! Nonsense! What have old ivy leaves got to do with your getting well? You're being silly, Johnsy.

JOHNSY: I'm not being silly. I've known it for days.

SUE: You're trying to frighten me. You're playing a game.

JOHNSY: It's not a game, Sue.

SUE: But the doctor said it was ten to one you'd be all well fast. Those are better odds than you get crossing a street in New York.

JOHNSY: Five.

SUE: *(Getting up quickly)* That's enough counting, Johnsy. Let me get you some soup. You need to eat to get well.

JOHNSY: I don't want any soup. There goes another. There are just four now. I want to see the last one fall before it gets dark. Then I'll go, too.

SUE: *(Bending over Johnsy, fixing her covers)* Johnsy! Please close your eyes. Don't look out of the window. I have to finish this drawing by morning and I need the light. If I didn't need the light, I'd pull the shade.

JOHNSY: Then tell me when you're finished. I want to see the last leaf fall. I'm tired of waiting. I'm tired of thinking. I want to go sailing down, down, down, like one of the poor, tired leaves.

SUE: Shut your eyes, Johnsy. Try to get a little sleep. *(A faint knock at the door. Sue answers it quickly and old Behrman enters.)*

SUE: Shhh! I think she's sleeping.

BEHRMAN: How is she?

SUE: Very sick.

BEHRMAN: What did the doctor say?

SUE: It's bad. It's very bad. *(She begins to cry.)*

BEHRMAN: Ah, doctors! She'll get well.

SUE: *(Shaking her head)* She doesn't want to get well. She says she is going to die when the last leaf falls off the ivy vine.

BEHRMAN: What leaf? What vine?

SUE: *(Pointing)* The vine on the backyard wall.

BEHRMAN: What kind of foolish talk is that?

SUE: I don't know. She keeps looking at the wall and counting the leaves. When the last leaf falls, she will die.

BEHRMAN: Foolish! Foolish! I have never heard such talk, as long as I am an artist.

SUE: Shhh! You'll wake her.

BEHRMAN: With all the rain and the wind! How long can a leaf stay up there on the wall?

SUE: *(Crying again)* I don't know.

BEHRMAN: Sh! Now you'll wake her up with your crying. There is nothing to cry about. *(He walks to the window, lowers the shade.)* Keep the shade down and dry your eyes. I think that maybe that last leaf will never fall from the wall.

A C T   T W O

ANNOUNCER: The second act opens in the same room, one week later, early in the morning. The window shade is down. Sue is drawing. Johnsy is just waking.

JOHNSY: *(Her voice much stronger than before)* Sue!

SUE: Yes, Johnsy?

JOHNSY: The window shade. Please pull it up.

SUE: *(Going to the window)* Sure. You're still waiting for that last leaf to fall.

JOHNSY: It must have fallen during the night.

SUE: *(Lifting the shade)* But it didn't.

JOHNSY: It's still there! Seven days now. How can it stay there with all the wind and the rain? A little leaf on an old vine? I just don't know how it does it!

SUE: It's there, isn't it?

JOHNSY: It's there, all right.

SUE: And you're getting better every day.

JOHNSY: I think I'm getting better.

SUE: That's what the doctor says.

JOHNSY: He can't understand that leaf, either. Why doesn't Behrman come to see me anymore? He must be too busy painting his master-piece. He's always working on his masterpiece, the poor old man. Ask him in to breakfast, Sue.

SUE: Not this morning, Johnsy.

JOHNSY: Why not? I'm hungry and I want Behrman to see me eat a big breakfast again. Maybe it'll inspire him. Ask him in.

SUE: I can't.

JOHNSY: Why not?

SUE: He's in the hospital.

JOHNSY: Oh, I'm sorry. I didn't know he was sick.

SUE: He's very sick.

JOHNSY: You should have told me.

SUE: There are some things you can't tell a girl who thinks she is going to die with the last leaf on an ivy vine.

JOHNSY: It didn't die. It didn't want me to die.

SUE: I didn't want you to die. Behrman didn't want you to die. *(Knock at the door)*

JOHNSY: Maybe it's Behrman.

SUE: *(Going to the door)* I wish it were. (Opens the door) Come in, Doctor. Good morning.

DOCTOR: Good morning. Well!

Good morning, Johnsy. You're looking really bright this morning.

JOHNSY: I do feel almost all well again, Doctor.

DOCTOR: Good. I think you are well again. It was that last leaf.

JOHNSY: It's still there.

DOCTOR: It'll be there for a long time.

JOHNSY: Nature is wonderful.

DOCTOR: Nature? Did you look at that leaf closely, Johnsy?

JOHNSY: I was waiting for it to fall.

SUE: *(Interrupting)* How is Behrman, Doctor?

DOCTOR: Didn't I tell you? He died last night.

JOHNSY: How terrible!

DOCTOR: He was an old man. All that cold rain and the wind were too much for him. It was a brave thing he did. He must have loved you like a father.

JOHNSY: But he was never out in the wind and the rain, Doctor. I don't understand. All he did was to paint pictures inside his little studio.

DOCTOR: You want to paint the Bay of Naples, don't you?

SUE: I told the doctor.

JOHNSY: I think it will be my greatest picture.

DOCTOR: Behrman painted his greatest picture just about a week ago, in the wind and the rain.

JOHNSY: What did he paint?

DOCTOR: Leaves flutter in the wind, Johnsy.

JOHNSY: *(Beginning to understand)* Oh! Of course…

DOCTOR: Have you ever seen that last leaf of yours move?

JOHNSY: Never.

DOCTOR: It couldn't. The first night that Sue pulled down the shade, Behrman got himself a ladder and some green paint. He went out into the rain and the wind. He climbed the ladder, and he painted the last leaf on the wall. There were no leaves at all left on the vine when Behrman climbed the ladder. That leaf you've been looking at is Behrman's. That last leaf is Behrman's greatest picture. It's his masterpiece.

----

1. RESPONDING TO THE SCRIPT

a. What do you think the leaves symbolize in this script?

b. At what point in the story do you begin to suspect the truth about the last leaf? What makes you suspect it?

c. Would you agree with the doctor when he describes the last leaf as Behrman's greatest picture? Explain your answer.

d. How do you feel about Johnsy at the end of Act One? At the end of Act Two?

2. WRITER'S DESK SHORT STORY SCRIPT

Henry Gilford wrote this script after reading a story by O. Henry. Many short stories and novels are brought to the stage, or made into movies, by scriptwriters. Can you think of a book you've read that was made into a movie? What was it? How was it changed? Was it strengthened or weakened by being adapted for film?

With a partner, choose a short story from this book. Work together to develop a script for a stage play or TV movie. As you write, remember that your audience should get the same message from watching your adaptation as they would from reading the story. You may need to include a narrator or announcer. (In movies this is known as the voice-over.) You may want to give the characters more dialogue than the original author has, to help develop the story. Include stage directions, and instructions for camera angles. Remember to credit your original source, for example, "Babysitting Helen" script by Jenna Redpath, based on a short story by Kathy Stinson.

3. VISUAL COMMUNICATION VIEWING PAINTINGS

Examine the painting of the Bay of Naples on page 316. Why do you think Johnsy wants to visit this place? What do you find appealing about the artist's interpretation?

Through the Internet or school library find a painting or work of art that is considered great, or a masterpiece. In your journal write a paragraph explaining your reaction to this piece of art. Discuss what it means to you, why you think it's famous, and whether you find it appealing. Remember to begin with a topic sentence, add supporting sentences to develop the topic, use connecting words to link the sentences, and finish with a strong concluding sentence.

HOW TO

PRESENT A PLAY

Goals at a Glance
- Work co-operatively to present a stage play. • Analyse oral presentations.

Start with the Script

The script tells who the characters are, what they look like, and what they say to each other. Usually scripts also include **stage directions** that describe where the action takes place; what the stage should look like and what special lighting and sound effects are required; and how the characters move and behave.

Some scripts contain very precise stage directions. Others, such as the script for "The Last Leaf," say very little about how the play should be brought to life.

If you are going to present a play, familiarize yourself with the script first to see how much detail it contains. Keep your audience in mind when you are making decisions about costumes, music, setting, and so on. For example, you might use one kind of background music if you were performing for children, but a different kind for an audience of classmates.

Divide Up the Tasks

To present a play, you and your classmates will have to decide who will take responsibility for the different tasks that are required.

Director: contributes to all decisions, co-ordinates all personnel, helps to shape the way the actors move and speak

Actors: perform one or more roles, bring the characters to life

Stage Manager: in charge of set construction, oversees lighting, sound, props, etc.

Lighting Technician: installs and or/operates lighting

Sound Technician: creates sound effects

Prop Manager: obtains and keeps track of all props

Costume Person: obtains and keeps track of all costumes

Make-up Person: designs and applies the actors' make-up

Prompter: helps the actors remember their lines in rehearsals and performances

PROCESS

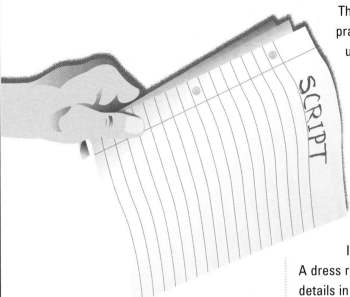

The actors should begin to learn and practise their parts while the others get underway with the set and other technical details.

The actors should first read their lines while sitting, then read them in position, then recite them from memory while moving on stage.

Incorporate props, sound effects, and so on into the rehearsals as they are ready. Everyone needs to practise, not just the actors!

Include a **dress rehearsal** in your plan. A dress rehearsal is a trial performance with all details in place.

Helpers: assist with set construction, scene changes, etc.

Plan the Process

Even if you are presenting a short play in a very simple way, you should take time as a group to create a plan. It should show the tasks to be done, who will do them, and when they will be completed. Read the script carefully as a group and discuss what will be needed to bring the play to life.

Make the key decisions at the beginning. Where will the presentation take place? Do sets have to be constructed or painted? What furniture and props are required? Will there be special costumes? Do you need lighting or sound effects or background music? Will actors wear make-up or masks?

Present Your Play

Actors should speak loudly so that everyone can hear.

Don't let a mistake stop the play. Ignore a flubbed line or a missed sound effect.

Members of the crew should remain quiet behind the scenes.

Self-Assessment

❏ Did each person have a clear role?
❏ Did you start by reading the script carefully and discussing it?
❏ Did you create a clear plan for your presentation?
❏ Did you include a dress rehearsal?
❏ Did you work as a team?

What were the strengths of your presentation? What were its weaknesses? List three ways your presentation could be improved.

PROCESS

Doing the right thing sometimes leads to wonderful new opportunities, as this young speechwriter discovered when he set out to…

Save South Moresby!

Speech by Jeff Gibbs

When I was sixteen, my friends and I were part of a successful campaign to save an ancient West Coast rain forest called South Moresby. Encountering those massive trees humbled me and made me understand that I was but one of billions of organisms on the planet. Working to see that forest officially protected taught me what committed individuals can achieve.

The empowering experience of that victory propelled me into a whole new world of friends, adventure, and hard work. South Moresby ultimately led me to live and learn from the indigenous people of the Amazon and Borneo rain forests, to tour schools with environmental presentations, and to leave university to initiate the Environmental Youth Alliance.

My two years with the EYA have been a life experience. I've crossed Canada ten times and travelled around the world, speaking to over one hundred thousand individuals in one hundred and fifty schools. The spark in people's eyes has kept me going.

I've seen the EYA grow from an office in my bedroom to a seventeen-thousand-member-strong organization with incredible youth leaders, dedicated staff, and wonderful volunteers. I'll probably be remembered as EYA's founder, but it's come about through the energies of many. To me, anyone who puts an effort into the EYA movement is a founder because they help bring the organization to the next level of success.

GOALS AT A GLANCE

- Examine the opinions of others.
- Model the selection to write a speech.

Here are some insights from my experience in the youth movement:

Around the world, youth are coming to the realization that excessive consumerism is at the root of today's environmental crisis. We've been brainwashed into believing that more material things will increase the quality of our life. But ironically, our greed, waste, and ignorance is destroying the very earth that gives us life. Many youth are changing their lifestyles; they are cutting back to help ensure a healthy planet.

Youth are beginning to think in a holistic, global way.
We are making the connections between environmental problems and such things as the media and consumerism, education and empowerment, poverty and population. The western world, of which Canada is a part, is home to only twenty percent of the earth's population, yet consumes eighty percent of its resources. As poor countries try to obtain our material wealth, the stresses on the earth's biosphere will be unbearable. For our own survival, we must set an example of living in balance with nature.

Most of our population is so removed from nature that they don't understand the full impact of their actions.
We allow TV to encourage us into a lifestyle of consumeristic values that disregard nature. What we really need to do is turn off the TV, go for a walk in the park, and more importantly, get out to places like South Moresby. We need to think more on our own and create the path we choose to follow. After all, we are not here for long and life is so precious.

The environmental youth movement is an education revolution. Today's youth aren't just staging protests. They are educating themselves about the problems, and thinking and acting on potential solutions. Many youth are committed to institutionalizing their idealism by going to university and pursuing careers that integrate their environmental concern.

My final comment is: *be bold and take risks, because that is how you stand to get the most out of life.* I almost didn't get involved with the EYA, because there was security in my studies and such an unknown outcome with this endeavour. Having done it, I have no regrets.

Why not join the Endangered Spaces campaign and protect your own South Moresby? Our earth can survive, but we need the bold actions of everyone. Sometimes the solutions may seem overwhelming, like the vastness of the ocean. But the ocean is filled by many small streams. Just remember you are one of those streams. ◆

1. RESPONDING TO THE SPEECH

a. What words would you use to describe the speaker? Use a web to develop a list of characteristics. Compare it with a classmate's.

b. What does the speaker expect his audience to do? What do you think you can do?

2. ORAL LANGUAGE EXAMINE OPINIONS

Are there any statements in this speech that you strongly agree or disagree with? Write these statements down, indicating your own position. Discuss these statements and your opinions with a partner.

3. WORD CRAFT UNDERSTANDING VOCABULARY

Are there any words or phrases within the speech that you did not understand? Reread the selection and use *context*—the meaning of the whole sentence and how the word is used—to help you figure out the meaning of unfamiliar words. Check a dictionary to see if you guessed the word's meaning correctly.

STRATEGIES

4. WRITING MODEL THE SPEECH

Reread this speech and think about its main idea, or message. Who do you think the audience is? What do you think Jeff Gibbs hoped to achieve with his speech?

Now prepare a speech of your own. Think of some topic you feel strongly about. Decide who your audience will be, and what you hope to achieve with your speech. Jot down some notes about the topic. Organize your notes into a logical presentation of the facts and ideas. Write a paragraph for each idea, elaborating on it, and supporting it with detail. Remember to use vivid images and a strong opening line and conclusion. Rehearse your speech until you're comfortable delivering it. Present your speech to your class, asking for feedback and questions.

SELF-ASSESSMENT: When you use a selection as a model, do you make a list of its features, and its strengths? Do you follow that list as you write?

Have you ever faced a turning point in your life?

What helped you get through it?

Consorting With Frogs

MEMOIR BY FARLEY MOWAT

Almost all young children have a natural affinity for other animals. I was no exception. As a child I fearlessly and happily consorted with frogs, snakes, chickens, squirrels, and whatever else came my way.

As a boy growing up on the Saskatchewan prairies, that feeling of affinity persisted—but it became perverted. Under my father's tutelage I was taught to be a hunter; taught that "communion with nature" could be achieved over the barrel of a gun; taught that killing wild animals for sport establishes a mystic bond between them and us.

I learned how to handle first a BB gun, then a .22 rifle, and finally a shotgun. With these I killed "vermin"—sparrows, gophers, crows, and hawks. Having served that bloody apprenticeship, I began killing "game"—prairie chicken, ruffed grouse, and ducks. By the time I was fourteen, I had been fully indoctrinated with the sportsman's view of "wildlife" as objects to be exploited for pleasure.

Then I experienced a revelation, which I described in *The Dog Who Wouldn't Be.*

It was in November of 1935 and my father and I were crouched in a muddy pit at the edge of a prairie slough called Wakaw Lake, waiting for daybreak.

The dawn, when it came at last, was grey and sombre. The sky lightened so imperceptibly that we could hardly detect the coming of the morning. We strained our eyes into swirling snow squalls and suddenly heard the sound of wings. Cold was forgotten. We crouched lower and flexed numb fingers in our shooting gloves.

My father saw them first. He nudged me sharply and I half turned my head to behold a spectacle of incomparable grandeur. Out of the storm scud, like ghostly ships, a hundred whistling swans bore down upon us on their stately wings. They passed directly overhead, not half a gunshot from us, and I was suddenly transported beyond time and space by a vision of unparalleled majesty and mystery. For one flashing instant I felt that they and I were one. Then they were gone and snow eddies obscured my straining vision.

After that it would not have mattered to me if we had seen no other living things that day, or fired a single shot. But the swans were only the forerunners of multitudes. The windy silence was soon pierced by the sonorous cries of seemingly endless flocks of geese that drifted, wraithlike, overhead. They were flying low that day, so we could see them clearly. Snow geese, startlingly white of breast, with jet-black wing tips, beat past while flocks of piebald wavies kept station on their flanks. An immense "V" of Canada geese came close behind. As the rush of air through their great pinions sounded in our ears we jumped up and in an action that was more of a conditioned reflex than a conscious one, we raised our guns. The Honkers veered directly toward us, and we fired. The sound of the shots seemed puny, and was lost at once in that immensity of wind and wings.

It was a pure mischance that one of the great geese was hit for, as we admitted to each other later, neither of us had aimed at them. Nevertheless one fell, appearing gigantic in the tenuous light as it spiralled sharply down. It struck the water about a hundred metres from shore and I saw with sick dismay that it had only been winged. It swam off into the growing storm, its neck outstretched, calling... calling...calling after the fast disappearing flock.

Driving home to Saskatoon that night I felt a sick repugnance for what we had done; but what was of far greater import, I was experiencing a poignant but indefinable sense of loss. I felt, although I could not then have expressed it in words, as if I had glimpsed another and quite magical world—a world of Oneness—and had been denied entry into it through my own stupidity.

I never hunted for sport again. ◆

---

1. RESPONDING TO THE SELECTION

a. Why do you think this particular flock of birds has such a profound effect on Farley Mowat?

b. How do you think Mowat's father will respond to his son's changing attitudes? Support your opinion with facts from the story.

c. How might a hunter respond to Mowat's words? With a partner, role-play a discussion or argument that he and a hunter might have.

2. MEDIA MAKER CARICATURES

Examine the **caricature** on page 326, and discuss it with a partner. How has the artist captured the subject of the selection? How is this image like and unlike other drawings or paintings? What can caricatures accomplish that other types of images cannot? What do you think the purpose of this drawing is?

> A **caricature** is a drawing that deliberately exaggerates the features or defects of a subject, reflecting the person's personality.

Draw a caricature of someone famous. First, find a photo of this individual, preferably a side view or profile shot. Examine the shape of the person's face and think about how the shape could be stretched or distorted for humorous effect. Exaggerate some of the physical features. For example, if the person is bald you could give him a high forehead; if she has glasses you could make them more prominent. Try a few sketches of the face, and experiment with the features and how they are exaggerated. In your final caricature include details that display the person's personality, interests, background, or profession, such as a guitar, the Rocky Mountains, or a camera.

SELF-ASSESSMENT: Compare your caricature to the photo of the celebrity. Reflect on how effectively you've captured personality, and exaggerated features.

3. WRITING NARRATIVE PARAGRAPH

On page 327, Mowat describes his experience as a revelation. Have you ever had a similar revelation? What happened? In your journal, write a **narrative paragraph** describing this experience. Include information about how you felt before your revelation, what exactly happened, and how you felt afterward. Try to use a variety of sentences, from simple to complex.

A **narrative paragraph** tells a story, using a change in speaker, place, time, or point of view.

REFLECTING ON THE UNIT

SELF-ASSESSMENT: LITERATURE STUDIES

As you worked on activities in this unit what did you learn about
• effective setting?
• using imagery?
• dynamic characters?
How did learning about these literary elements help you to understand or appreciate the selections?

VISUAL COMMUNICATION

Create a collage that illustrates several of the important themes or topics covered in this unit. Your collage should make a statement or take a stand on the topic. Somewhere in your collage, include a sentence or two that summarizes what it is that you want to say about the unit.

WRITING

Write an original poem or paragraph in response to any aspect of this unit. Find or create an illustration to go with your creative writing.

ORAL LANGUAGE

Choose two characters from two different selections in this unit. With a partner, develop a dialogue in which they share with each other what it is that they did that made a difference.

GLOSSARY

Adjective An adjective is the word that describes a noun or pronoun: *He felt a sharp pain. Her icy green eyes stared at the stars. He looked cold.* Adjectives as well as describing, can also limit a noun: *I saw two movies on the weekend.*

Alliteration Alliteration involves the repetition of the same first sounds in a group of words or line of poetry: *The sun sank slowly.*

Anecdote An anecdote is a brief story that retells an incident or event. Like a story, it could be sad, funny, or adventurous, and often has a plot, characters, and setting.

Antagonist An antagonist is the person or thing in a story fighting against the main character or protagonist.

Assonance Assonance is the repetition of similar vowel sounds. It is a partial rhyme in which the vowels are similar but the consonants are different: *pear/bear, care/dare.*

Caption A caption is an explanation or title accompanying a picture. Captions are most often used in newspaper and magazine articles.

Caricature A caricature is a drawing that deliberately exaggerates the features or defects of a subject, reflecting the person's personality. Caricatures are often used in newspaper editorial pages.

Clause A clause is a group of words that has a subject (a noun) and a predicate (a verb and sometimes adjectives, adverbs, and phrases).

An **independent** or **main clause** is complete thought and stands alone as a sentence: *I shut the door. The cat ran into the street.*

A **dependent** or **subordinate clause** is not a complete sentence and doesn't stand alone as a sentence: *Although she missed the bus. Whenever Jack got the chance.*

Comic Strip A comic strip is a series of drawings, especially cartoons, that tell a funny story, an adventure or a series of incidents. Comic strips involve recurring characters.

Conflict Conflict is a problem or struggle in a story that the main character has to solve or face. Conflict is created in four classic way: human against self, human against human, human against nature, human against society. Writers may choose to use more than one conflict in a story, which can create an exciting plot.

Conjunction A conjunction is a word that connects other words, phrases, clauses, or sentences. There are three types of conjunctions.
- co-ordinating conjunctions *(and, or, nor, for, but, so, yet): Carla and I are best friends.*
- subordinating conjunctions: *(whenever, after, if, since, because, before, unless): I break out in a sweat whenever I get on an elevator.*
- correlative conjunctions *(but...and, either...or, neither...nor, not only...but also): My watch is neither on my wrist nor by my bed.*

Dialogue Dialogue is a conversation between characters. In narrative, every time a new character speaks a new paragraph is used. Quotation marks are used to indicate that dialogue is beginning and ending.

Ellipsis Points [...] Ellipsis points are a series of dots used to show that something has been left out. Use ellipsis points as follows.

- to show that one or more words have been left out of a quotation.
- to indicate that a sentence or thought has been left unfinished.

Five W's The five W's of journalism are the five questions that every newspaper or magazine article should answer: who, what, where, when, why (and sometimes how). By the end of the article, the reader should know who was involved in the story or event, what happened, where it happened, when it happened, why it happened, and how it happened.

Flashback A flashback is an event or scene that took place at an earlier point in a story. Writers use flashback to explain something that is presently occurring in the story. Flashbacks can also explain a character's motivation and help to clear up any unanswered questions in the plot.

Foreshadowing Foreshadowing is a writing device used to give a hint about what is to come in a story. The hint, however, should not be too obvious to the reader because it will give the plot away and affect the suspense. Foreshadowing is used mainly in mysteries and suspense stories, but can be used in other genres as well.

Headline A headline is the words printed at the top of an article in a newspaper or magazine to indicate what the article is about. The headline should be kept short (only two or three words), and yet should concisely indicate what the story is about.

Imagery Imagery is a technique poets and writers use to describe and appeal to the senses. There are many types of imagery including simile, metaphor, alliteration, and personification.

Irony Irony is using a word or phrase to mean the opposite of its normal meaning. *Calling a small bungalow a mansion is irony.* One of the most common types of irony is dramatic irony. Dramatic irony occurs in a situation in which the audience knows something which the character does not.

Lead A lead is the opening paragraph of a newspaper or magazine article. The lead should contain as many of the answers as possible to the five W's of journalism: who, what, when, where, and why.

Legend A legend is a story from the past that has been widely accepted as true. For example, the stories of King Arthur and his knights of the Round Table and Robin Hood are thought of as legends and not history. Sometimes legends explain natural facts such as how mountains were formed and often include magical elements.

Logo A logo is an identifying symbol or image, sometimes including a name or word, used in advertising. Most companies have a logo that is instantly recognizable to the consumer. For example, Nike's swoosh, or McDonald's M.

Memoir A memoir is the recording of a person's own experiences, and involves the retelling of memorable experiences from that person's life. Each experience is told like a story, and is written from the first person point of view (*I, me, we, us*).

Metaphor A metaphor is a writing device in which a word or phrase that ordinarily means one thing is used to describe something else, suggesting that some common quality is shared by the two: *a heart of stone, copper sky*. As well as painting vivid pictures for the reader, metaphors help to make abstract ideas more concrete, add emotion, and show the writer's feelings.

Mood The mood or atmosphere is the feeling that pervades a piece of writing or work of art. *The mood of Frankenstein is sombre and dark*. Mood is created through description and through the plot and the setting.

Myth A myth is a traditional story about superhuman beings, such as gods, goddesses, heroes, and monsters, usually explaining the origin of natural events and forces, and cultural practices. Some myths teach values, such as humility.

Narration Narration is the telling of an event or series of events. Narration is used in all types of writing including narrative, plays, and poetry.

Narrator The narrator is the person or character telling a story. See point of view.

Noun A noun is a word that refers to people, places, qualities, things, actions, or ideas. *When Joe was at the library in Guelph, curiosity caused him to read an article that claimed fear could be cured by meditation.*

Paragraph A paragraph is a group of sentences that develop one aspect of a topic, or one phase of a narrative. The sentences in a paragraph should be clearly related to each other. Sometimes, especially in essays, the aspect or point being developed is expressed in a topic sentence, and the other sentences in the paragraph expand on this statement.

A **descriptive paragraph** describes a person, place, thing, or idea.

A **narrative paragraph** tells a story by sharing the details of an event or experience.

A **persuasive paragraph** expresses the writer's opinion about a topic or subject and tries to convince the reader to agree with it. A topic sentence is often used to state the point of view. Accompanying sentences attempt to prove the topic sentence.

An **expository paragraph** gives step-by-step instructions about how to do something. It may give directions and explain ideas. Transitional expressions such as *first* and *next* are often used to show sequence and order in this type of paragraph.

A **dialogue paragraph** is used mainly in stories. Dialogue is the words spoken by characters in the story. Every time a new character speaks a new paragraph is used. Dialogue paragraphs are enclosed in quotation marks.

Personification Personification is a literary device that gives human traits to non-humans: *The stream gurgled.* Personification is used most often in poetry and narrative writing but can be used as a technique in print ads.

Phrase A phrase is a group of words, used together in a sentence, that does not have a subject and a verb:
Marcella spoke *for the first time.*
   (prepositional phrase)
Thinking fast, I covered my ears
   (participial phrase)
Catrina wants *to be a scientist.*
   (infinitive phrase)

Plot The plot is the events in a story that make up the action. The plot in a story usually has five elements: the exposition (set-up), rising action, climax, falling action, and resolution.
- The **exposition** sets up the story by introducing the main characters, the setting, and the problem to be solved.
- The **rising action** is the main part of the story where the full problem develops. A number of events is involved that will lead to the climax.
- The **climax** is the highest point of the story where the most exciting events occur.
- The **falling action** follows the climax. It contains the events that bring the story to the conclusion.
- The **resolution** is the end of the story when all the problems are solved.

Point of View Point of view refers to the position from which the events of a story are presented to us. There are two main points of view: first person and third person narrative.
- **First person** means the story is told through one character's eyes and the

events are coloured through that character's experience.

- The **third person** point of view means the story is told by an onlooker or narrator. There are two third person points of view: **Omniscient** and **limited.** In the omniscient point of view, the narrator knows everything about all the characters and the events, and can shift from character to character. In the limited point of view, the author may choose to tell the story through one character or a group of characters' eyes.
- Many modern authors also use a "multiple point of view" in which we are shown the events from the position of two or more different characters.

Pourquoi Tale A pourquoi tale is a traditional story that explains why a natural phenomenon came to be. For example, *The Magic Millstones* explain why the sea is salt. Sometimes pourquoi tales involve superhuman beings such as gods and supernatural occurrences.

Pronoun A pronoun is a word that replaces a noun or another pronoun. There are many different types of pronouns, and most of them cause no problems.

Protagonist The protagonist is the main character in a story. The story is usually told from this person's point of view.

Rhyme Rhyme is the repetition of sound in different words, especially at the ends of words. For example, *see* rhymes with *bee*. Rhyme is one of the main techniques used in poetry.

Rhyme Scheme A rhyme scheme is the pattern of end rhymes used in a poem. The rhyme scheme is usually indicated by letters, for example, *abba abba cde cde* and *abab cdcd efef gg* are both rhyme schemes for a type of poetry called a sonnet.

Rhythm Rhythm is the arrangement of beats in a line of poetry. The beat is created by the accented and unaccented syllables in the words used in the line.

Run-on Sentence A run-on sentence is formed when two sentences run into one another. To fix a run-on sentence, add the proper punctuation, or change the wording to make it a single sentence.
Run-on: *The sky is clear it is spring at last.*
Better: *The sky is clear; it is spring at last.*
OR
The sky is clear, and it is spring at last.
OR
The sky is clear because it is spring at last.
You call two sentences separated by a comma a comma splice. Fix the comma splice the same way you would fix a run-on sentence.

Satire A satire is a type of writing that uses humour and irony to point out what is wrong with an organization, person, or society. Jonathan Swift's *Gulliver's Travels* is a satire.

Science Fiction A science fiction story takes readers to other worlds or to other times. Science fiction writers sometimes base their stories on scientific facts or scientific possibilities that haven't been proven yet. Plots often deal with the impact of science and technology on humans and the world. Popular science fiction themes include space travel, time travel, advanced technology, and life in the future.

Script A script is a story written to be performed as a play or developed into a movie or television show. The script tells a story with setting, plot, and characters. The story is told through dialogue between characters and through narration as well. Characters are usually listed on the left side of a script and their "lines" are included beside the character name. Scripts also contain stage directions that give instructions for setting up the stage and for the actors.

Semicolon [;] Use a semicolon to separate two related sentences: *I love watching television after school; it relaxes me.*

- A semicolon may also be used along with a co-ordinating conjunction (*and, or, nor, for, but, so, yet*) to join main clauses, if one or more of the clauses already contains a comma: *I threw on my coat, picked up my wallet, and raced to the bus stop; but the bus had already left.*
- Semicolons are also used to separate items in a list, when one or more of the items contains a comma: *Walter has lived in Tokyo, Japan; London, England; and Estavan, Saskatchewan.*

Sentence A sentence is a group of words that expresses a complete thought. Every sentence needs a subject and an action.

A s**imple sentence** has one subject and one verb: *Yukio's house has five bedrooms.*

A **compound sentence** has two or more main clauses (that is smaller sentences that can stand alone). The sentences are usually joined together by a semicolon, or by a comma or semicolon followed by *and, or, nor, for, but, so,* or *yet: Yukio's house has five bedrooms, and the yard is huge.*

A **complex sentence** has a main clause that can stand alone as a sentence, and one or more subordinate clauses that cannot stand on their own as sentences. In the following example of a complex sentence, the main clause is underlined, and the subordinate clause is in italics:
<u>Yukio's house</u>, *which he built himself,* <u>has five bedrooms.</u>

Sentence Fragment A sentence fragment is a group of words that is set off like a sentence, but lacks either a verb or a subject. Sentence fragments are acceptable in informal writing, dialogue, and spoken English, but are not appropriate in formal writing:
Fragment: *We went to the game. Josh and I.* (lacks a verb)
Revised: *Josh and I went to the game.*

Setting The setting is the place and time where a story takes place. Setting plays an important role in many types of stories: science fiction, historical fiction, fantasy, and adventure stories.

Simile A simile is a comparison of two different things using the words *like* or *as: My ears buzzed like a mosquito.* Similes are used in both prose and poetry.

Slogan A slogan is a short, catchy phrase used by a business, club, political party, company, and so on to advertise its product or purpose. Slogans are most often used in print ads and radio and TV commercials. Along with a logo, a good slogan will instantly bring the product it advertises to the consumer's mind.

Stanza A stanza is a group of lines of poetry arranged according to a fixed plan. Stanzas usually contain the same number of lines, meter, and rhyme scheme. The term stanza is most often used to refer to groups of four lines or more. The four line "quatrain" is the most common. In free verse, a poem may be organized by stanzas, but will not have a regular rhyme scheme.

Stereotype A stereotype is an oversimplified picture, usually of a group of people, giving them all a set of characteristics, without consideration for individual differences. Avoid stereotypes in your writing. Try to create fresh, real characters.

Symbol/Symbolism A symbol is a person, place, thing or event that is used to represent something else. For example, a rainbow is often used as a symbol of hope.

Tone Tone is the atmosphere or mood of a piece. It can also refer to the author's attitude or feeling about the reader (formal, casual, intimate) and his subject (light, ironic, solemn, sarcastic, sentimental).

Verb A verb is a word that expresses an action or a state of being. Verbs that express a state of being are sometimes called linking verbs, because they link the subject to another word that describes the subject.
Action verb: *Sunil <u>ran</u> to school.*
Linking verb: *Mariko <u>seemed</u> tired.*
The verb *be* is the most common linking verb, but verbs like *seem, appear, feel, smell,* and *look* can act as linking verbs.

ACKNOWLEDGMENTS

Every reasonable effort has been made to trace owner-ship of copyrighted material. Information that would enable the publisher to correct any reference or credit in future editions would be appreciated.

3 "Lines for a Bookmark" by Gael Turnbull from *Trio* (Contact Press, 1945)/ 10-12 "Mystery of Mysteries" from *It was on Fire When I Laid Down on It* by Robert Fulghum. ©1989 by Robert Fulghum. Reprinted with permission of Villard Books, a division of Random House, Inc./ 13-20 "The Jade Peony" by Wayson Choy. Reprinted with permission of the author./ 22 "Who Am I" by Felice Holman from *Sound of Thunder* edited by I. Mills./ 23 "And I Remember" by Afua Cooper reprinted from *Voices: Canadian Writers of African Descent*, edited by Ayanna Black. Published by Harper CollinsPublishersLtd,. ©1992 by Ayanna Black./ 24 From *Soda Jerk* by Cynthia Rylant, illustrated by Peter Catalanotto. Text ©1990 by Cynthia Rylant. Illustrations ©1990 by Peter Catalanotto. Reprinted with permission of Orchard Books, New York./ 25 "Wanted: Someone Who Cares" by Shawna Lynne Danielle Panipekeesick from *Writing the Circle* edited by Jeanne Perreault and Sylvia Vance/ 28-31 "Going Back Home" from *Going Back Home: An Artist Returns to the South* story interpreted and written by Toyomi Igus./ 33 "Acceptance" by Vidhya Sridharan. Reprinted by permission of the author./ 35-42 "On the Sidewalk Bleeding" by Evan Hunter. ©1957, 1985 by Evan Hunter. Originally published in *Happy New Year, Herbie, and Other Stories*. Reprinted with permission of the Author./ 44 "The Road Not Taken" by Robert Frost from *Out and About: Poems of the Outdoors*./ 46-56 "Borders" from *One Good Story, That One* by Thomas King. Published by HarperCollins PublishersLtd,. ©1993 by Thomas King./ 62-67 "Kath and Mouse" by Janet McNaughton. Reprinted by permission of the author./ 72-75 "Thank You, Ma'am" from *Don't You Turn Back* by Langston Hughes./ 77-84 "A Sunrise on the Veld" from *African Stories* by Doris Lessing./ 87-92 "Coffee, Snacks, Worms" by Karleen Bradford. Reprinted by permission of the author./ 84-99 "G. Trueheart, Man's Best Friend" by James McNamee from *Over the Horizon and Around the World in Fifteen Stories*./ 102-103 "Bus Stop" by W. D. Valgardson. Reprinted by permission of the author./ 106-117 "The Leaving" by Budge Wilson from *The Leaving* by Budge Wilson. ©1990 by Budge Wilson. Originally published by House of Anansi Press Limited. Reprinted by permission of Stoddart Publishing Co. Limited, Don Mills, ON./ 122-125 "The Day the Martian Landed" from *Farewell to the Twentieth Century* by Pierre Berton. ©1996 Pierre Berton Enterprises Ltd./ 127-139 "Moon Maiden" by Alison Baird. ©1998 Alison Baird taken from *What If...? Amazing Stories Selected by Monica Hughes* published by Tundra Books./ 141-143 "Who's Out There?" from *As It Happened* by Barbara Frum. Reprinted by permission of the estate./ 145-148 "Radical Robots" by YES Mag with John Garrett from *YES Mag* (Summer 1998, Issue 10)./ 150 "Shooting the Sun" by Amy Lowell from *The Complete Poetical Works of Amy Lowell*. ©1955 by Houghton Mifflin Co. © renewed 1983 by Houghton Mifflin Co., Brinton P. Roberts and G. D. Andelot Belin, Esq. Reprinted by permission of Houghton Mifflin co. All rights reserved./ 152-158 "A Major Malfunction" by Michael Kilpatrick from *The Blue Jean Collection* (Thistledown Press, 1992)./ 162 "High Flight" by John Gillespie Magee, Jr. Reprinted by permission from This England Books./ 163 "Fueled" by Marcie Hans./ 164-168 "Undersea Science" by Thomas Potts from *YES Mag* (Spring 1998, Issue 9)./ 170 "The Choice" by W. Hilton-Young./ 174-175 "The Gift of Stories, The Gift of Breath" from *Four Ancestors: Stories, Songs, and Poems from Native North America* by Joseph Bruchac./ 176-179 "The White Stone Canoe" by Henry Rowe Schoolcraft from *The Fire Plume: Legends of the American Indians* edited by John Bierhorst. ©1969 John Bierhorst./ 181-186 "Savitri and Satyavan" from *Seasons of Splendour: Tales, Myths & Legends of India* by Madhur Jaffrey. Text ©1985 Madhur Jaffrey./ 188-191 "The Magic Millstones: Why the Sea is Salt" from *The Book of Creation Stories* retold by Margaret Mayo and illustrated by Louise Brierley first published in the UK by Orchard Books, a division of The Watts Publishing Group Limited, 96 Leonard Street, London EC2A 4XD./ 195-197 "Water, Moon, and Sun" from *Realms of Gold: Myths & Legends from Around the World*. Text © Ann Pilling 1993. Reprinted by permssion of Larousse Kingfisher Chambers Inc., New York./ 199-200 "That Wascawwy Wabbit: Bugs Bunny as Trickster" from *Myths Within* by David Creighton./ 203-207 "The Legend of the Panda" by Linda Granfield. Taken from *The Legend of the Panda*. ©1998 Linda Granfield: text, Song Nan Zhang: illustrations. Published by Tundra Books./ 209-215 "Paris and the Golden Apple" by Eth Clifford in *The Magnificent Myths of Man* edited by Thomas Hoobler and Dan Fisher./ 220-223 "When Movies Cost a Nickel" (originally entitled "The Golden Age of Laughter") from *Never Sleep Three in a Bed* by Max Braithwaite. Used by permission, McClelland & Stewart, Inc. *The Canadian Publishers*./ 225-227 "Hollywood's New Rules for Car Chases" from *Farewell to the Twentieth Century* by Pierre Berton. ©1996 Pierre Berton Enterprises./ 228-233 "Trick Shots" by Ian Graham./

ACKNOWLEDGMENTS • 335

235-236 "Based on the Novel" (originally entitled "Don't Wait for the Movie") from *More Than Words Can Say* by Gordon Korman. Reprinted with permission of Gordon Korman Enterprises Inc./ 238 "The Day the TV Broke" by Gerald Jones. Reprinted by permission of *The Saturday Review* ©1979, General Media International, Inc./ 240-241 "Good News" by Joseph Schrank./ 243-244 "How We Make the TV Show: Behind the Scenes at *Street Cents."* Reprinted with permission of Barbara Kennedy./ 247-248 "Drink Milk, Love Life" from the Milk Marketing Board./ 250-251 "The Two Sides of Advertising" from *Break for Commercials: An Examination of Advertising Techniques* by Edith Rudinger and Vic Kelly./ 252-257 "What's the Message? Print Ads from Canadian Magazines."/ 258-260 "How to Create Print Ads."/ 261-263 "Twisting the Familiar" from *The Popcorn Report* by Faith Popcorn./ 264-267 "The Internet: The Newest Medium by Catherine Rondina./ 272 "If I Can Stop One Heart From Breaking" by Emily Dickinson. Reprinted by permission of the publishers and the Trustees of Amhurst College from *The Poems of Emily Dickinson*, Thomas H. Johnson, ed., Cambridge, Mass.: The Belknap Press of Harvard University Press. ©1951, 1955, 1979, 1983 by the President and Fellows of Harvard College./ 273-286 "And the Lucky Winner Is..." by Monica Hughes. Reprinted by permission of the author./ 288-290 "Signposts on the Journey" (originally entitled "Son Provides a Real Buist of Pride") by Steve Buist, *The Hamilton Spectator* (November 2, 1998). Reprinted by permission of *The Hamilton Spectator.*/ 292-295 "The Long Journey" by Sue Mann./ 296-298 "Halting Hatred" by Shaun Chen from the *Toronto Star* (Tuesday, March 23, 1999), pp. E1, E3. Reprinted by permission of Young People's Press./ 300-305 "Babysitting Helen" by Kathy Stinson from *Takes: Stories for Young Adults*, R. P. MacIntyre, ed., (Saskatoon, Saskatchewan: Thistledown Press, 1996). Reprinted by permission of Thistledown Press./ 308 "Shoes" by Sylvia Hamilton from *Fiery Spirits: A Collection of Short Fiction and Poetry by Canadian Writers of African Descent* Ayanna Black. Published by HarperCollins*PublishersLtd*. ©1995 by Ayanna Black./ 310 "Birdfoot's Grampa" from *Entering Onandaga* by Joseph Bruchac./ 313-318 "The Last Leaf" based on a short story by O. Henry from *Plays for Reading*. ©1966 by Henry Gilford. Reprinted with permission of Walker and Company, 435 Hudson Street, New York, NY 10014, 1-800-289-2553. All Rights Reserved./ 322-324 "Save South Moresby!" (originally entitled "Moving On") by Jeff Gibbs from *Environmental Youth Alliance Newsletter*, Vol. 2, No. 4, 1991./ 326-328 "Consorting With Frogs" (originally entitled "How I Became a Non-Hunter") by Farley Mowat.

Photo Credits

8-9 © King Features Syndicte, Inc.; 11 S. Camazine /Publiphoto; 22 David Noton/Masterfile; 33 Vicky Kasala/Image Bank; 44-45 Andrew Judd/Masterfile; 46, 47, 49 Pete Turner/Image Bank; 58-59 © King Features Syndicte, Inc.; 70-71 Rodrigo Moreno; 73 Photodisc; 77, 84 K.&K. Ammann/Masterfile; 101 top right from Homeward Bound/Buena Vista/The Kobal Collection; 101 bottom left from Benji/Mulberry Square/The Kobal Collection; 107 At the Window by Ken Danby/Mill Studios Corporation; 111 Boy on Fence by Ken Danby/Mill Studios Corporation; 120-121 John Foster/Publiphoto; 141 John Reeves; 146 © Agence France Presse/Corbis-Bettmann; 147 © John Garrett; 148 left, right © NASA; 150 Richard Coomber/Masterfile; 158 Bruce Weaver/CP Picture Archive; 162-163 Lynnette Cook/Publiphoto; 165, 166, 168 National Undersea Research Center at the University of North Carolina at Wilmington; 172-173 Scholastic Canada Inc., Anness Publishing Limited, Harry N. Abrams, Inc., Kingfisher Books; Ray Boudreau; 177 J.P. Fruchet/Masterfile; 182-183 Illustrations copyright © 1977 by Helen Cann. From *Fathers and Daughter Tales*, published by Barefoot Books Ltd.; 199 Dr. Stephen Thorson; 211 © Normand Cousineau. *From Atalanta: The Fastest Runner in the World*, reprinted with permission of Annick Press Ltd.; 221, 222 Culver Pictures Inc./Superstock; 226 from Lethal Weapon/Warner Brothers/The Kobal Collection; 228 British Film Institute; 229 both The Ronald Grant Archive; 231 top Aquarius Library; 231 bottom British Film Institute; 232 British Film Institute; 233 North Parsons; 236 top from My Left Foot/Granada/Miramax /The Kobal Collection; 236 bottom left © 1995 Paramount Pictures; 236 bottom right © 1987 Twentieth Century Fox; 245 from *Street Cents*, with permission of Canadian Broadcasting Corporation; 246 United Features Syndicate, Inc.; 245, 247, 248 Ian Crysler; 247-248 Milk Marketing Board; 252 Tourism Newfoundland & Labrador; 253 Tourism Yukon; 254 Singapore Tourism Board; 255 World Wildlife Fund Canada; 256 courtesy of Nikon; 257 Canadian Pacific; 265 The Aboriginal Youth Network; 272 Marc Romanelli/Image Bank; 288-289 Eye Wire Studios; 293, 296 K. Beatty/The Toronto Star; 298 R. Eglinton/The Toronto Star; 308-309 Jane Sterrett/ Image Bank; 310, 312 Wisniewski/Masterfile; 316 Le Port de Capri by Constantin Gorbatoff/Christie's London /Superstock; 323 David A. Ponton/Masterfile.

Illustrations

Front cover, 270-271 Brian Deines; 10-11, 70-71, 120-121, 172-173, 187, 218-219, 270-271 Peter Cook; 13,17, 20 Bernadette Lau; 36 Alex Murchison/3 in a Box; 60-61, 104, 160, 192,194, 250, 320, 321 Clarence Porter; 67 Dominic Bugatto/3 in a Box; 88-89 Terry Shoffner; 97 David Rolfe/ 3 in a Box; 123, 126 Barbara Spurll; 132, 137 Peter Lacalamita/3 in a Box; 156 Scott Galley/3 in a Box; 218-219 Steve Munday/3 in a Box; 275, 283 Peter Yundt/3 in a Box; 293 Patrick Fitzgerald; 300, 304, 305 Stephen Taylor; 326 Charles Weiss.